UNIVERSITY OF SOUTHAMPTON

MONOGRAPH SERIES No. 1

THE IRON AGE AND ITS
HILL-FORTS

Southampton, 1971

THE IRON AGE AND ITS HILL-FORTS

Papers presented to
SIR MORTIMER WHEELER
on the Occasion of his Eightieth Year
at a Conference held by the
SOUTHAMPTON UNIVERSITY ARCHAEOLOGICAL SOCIETY
5th – 7th March, 1971

Edited by
David Hill and Margaret Jesson

This volume is made possible by a grant from the
Committee for Advanced Studies of the
University of Southampton

Published by the
Southampton University Archaeological Society
for the
Department of Archaeology, University of Southampton
1971

Printed by
The Millbrook Press Limited, Southampton

CONTENTS

LIST OF LINE ILLUSTRATIONS

LIST OF PLATES

(between pages 148–149)

LIST OF SUBSCRIBERS

Mr. and Mrs. P. V. Addyman
Leslie Alcock
F. G. Aldsworth
David Alexander
D. F. Allen
Patricia Allin
Ilid E. Anthony
Paul Ashbee
Professor L. J. Austin
Richard Avent
Mr. and Mrs. Aylmer
   Aylmer-Kelly
A. W. B. Aylmer-Kelly
Gordon J. Aylward

Linda Babb
Adrian V. Babbidge
Miss A. L. Bacon
Colin Baddeley
David Baker
M. P. Baker
J. H. Ball
K. E. Barber
Dr. L. H. Barfield
Mr. and Mrs. Jeremy Barker
Belinda Barratt
J. Barrett
J. D. Bateson
E. A. Baxter
Mrs. J. Beale
M. G. Bell
Mrs. H. M. Bennett
Joyce Benson
Miss P. Beswick
Martin Biddle
M. W. Bishop
C. E. Blunt
J. Bosanko
Mrs. F. H. Bourdillon
Maryann Bowen
Nick Bradford
J. W. Brailsford
Sylvia J. Bremner
C. Stephen Briggs
A. E. Brown
Christopher Patrick Brown
Iain G. Brown
Mary Browne
Hilary J. Bruce
J. Bryan
W. T. Bryan
P. C. Buckland

Annette Budden
Mr. and Mrs. C. J. Budden
Mrs. P. V. M. Bullman
G. R. Burleigh
Miss Gilian Burn
I. C. G. Burrow
F. W. Butler

David H. Caldwell
Robin K. Campbell
Mrs. M. P. Canham
Mrs. E. Canter
Miss Phyllis M. Carter
John Casey
J. Caton
Mr. and Mrs. T. M.
   Cave-Brown-Cave
A. J. Challis
Mr. and Mrs. T. C. Champion
H. P. A. Chapman
Mary E. Chick
Peter Clack
M. H. Clapham
Ann Clark
D. V. Clarke
Giles Clarke
Miss P. V. Clarke
J. H. Cleland
B. Clements
Dr. Joanna Close-Brooks
Marta Cock
M. Cockle
Miss R. Collier
A. E. P. Collins
John Collis
Linda J. Cook
T. D. Cook
J. X. W. P. Corcoran
Peter O. Couldrey
Dr. and Mrs. E. Course
John D. Cowen
R. M. Crane
Miss M. D. Craster
J. B. Cresswell
Professor R. A. Crossland
R. N. Cuff

M. W. Dacre
Glyn Daniel
Peter Danks
D. Gareth Davies
Glyn Hope Davies

G. M. R. Davies
Jeffrey Davies
Miss P. M. Davies
J. C. Day
Alan Deacon
Mrs. K. de Brisay
P. J. W. de Grouchy
Éamonn de hÓir
Mrs. S. de hÓir
Miss Anthea V. Diver
Brian Dix
Miss Josephine P. M. Dool
G. Dowdell
John H. Drinkwater
Patricia Drummond
James Dyer

Barbara Eastwood
S. R. Eccles
W.Cdr. T. W. Ellcock
Mrs. A. Ellison
George Eogan
D. Morgan Evans
R. D. G. Evely

Bernard Fagg
J. and J. Fairclough
Rodney Fanthorpe
M. E. Farley
J. E. Farmer
R. A. H. Farrar
Clare I. Fell
K. J. Field
N. H. Field
Zachary P. Finklestein
B. H. W. Finlaison
T. M. Finnie
Michael E. Fisher
Andrew Fleming
Mrs. Fortescue
P. J. Fowler
Lady Aileen Fox
Susan Frankenstein
S. P. L. Freeman
Professor S. S. Frere
E. D. Fry
Malcolm F. Fry
Fil. Kand Birgitta Frykman

N. G. Gammer
Peter S. Gelling
A. V. B. Gibson
A. J. Gilmour

Miss Betty Gobel
Michael C. S. Godfrey
Roger Goodburn
Philip Goodwin
Daphne Gould
L. C. B. Gower
James A. Graham-Campbell
Annie Grant
Miss E. Grant
Lt.-Col. G. E. Gray
Christopher John Sparey Green
Martin T. Green
Mr. and Mrs. R. G. Greenaway
Peter Greening
Dr. John Greeves
T. A. P. Greeves
Tony Gregory
Vincent L. Gregory III
Jane Griffiths
N. A. Griffiths
Mrs. W. R. Groves
Graeme C. Guilbert
P. E. Gunstone

Patrick J. Halloran
Miss A. E. Hamlin
N. D. C. Hammond
The Viscountess Hanworth
L. S. Harley
Miss J. Harman
A. E. T. Harper
A. R. Harper
R. C. Hart
David Harvey
Professor Christopher Hawkes
Richard Haworth
Miss Sandra Haworth
Elizabeth Hemingway
Stuart Henderson
Margaret Herdman
D. J. Heys
Mrs. P. Hibberd
Edward A. K. Higginbotham
Mary C. Higham
David Hill
Roger A. Hills
Mervyn D. Hinge
Brian Hobley
E. W. Holden
Raymond Holt
Brian Hope-Taylor
Mr. and Mrs. N. M. Hopkin
John Hopkins
Graeme K. Horner

Paul Horton
S. W. Howard
G. Howe
Michael Hughes
Miss M. Hunt

P. J. Isaac

L. H. Jeffery
Stanley Jepson
Margaret Jesson
C. E. Joel
F. B. Johnson
D. E. Johnston
Dilwyn Jones
Elizabeth A. T. Jones
J. D. Jones
M. J. Jones
M. U. Jones
Richard Jones

Mrs. Anne Kahane
Miss Clare Kahane
David H. Kennett
M. A. Kent
Robin Place Kenward
J. B. Kenworthy
Kathleen M. Kenyon
J. K. Knight
G. C. Knowles

John Laidlaw
Lloyd R. Laing
R. G. Lamb
Mr. and Mrs. P. A. Langmaid
Cherry Lavell
A. J. Lawson
John Leach
Ralph D. S. Leake
Francis Lee
David Leigh
Geoffrey D. Lewis
J. B. Lightfoot
J. H. Little
R. G. Livens
C. A. Lovegrove
A. W. G. Lowther
L. Luckett

M. R. McCarthy
Jean Macdonald
J. G. McEwen
Ronald Macfarlane
J. C. McGovern
Arthur Macgregor

Mrs. E. L. Machin
D. F. Mackreth
D. G. Macleod
J. C. McPeake
P. D. Macrae
Sir Max Mallowan
John Marjoram
J. R. Marjoram
J. Marjot
W. Marsh
E. A. Martin
P. J. R. Mason
Leslie G. Matthews
Jeffrey May
Lesley A. Maynard
Joyce Medcalfe
Marion Meek
John A. Meer
J. V. S. Megaw
A. G. Mein
H. E. L. Mellersh
Ralph Merrifield
Roger Miket
Mrs. Henrietta Miles
A. G. Eric Millington
J. H. Money
J. E. T. Monnington
Mrs. Gwen E. Montagu
C. N. Moore
W. R. G. Moore
Elizabeth J. Moreland
M. Morris
A. Morrison
Frances Moss
Frank Moss
Miss Mary-Jane Mountain
R. Mowat
C. R. Musson
Dr. J. N. L. Myres

T. G. Newman
Mr. and Mrs. Niblett
D. C. Nicoll
G. R. Nicoll

P. T. Oborn
B. J. O'Connor
W. A. Oddy
Miss M. O'Gorman
Miss M. S. Oliver
Mrs. E. Owen

David J. R. Palmer
C. R. Partridge

Miss A. Patrick
C. O. Peabody
K. J. Penn
Dr. B. T. Perry
Bernard Phillips
D. C. Phillips
Stuart Piggott
Gladys Pike
Michael Pitts
Miss Georgina Plowright
K. Lloyd Plumridge
Mrs. J. M. Popplewell
C. F. R. Potter
F. L. Preston
S. J. Price
R. D. Pringle
L. A. Probert
F. M. M. Pryor
J. Przybyla
G. Pulzer
D. F. Purcell
Brian Pybus

Sarah M. G. Quain

P. A. Rahtz
Ian Ralston
Adrian B. Rance
Bernard Rawes
Miss Barbara Read
G. M. Reed
Miss Mary Wharton Reed
Kenneth G. H. Reedie
Joyce Reeves
Colin Renfrew
D. F. Renn
Brian Rich
Peter Richards
David Ridgway
Mr. and Mrs. J. M. Roberts
P. H. Robinson
Joan Robson
W. J. Rodwell
A. E. Rollings
Alan Rowe
J. H. Rumsby
R. A. Rutland
Etienne Rynne

Dr. J. K. St. Joseph
Edward Sammes
Miss Elizabeth Sampson
Helen E. Sandford
Alan Saville
H. N. Savory
William Say
J. J. Schwieso
A. R. L. Selkirk
M. L. Shackley
Ian A. G. Shepherd
J. G. T. Sheringham
Miss Sue Sidney
Veronica Simmons
Miss M. J. Skelding
Moira Skinner
Clyde Curry Smith
Miss C. Deland Smith
R. F. Smith
Grahame J. Soffe
Anne Sowerbutts
Mansel G. Spratling
D. S. Stafford
P. H. Stanier
D. W. A. Startin
J. B. Stevenson
D. S. Stewart
Fionna C. Stewart
J. A. Sugden
G. Summers

E. J. Talbot
Alison Taylor
R. M. Taylor
C. F. Tebbutt
Professor Charles Thomas
Nicholas Thomas
Stanley Thomas
F. H. Thompson
Isobel Thompson
Jenny E. Thompson
Miss Lisbeth M. Thoms
Robert G. Thomson
Lilian Thornhill
John R. L. Thorp
Mrs. Mary Tisdall
Mrs. Brenda L. Toller
Fay Tracey

A. E. Truckell
Philip Twentyman
A. Tyler
Mrs. Edith Tyson

F. M. Underhill

A. Van Doorselaer
Major and Mrs. H. L. Vatcher
D. J. Viner
Blaise E. Vyner

Peter Wade-Martins
J. M. Wagstaff
G. J. Wainwright
Marion B. Walker
T. W. Walker
G. J. Wall
Alec P. Warden
Anne M. Wardman
John Ward-Perkins
Kathleen Warner
Malcolm J. Watkins
Mrs. C. Weber
Dr. Graham Webster
V. R. Webster
Frances Welsh
Lynda Whalley
P. M. White
P. W. Whitaker
Gladys G. Wilkins
Eurwyn Williams
J. R. Williams
Mrs. T. Willis
Andrew J. Wilson
Kenneth and Peggy Wilson
M. Winsch
Ann Wintle
A. G. Woodcock
Miss P. Carr Woods
H. N. Wright

E. M. Yonge
Susan Young
B. A. Yule

Un Etudiant en Histoire
A Member, Archaeological
    Centre, Bournemouth

INSTITUTIONS

Bangor, University College of North Wales Library
Bath, King Edward VI School
Belfast, Queen's University Library
Belfast, Ulster Museum, Department of
Antiquities
Birmingham University, Department of
Extra-Mural Studies
Bournemouth Archaeological Centre
Bradford, Cartwright Hall Museum
Bristol City Museum
Bristol University, Department of Extra-Mural
Studies

Canterbury, Royal Museum and Public Library
Cardiff, National Museum of Wales
Carisbrooke Castle Museum
Cheltenham Art Gallery and Museum
Christchurch, Red House Museum
Colchester and Essex Museum
Copenhagen, Royal Library
Council for Kentish Archaeology

Doncaster Museum and Art Gallery
Dorset County Library
Dorset Natural History and Archaeological
Society
Dublin, Department of Education
Durham University

Edinburgh, National Museum of Antiquities of
Scotland
Exeter City Museums
Exeter, Saint Luke's College
Exeter University Library

Frankfurt, Romisch-Germanische Kommission
des Deutschen Archäologischen Instituts

Göteborgs Archeologiska Museum
Guildford Museum

Hampshire County Library
Hampshire County Museum Service
Hythe Borough

Ipswich Museum

Kidderminster Public Library
Kingston upon Hull College of Education
Kingston upon Hull Museums

Leeds City Museums
Leicester, Newarke Houses Museum
Leicester University Library

Letchworth Museum and Art Gallery
Lincoln City Libraries
London, British Museum
London, Guildhall Museum
London, Horniman Museum and Library
London University, Institute of Archaeology
Luton Museum and Art Gallery

Maidstone Museum and Art Gallery
Marburg University, Vorgeschichtliches Seminar

Norwich Corporation Museums Department
Nottingham University Library

Oxford, Ashmolean Museum
Oxford University, Institute of Archaeology

Poole Borough Libraries

Reading, Berkshire College of Education
Reading Museum and Art Gallery
Rome, British School

St. Albans, Verulamium Museum
Salisbury and South Wiltshire Museum
Scunthorpe Museum and Art Gallery
Sheffield City Museums
Sheffield University Library
Shrewsbury Borough Museums
Somerset Archaeological and Natural History
Society
Southampton City Museums
Southampton, Ordnance Survey, Archaeology
Department
Southampton University, Department of
Extra-Mural Studies
Southampton University Library
Stafford College of Further Education
Stoke-on-Trent Museum

Totton College

Wellington, The Blessed Robert Johnson
Catholic Secondary School
West Kent Border Archaeological Group
Weston-super-Mare Public Library and Museum
Wiltshire Archaeological and Natural History
Society
Winchester City Museums
Worksop Public Library and Museum
Worthing Museum

Yorkshire Museum

Bauermeister Booksellers, Edinburgh, Scotland
B. H. Blackwell Ltd., Oxford
K. J. Bredon's Bookshop, Brighton
A. Brown & Sons Ltd., Hull
Dillon's Q.M.C. Bookshop, London
Holt Jackson Book Co. Ltd., Lytham St. Annes
Librairie R. Didier, Nancy, France
W. P. Van Stockum N.V., Booksellers, Den Haag, Holland
The Swindon Bookshop Ltd.

Dedicatory Address
by the Chairman of the Conference

IT IS a truism to say that Sir Mortimer Wheeler needs no introduction from me. He is, in fact, one of the best-known figures of our time, not only in the particular field of archaeology, but also in fields as diverse as those of the administrator, of the author, of the entertainer (in the best sense of the word) and of the soldier – and that not merely, like Edward Gibbon, in the Hampshire Militia, but in the Royal Regiment of Artillery, whose motto might well be his own: *Ubique, quo fas et gloria ducunt.*

The element of *gloria* is essential, not accidental, for Sir Mortimer is the modern representative of Renaissance Man. But long before Renaissance Man evolved, the Greek historian Polybius had taught us that only a man who has made history can satisfactorily write it. And if I were asked to explain how Sir Mortimer has made his most signal contributions to archaeology, I would say that it was by the application to it of the skills of the soldier and the administrator – strategy and tactics (plus a touch of ruthlessness) on the one hand, but a proper regard for the supporting services on the other.

As a matter of fact, this assessment is based on personal experience. The first excavation in which I was ever involved took place in a field beside a river. When we arrived, we were conducted to a sort of clearing in the four-foot-high grass and told to dig *here*. This we did, undisturbed by any further information or advice, for all the world like Martin Tupper on Farley Heath, with his

> Surrey serfs, turning the turfs,
> The merry livelong day.

And when evening came, we mounted our bicycles and rode away. I am still not sure what it was all about (though I suspect that it had something to do with the Bronze Age) and I cannot remember who was supposed to be directing the operation – which is probably just as well.

But the second excavation in which I was involved was at Maiden Castle, and here the contrast was complete. No question here of not knowing what we were about: from the first we were *told* – indeed we were given (or more probably sold) the interim reports for the preceding years, which had, of course, been promptly produced; and thereafter we were compelled to keep abreast of developments. The most serious crime – and the only one which invoked those spectacular rages – was to appear at a loss when asked the question: 'Now what are you doing *here*?' and we students were put on a roster to show visitors round the excavations and explain what was going on to them – surely the best way of setting one's own thoughts in order. Work began at 9 o'clock sharp and ended at 5, unless some important operation required one's attendance until dusk; and at a quarter to 5 a whistle blew to warn us to clean up, so that all cuttings were left in immaculate order. Anyone who was consistently late for work was politely but firmly asked to leave: in those days, of course, we were all unpaid volunteers.

There were relaxations – skittles matches in Dorchester (I suspect now that this was a form of 'organised sport', though it didn't feel like it at the time), mackerel fishing in Weymouth Bay (this helped the commissariat) and even poetry reading in the dusty school-house at smokefall. But over all there ranged the giant figure of the Keeper, striding purposefully from site to site, newly-alighted, it might seem, from Rugby Chapel. I think that the analogy with Thomas Arnold is fair, because there was probably an element of paternalism in all this, which might not appeal to the modern generation of students. But there was no doubt at all about the sense of participation.

In retrospect, I think that we were particularly fortunate in joining the Wheeler Circus in 1937, for not only did we know Maiden Castle at its most purposeful, but, as soon as we had been absorbed into it, any tendency to insular parochialism was firmly strangled at birth. The very next year the whole caravan crossed the Channel, to M. Giot's country, and the big top was re-erected first at le Camp d'Artus, Huelgoat, and then at le Petit Celland, near Avranches, while a subsidiary one-ring affair was staged at Kercaradec, near Quimper, and from time to time we were sent in flying columns all over Brittany. Thus we were taught that while archaeology, like charity, may begin at home, it must not end there.

The following year the process was repeated in Normandy, but operations there were cut short by the onset of war. That war, and the very distinguished part which Sir Mortimer played in it, is not our immediate concern, nor again is his great work in organising the archaeology of the whole sub-continent of India – ludicrous as it is to pass over such an achievement in so few words. But in 1950 he was back at work again on our own hill-forts: first at Bindon, where he characteristically 'borrowed' a sergeant and five men to produce what is still our most reliable evidence for what was actually involved in the construction of a rampart, and then at Stanwick, which he showed to be the scene of the last stand of the Brigantes.

Lydney, Prae Wood, Wheathampstead, Maiden Castle, Huelgoat, Kercaradec, Avranches, Fécamp, Duclair, Bindon, Stanwick – each of them was in its day a classic of its kind. Of course great changes have taken place since then in archaeology, and not least in the study of the Iron Age. New techniques have been developed, new discoveries made, and some of Sir Mortimer's own formulations have been superseded. This does not distress him, for he has read his Plato and he knows that the dialectic of knowledge proceeds by destroying hypotheses. But this does not mean that they are merely alms for oblivion, since the golden atoms of evidence from which they were formed remain, as bright as ever, for use in the newer (and no doubt equally transitory) constructions.

And of course Stanwick, though it remains, at present, his latest work on the British Iron Age, does not mark the end of the story. The Elder Pliny tells us that in one of his later books (now lost) Livy wrote that he had already achieved enough of glory and could have retired to leisure, but that his restless spirit, his *animus inquies*, fed upon his work. So also has it been with Sir Mortimer. In the intervening years he has ranged over three continents, founding an institute here, initiating research there, and in the meantime instructing and delighting us with books: books on India, books on Africa, books on the meaning as well as the practice of archaeology, and books above all on life. Still his *animus inquies* drives him on: long may it continue to do so.

Ladies and gentlemen, it would be idle to attempt to recount all his achievements and the honours he has earned; they fill a column of *Who's Who* and might perhaps best be summarised in the Roman statue-base formula: *Omnibus honoribus in patria sua functus*. Instead, I will simply turn to him and say: 'Sir, we are delighted to have you with us this evening, and we hope that you will do us the honour of assuming the patronage of this our conference.'

A. L. F. RIVET

Southampton, 5th March, 1971

EDITORS' NOTE

These papers are edited on behalf of the Southampton University Archaeological Society, whose enthusiasm and hard work made possible the realisation of the conference.

David Hill and Margaret Jesson

FENCE, WALL, DUMP, FROM TROY TO HOD

By C. F. C. HAWKES

1. PROLOGUE AT GERGOVIA: CAESAR AND ARCHAEOLOGY

'MADE uncommonly strong by its position and its works': thus would Caesar tersely note that a hill-fort facing him, in Britain or Gaul, was especially worth remark. At Gergovia, where the Arverni (of the central-French Auvergne) faced and then repulsed him, from its southerly defences, the Anglo-French excavations of 1934 let me section those defences – wall on rock-cut scarp – myself. But my displaying the work to visitors from the region's learned society, as fitting Caesar's account, and also his date through a stratified amphora, rightly provoked their leader into questioning what it meant. Rightly, because what sealed the piece of amphora, down the scarp, was the fall of the wall-face on to it; later, of course, than Caesar's repulse. The coins from the site do imply that the wall was built not very much sooner; but its fall coming only later entirely fits my amphora's form, namely Dressel 1B, which can continue to Augustus (Peacock here, pp. 161–88). And although such defences might be rendered ineffective, by whatever means suited the Roman order after the conquest, yet Gergovia kept a gateway, and had an occupation flourishing, well on through early Gallo-Roman times.

Finding actual events of history at such an oppidum, in fact, may need more work, besides more luck, than at first appears. It is anyhow not the only thing to be aimed at by a dig. While to get any hill-fort dated is of course the prime objective, this alone is not enough. What was its setting, its social meaning and purpose? These questions, finally, send one back to the facts of its actual structure: the barrier or fence, the rampart or wall, the bank or dump and the scarp or ditch or ditches; their materials, entrances, size of space enclosed; and the choice of ground and situation. Its works and its position, Caesar's *opus* and *natura*, tell of its strength indeed; but of more than that, if we think of them and study them as we ought. Hence my blunt title. Hod is Hod Hill in Dorset. We shall soon be starting at Troy. But I have one point to be touched on first.

2. FORT SITES AND SANCTITY: OLDER RELIGION

Among Gergovia's Roman buildings were temples. Two, within an enclosure cleared in 1934, were of the familiar Romano-Celtic type with portico, and square. Sanctification of their area can well have been post-conquest. But was nothing done, at all, when the fortress was built, to invoke or to renew divine favour? It had certainly had a previous prehistoric occupation, apparently unfortified (cf. end of part 3); but if we know too little of that, may there not be other cases, where pre-Roman fortification and religion went together? In Britain, in the earthwork-protected enclosure at Heath Row (within the area of London Airport), lay the emplacement of a porticoed rectangular temple, timber-built, of the Iron Age, as the pottery all declared. Prior to that, the site disclosed two Neolithic pits. And whether or not there was here a sanctity already as old as that, we have a much more striking case that is indisputable: Maiden

B

Castle. The renowned Dorset fortress, when 300 years disused, had a Romano-Celtic temple built beside its eastern summit, just where its strangest older feature, the Neolithic Long Mound, ended on a ritual pit, near a ritual burial and others. May not the 'Bronze Age hiatus', between those older times and the Iron Age, be peculiar to this site, as being made so sacred by the Mound, along the whole 550 metres of its crest, that it repelled all secular uses till the fort came to be built?

Note that the fort in its primary form, around the eastern summit only, though cutting the Mound and its cursus-like lateral ditches into two, yet enclosed the point it was aimed at, with the ritual pit and burials. It rather recalls, in Ireland, the famous sacred site of Tara, where the Neolithic 'Hostages' Mound' with its burials is aimed at directly by the so-called 'Banquet-hall', long and straight and seen as cursus-like by Piggott, despite an Iron Age intrusion (the 'Fort of the Synods') and the enclosing of the Neolithic mound by the 'Fort of the Kings'. And though the great expanse of holy ground around Stonehenge, with its cursus and mass of pre-Iron Age burials, never received a fort any nearer than its edge – that miscalled 'Vespasian's Camp' on the west of Amesbury Abbey Park – yet it gives, in the Wilsford Shaft, a clue for our tracing older religion in later Celtic. What Piggott has written needs here no repeating: of the like deep shafts in quadrangular Iron Age enclosures, east of the Rhine, and analogies spread through France ranging back to the previous Bronze Age, but including associations with square Romano-Celtic ground-plans. What I would add to this is the prospect of such shafts being found in hill-forts. We may soon be hearing of a first British instance. And in Germany, in the western part of the lands of the Lausitz culture (sometimes called the Lusatian), around the middle Elbe, the strongly-ramparted fort of that culture at Lossow, on a low-lying promontory (flanked by water), has been found to contain shafts of the kind in quite surprising numbers, as though the fort became, or always was, entirely a sacred place. I shall soon be reverting to Lausitz-culture forts, as significant further, if indirectly, for Britain; meanwhile, of the factors affecting choice of site to fortify, when fortifying came in (Cunliffe here, p. 57 ff.), I have made a point of stressing the religious because we all, at home and for much of the Europe that was Celtic in the Iron Age, are seeing that Celtic religion can contain much older things. So may Celtic forts. And now I pass to the forts themselves.

3. MATERIALS FOR PROTECTION: COMMUNITY SITES AND HILL-TOPS

Rock or cliff, water or marsh, could of course protect early dwellings where their natural advantage might be taken. Yet we probably think too little, even for sites on open plains, of protection from animal prowlers, obtained without leaving clear traces in the ground. Dogs, guarding village or home as now, had then doubtless often more to face from predators; cutting thorn for a barrier would help, and so would planting it, live, for a hedge – which nevertheless would grow with gaps, so call for some aid from fencing. Wattling a fence, like basketry, must have been a widespread Neolithic craft; but where the country gave you stones, you did better with a wall, and the proof is of course the early one at Jericho. Wall-stones, however, to be good and plentiful enough, need quarrying; their weight is a strain on transport; they may have to be brought from far. And though growth of large communities and social organisation, in the East's alluvial river-lands, led so early to the rise of towns, yet building them walls, like houses, needed the alluvium's own materials: the reeds and the mud that gave the builders of towns their inexhaustible supplies of mud-brick. Mud-brick and urbanism throve there together, while away towards Europe there was far less of either. Mediterranean lands, despite their having easily-worked limestone, could in early conditions not support communities so large; thus the walled and full-sized town, on their European coasts, will hardly concern me here before our knowledge becomes historical. In Anatolia, Çatal Hüyük too, and towns besides and after it, send one on towards Europe with their urbanism left behind. All our farming-settlements, small or large, were really villages. And while the climate-limit for mud-brick, in the plains, is reached in Hungary, the loess and other farming-lands spread variously on, suiting always wood and wattlework and earthwork.

So here, perhaps too tardily, I come to the bank or dump. To form a good barrier together with the ditch, from which its earth is scraped (Shaw 1970) or dug, it ought to be massive, or else the ditch should be wide, or a double one or multiple, and in any case it will gain from anything added to its height. A hedge to be grown along its top, or a wattled fence to be set there, can be slighter because of the elevation, and the protection given by the ditch, making it hard to climb or leap. Granted this aid, its effectiveness is got by work requiring no great skill; once compacted, it is easy to maintain, yet its digging, unless in rocky ground, can be quick. It thus has certain advantages compared with fence or wall; and with either, as we shall see, you can advantageously combine it.

Town and village, large and small, I call community sites. What any could hold for religion, is a matter I shall here pass by. Temples of course are things of the East, and its urbanism embraced them; what villages up to Central Europe had, seems more domestic; it has certainly left us nothing like the sacred sites of the West. Neolithic or Early Metal Age community sites, in any case, with a farming economy, are normally not on hill-tops. Physical conditions of some special kind excepted, one finds them in intermediate country, plains, or valleys or water-sides; somewhere, at all events, near their farm-land. But hill-tops stand for safety. You can live up above your farm-land. And at least by Late Neolithic times, such sites had started to be chosen. Are such settlements then to be reckoned true community sites, or not? If protected further by defences – strong through works besides their position – did these protect all the people or only some, leaving out the others? And so we come, east and north and west of the northern Aegean, to the early 'acropolis' sites containing porched-hall houses, the 'megaron' type, which indeed has analogues as far as Middle Europe, but at first was Anatolian, and in Aegean lands was specialised for a central role in fortified sites, not enclosing all their community but commanding it. Such summit-sites need not be centred on a 'megaron', even within defences that accentuate their strength, but its presence, as the grandest form of building inside them, can accentuate their character of citadel rather than city, not hill-town or village so much as hill-fort. Troy, from its very first phase, was just such a citadel, perched on the edge of the Hissarlik hill; it has the 'megaron' in anyhow its second phase; its works were those of a fortress, never large but extremely strong. The labour of their construction implies a community more numerous, and readier for heavy toil, than the lords who possessed the treasures of precious metalwork found in hoards there. So I take Troy as a symbol and embodiment of power, which dominant social groups could hold over larger group populations, topographically secured by the strength of fort-citadels. The sites of these I here call citadel sites, in a distinction from community ones which I stress as something important. 'Hill-fort', in modern English usage, blurs the two.

Away from such concentrations, on Europe's plains from eastern to northern, west towards Flanders along the outside of the continent's mountain spine, in the same span of time, Neolithic to Early Metal, populations were spread in which a power much simpler, to be guessed only from burial forms and rarely-discovered cattle stockades, came to be exercised by a range of groups, in ways we can see more clearly in the Bronze Age. On and within the mountain spine, indeed, in the Late Neolithic already, cruder versions of the Aegean area's citadels may be found on hill-tops. Within it, in Croatia, is the strong little 'burg' of Vučedol. In the Bohemian hills is Homolka (of Řivnac culture): too small to be communal, with its six or seven little huts, it is strongly placed on a summit, within a post-and-wattle fence, standing along a dump bank raised from a ditch or scarp, with narrow fenced lanes across for entry. In South-western Europe again, far less rustic, and walled in stone, with bastions and other details pointing to links with the East Mediterranean, we have the rare but impressive citadels often credited to 'colonists', like that at Zambujal near Lisbon, where excavation is now proceeding. But whether or not their example, or report of such forts more vaguely, spread north into France or farther still, to affect the design of earthwork, Neolithic and Beaker enclosures here (as already indeed in Italy) still appear merely communal, using ditches sometimes multiple, but apparently banks of rubble or earth in dump-work. The westerly lands with these, and the eastern and central with works more varied, some not communal but simplified-citadel, alike make contrast with the plains across the north, where dominance did without fortifications we can recognise. From those plains nevertheless, various groups did pass, through the mountain spine, into Central and Western/Central Europe; and by Early Bronze times, and on through much of the second millennium, we see the result of this and other moves in a cultural range, which loosely, from its Middle Bronze-Age barrows, is known as 'Tumulus'. And in this again there are hill-top sites, which again may be viewed as citadels, but in any case, as far as is known, without fortifications. Hedges or fences or piled-up stones are gone, or have lost identity; pottery and other finds may abound, as at Reusten in Württemberg (the most fully published); but otherwise we seem to have the hills without the hill-forts. I believe we may perhaps have such Bronze Age sites on hills in Britain too. How then did the hills get their hill-forts after all?

4. SETTLED FOLK AND CITADEL: BRONZE TOWARDS IRON AGE

When Troy, from its first and second phase, attained at last its sixth, this citadel lasted alongside those of Mycenean Greece. Fortifying in stone had come there too; but the masonry and the size of the great Mycenean walls, or of the Trojan, must not let us fancy them now the walls of towns. At Mycenae, through its first 200 years of occupation, we know nothing of how it may have been defended. The citadel wall has not been shown to be earlier than the fourteenth century; and the hill-top within was just a large-sized citadel, an acropolis matching the greater power and wealth that its rulers commanded. The 'palace' and all its resources, material, treasure, labour force and armed force, was still not a town in the community sense: the people it ruled were outside it, around below, where their clusters of chamber tombs, humbler than the few great royal ones, point to their having dwelt in open village-like settlements. No walled 'lower town' appears till classical times (fourth century). Thus Mycenean walled sites, whether large like this or smaller, were socially still citadel sites, the castles of a ruling class. And farther up inside Europe, where there were 'mini-citadels' earlier, there are fortified sites that support the idea of a sequence, similar socially, amongst and within the highlands and hills that rise to the Carpathian Ring. By its bend from east to north, perhaps the greatest yet explored of them is Sarata Monteoru. When its publication comes, the idea should gain context. Transylvania, Slovakia, and Hungary westward, have Middle Bronze fortification, a well-known case being Barca. Farther on, however, both sides of the Danube, and over and past the Main and Rhine, what are found then instead are those hill-top sites, like Reusten, which afford no traces of defence works. The change that brought hill-fort building westward, to Alpine foreland, middle Elbe, and farther on, came with the turn of the second and the first millennium, when Mycenean power had collapsed.

Through that time of trouble and movement, Mediterranean and European, from before 1200 B.C. towards 1000, Continental archaeology faces much that stands for change, in economy, burial-customs, industry and armament. 'Urnfield culture', like 'Tumulus', is a loose term only. But with its seeming so certain that Europeans now had drawn, in bronze-work anyhow, on Mycenean leavings, one can all the more readily credit the like in fortification. Gaps in time and space will be slow to fill, undoubtedly. Yet at least it is clear today that one need not wait for the resurgence, towards 800, of East-Mediterranean peoples' enterprise, to recognise hill-forts far across Europe. Astride and beyond the mountain spine, from the Oder west to the Elbe, one has the Lausitz culture, noticed above for the fort with the shafts at Lossow. Started, as a culture of urnfield type, appreciably prior to 1000, it has pottery and metalwork abundantly sufficing for distinction of its earlier phases from its later. The later, contemporary with the Mediterranean enterprise, and with thrusts from the east of folk with fast horsemanship and wagonry, come towards 800 and end well within the Iron Age. It is earlier than all that, as C14 will help to show us, that Lausitz people have now to be seen as first constructing hill-forts. And the work of Werner Coblenz, from his headquarters at Dresden, has for something more than a dozen years been showing what these were like.

The Schafberg at Löbau – one example out of a number – on the flattish summit of a very steep hill, is a citadel-fort in a typical situation; fig. 1, *d* shows its wall among the several massive forms of fortification reconstructable at these sites from the work of Coblenz and others. The materials were stout timbers, earth, rubble and masonry; their remains allow all to be reckoned as of formidable height. At Niederneundorf (*c*), the wall was all of timber, with deep-set uprights, and with two protective rows of stakes in front as *chevaux de frise*; from this kind of thing was developed the timber 'box' construction, as attested in the later phase at Biskupin, the Polish marsh-fort (*b*). But at Sörnewitz (*a*), the construction used a fence as facing for a rampart, timber-laced only at the bottom and otherwise of earth, piled dump-wise, with also an earth slope piled in front, to protect the fence's base. Lausitz engineers thus commanded all

9

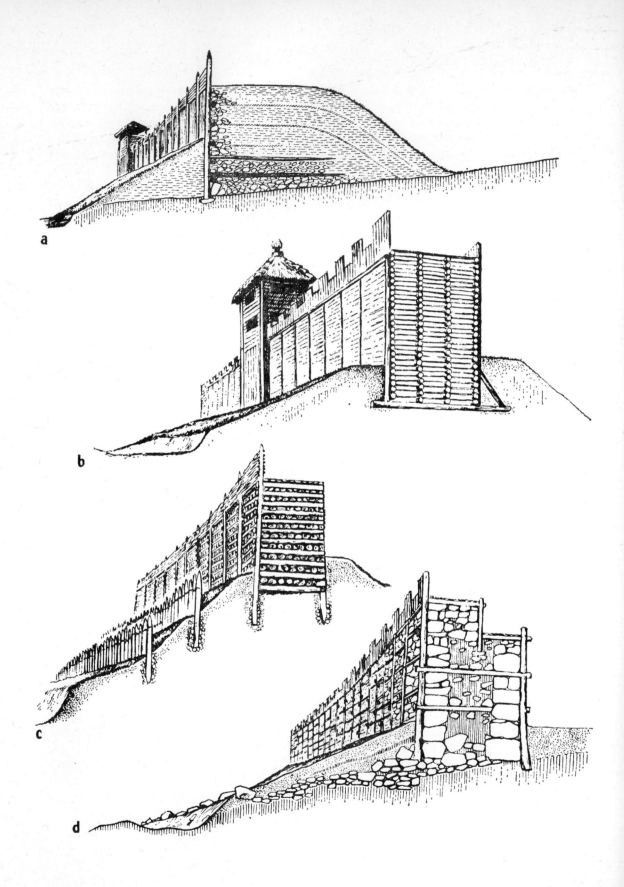

a

b

c

d

three methods: fence, wall, and dump. They could use them all on a massive scale. The amount of timber to be cut and then seasoned, carried into place on summits, and erected with earth and rubble and in some cases masonry, shows a social power over labour, skilled and unskilled alike, which is consistent only with a rigorous and warlike ruling class. And as the methods were alternative, or greater could succeed to lesser – this had been so at Löbau – each could be used in accord with circumstance: if wall too laborious, then fence alone or dump alone. This inference is only rational; and there is more to bear it out. Meanwhile you have here, around the Saxon Elbe, in the period following Mycenae and Monteoru, a Lausitz-culture province that can scarcely have been the only one, where a Late Bronze ruling class had set itself on hill-forts. Settled folk, the cultivators known from village cemeteries – the usual Lausitz urnfields – lived below, out on the land. The forts are plainly citadel sites, both the smaller and also the larger. If the ground allowed, and the controlling power was big enough, more could be given room to live, or to bring their beasts inside. But the larger the site, the more work it meant to build defences; so a full-scale wall, round a site at all extensive, means a power pretty big within its region. Along the Danube or south of it, by the Alps, there may be more such; but there, archaeology has so many forts of the Iron Age, Hallstatt and La Tène, that we have to wait for a longer sequence. Yet the Lausitz forts are not too remote to have interest for Britain.

5. THE CONTINENT AND BRITAIN: SCOTLAND, NORTHERN ENGLAND, SOUTH

The Elbe flows to the North Sea, with Britain off beyond. Or by land, travelling west across the Saale, one meets the Weser, again with a North Sea mouth, in Lower Saxony. Both, when they leave the hills, cross plains with no more forts. Yet Lower Saxon culture there was influenced by Lausitz; and the hills that are left by the Weser, and its confluent the Leine, on their course north to the plain, have hill-forts too. On the rim of Lower Saxony here, round Göttingen, modern field-work has distinguished, from Early Medieval ones, some forts of the Early Iron Age, all on citadel-suiting sites. Up on steep hill-tops, well above the spring-line, and affording no traces of community occupation, they could serve for occasional refuge, yet do not appear likely to have ever been undertaken unless some power or stress demanded. Neolithic traces occur, but are sparse; so indeed are those of the Iron Age, yet these date the fort-works: ditch and bank, still not enough dug. At least there is something here, well away from Danube, Main or Rhine, which gives one more than the fort-less summits used by Bronze Age people previously. And the British Isles had had links with Lower Saxony long already; they even stretched to the Elbe, so we need not feel we are

Fig. 1 (*left*). Lausitz culture, types of fort-wall building (after Coblenz 1970)

a. Earth dump rampart, with rubble base, timber-laced, and fence-like vertical timber face (example: Sörnewitz, Middle Germany).
b. Timber wall of triple 'box' construction, late Lausitz phase (example: Biskupin marsh-fort, Poland).
c. Timber wall, log-bodied, with rows of stakes as *chevaux de frise* (example: Niederneundorf, Middle Germany).
d. Wall with timber-laced earth and rubble core, faced vertically with timber-framed masonry blocks (example: Schafberg at Löbau, Middle Germany; also Pfaffenstein).

From Actes du VIIme Congrès International des Sciences Préhistoriques et Protohistoriques, Prague 1966 (ed.) J. Filip, tome I 1970, 717, fig. 2.

too far out. Some kind of impulse oversea may thus seem thinkable, whether movement of force or flight, or word of mouth through seamen or traders, which could bring North England, and Scotland too, the idea and practice of fence, wall, or dump, to be started afresh for defence of sites on hills, in what here was then still the Bronze Age.

Our subject being Southern Britain here, and not the North, I need not stray to repeat what Northern work in the field has long been telling us, and tells us now with the added strength imparted by C14 dates. Fenced or palisaded sites, timber-laced wall-forts, walls all of stone around forts or little farms, viewed in the past as all of Southern derivation, stand today in Scotland and Northern England as a challenge. Were they foreign-inspired at first, or something Southern after all, or miraculously spontaneous, like the birth of a Northern Athena? And as any such fort, if to be built with saving of labour, may be placed on a cliff or promontory, thus sparing half its circuit, I will recall that in north-east Yorkshire two such sites have been tested by digging: Eston Nab, jutting out from Cleveland high above the vale of smoky Teesside, and Boltby Scar on the Hambleton Hills, looking down on the Vale of York. My reaction to Frank Elgee's pottery from Eston was to compare it with the sherds from the Heathery Burn Cave: as has since become clearer, seventh century B.C. At Boltby, which need not be all that different, George Willmot found a pair of fine gold basket ear-pendants, a thousand years older, laid sealed beneath his rampart. So would one pass, if this were the place and time, across the Vale to Huddersfield, and to the recent work at Almondbury by Dr. W. J. Varley. But here and now, these few words may perhaps suffice. We have still enough to excite us from new digging in the South.

Ivinghoe, Rainsborough, Leckhampton, Crickley Hill, and Blewburton close to the Thames on its spur of the Berkshire chalk, all have been showing, from recent excavation, that forts in the South start early. The seventh century is not too soon. Blewburton also has recalled to mind that a palisade-enclosure, not identical in circuit with the fort's, may be found preceding it. And such early forts are walled, the wall timber-laced in chalk or in rubble-filled stone. If their builders brought or learnt their methods from the Continent, in parallel with the Northerners, the source could be the Ardennes: continuation westwards of the Hunsrück and Eifel, where such building reached farthest down the Rhine from the Alpine foreland. The Hunsrück-Eifel culture inherited this, with much else, from the Urnfield, to pass, through the seventh century and sixth, into an Iron Age spreading from the Hallstatt. By then, these lands were linked with Iron Age Italy; from its own side of the Alps were brought the beaten-bronze situlas, so frequent in the sixth and fifth centuries on the Rhine, whence their rendering in pottery spread to Britain. And the forts, even if citadels still, could be now more often larger, as the social force of power over communities grew stronger with the resources of an economy using iron. The famous Heuneburg, over on the uppermost Danube, is just such a major citadel, with its timber-laced walling varied in part by a borrowing from the South: a stone-based wall built of mud-brick. Mud-brick, the material of the old Oriental urbanism, had come in beside masonry now in the 'Orientalising' process, which affected the culture of the Greeks through all this time of their westward enterprise. From Italy, and the coast about the Rhone, there came the trade with the Hallstatt world inland, which the Heuneburg attests. At Hallstatt itself, established earlier in the story, rather before 700, the citadel remains unknown to us, but it must underlie what is called the Rudolfsturm, the former small castle overlooking the cemetery and the way to the salt-mines which make the site's renown. Two centuries later, when it was largely superseded by the Dürrnberg salt works, still in Austria but more westerly, what dominated this was a hill-fort far larger, in the manner of the La Tène culture then about to arise. And Mediterranean urbanism, meanwhile, had acquired the strength to give its towns, its full community-sites, their embracing circuit of walls. At last the citizens dwelt inside, not down outside the stronghold; and the walled town, added to a citadel or taking the place of one, appeared just as in the East or Greece, in Italy and southernmost Gaul and Spain.

The problem then for the La Tène world, of the Celts beyond that urbanism, was how to match it in the forms of its own tradition, that of hill-forts traditionally citadels. Walling these at the size of towns, in timber-laced structure or in its 'Gallic wall' version, meant a huge social effort – quite frequently undertaken, as at Manching in Bavaria, but often in part commuted by fortifying a promontory instead of the whole circumference. Bavarian Kelheim illustrates this, and so does the Atlantic seaboard, in the 'cliff castle' promontory forts of Brittany and South-west Britain – to which those of Southern Ireland, despite their present lack of dating-evidence, surely should be added. But between the ocean coast and the Vosges or Rhine and regions east, the problem in Northern Gaul was met by the old alternative to walls: dump ramparts. Thence came the massive defences of Vieux-Reims, of Vieux-Châlons, and their like; and thence, by further enhancement, was devised the 'Fécamp' dump-ramparted model, with its very broad ditch, which discomforted Caesar. Britain, with little closely similar to that, has yet a big range of dump-ramparted forts: with ditches and ramparts multiple, or ditch between two ramparts, or single rampart often covering the line of an older timber-laced wall. And Hod Hill in Dorset, under Richmond's eye, showed that along the dump's crest there could still be a wall, or at least a flint parapet. It was the nearest to urbanism that hill-fort building could get. The exploring of all these forms of it has owed most, in his times, to Mortimer Wheeler. And with that salute, I end this introduction to 'The Iron Age and its Hill-forts': from fence, to wall, to dump.

BIBLIOGRAPHY

PARTS 1–2. PROLOGUE; FORT SITES AND SANCTITY

Gergovia

Brogan, Olwen, and Desforges, E. 1940. 'Gergovia', *Arch. J.*, 97, 1–36; my section, 6–8, figs. 2–3, pl. IIB.

Hawkes, Christopher. 1935. 'Fouilles à Gergovie' (introd. P. F. Fournier), *Revue archéologique* 6 sér., 5, 221–3, 227–30.

Features connoting sanctity

Piggott, S. 1968. *The Druids*, London (Thames & Hudson). Here especially 71 ff. and 80 ff.

Schwartz, K. 1962. Includes: 68, fig. 34, fort and shafts at Lossow (Middle Germany: Coblenz 1958 below, part 3) in longer study for which see Piggott 1968, giving ref. at 202.

Wheeler, R. E. M. 1943. *Maiden Castle, Dorset*, London, *Research Report, Soc. Antiquaries* 12. Here: 19–27, 72–9, 122–35.

PART 3. PROTECTION: COMMUNITY SITES AND HILL-TOPS
(*Neolithic to Middle Bronze Age*)

Near East, Aegean, Mediterranean, Peninsular

Blegen, C. W., Caskey, J. L., and Rawson, M. 1950–1. *Troy*, vols. I, II, Princeton, N. J., University Press (for University of Cincinnati Archaeological Expedition). See reviews by V. G. Childe 1951, 1952, *Antiquity* 25, 51; 26, 158; and Blegen 1964 (below).

Kenyon, K. M. 1960–5. *Excavations at Jericho*. 2 vols. Jerusalem (British School of Archaeology).

Mellaart, J. 1967. *Çatal Hüyük: a Neolithic town in Anatolia*, London (*New Aspects of Antiquity* series).

Sangmeister, E., and Schubart, H. 1965 onwards. 'Grabungen in der Kupferzeitlichen Befestigung von Zambujal/Portugal'. Serially in *Madrider Mitteilungen* 6, 8, 10. Heidelberg.

Savory, H. N. 1968. *Spain and Portugal*, London (Thames and Hudson). Here: 152–60, 165, 193–5.

Schubart, H. 1970. 'Die Kupferzeitliche Befestigung von Columbeira/Portugal.' *Madrider Mitteilungen* 11, 59–73. Heidelberg.

Theocharis, K. 1968. *Praktika 1968*: 24–30 (also 1962, 1963, 1966); shows that among Greek 'acropolis' sites with porched-hall 'megaron' houses, in Thessaly not only Dimini, but also Sesklo, had multiple-ditched defences. I owe this reference to Miss Chr. Soutinou.

Trunp, D. 1957–1963. Papers British School Rome 25 and 31, on the hill-settlement of La Starza at Ariano Irpino.

Whitehouse, Ruth. 1968. 'Settlement and Economy in Southern Italy', *Proc. Prehist. Soc.* 34, 332–67. Here: 344–6, 351–3, 354 ff.

Europe, South-eastern to West-central

Piggott, S. 1965. *Ancient Europe*, Edinburgh. Here: 52 f., 58–9, 68–9, 74 f., 85–7, 108–9, 121, 140, 161, 210; may be supplemented especially from the following:

Berciu, D. 1967. *Romania*, London (Thames and Hudson). Here: 49–59 ff., Middle and Late Neolithic (on Vădastra, cf. *Act. VII Congr. Internat. Sc. Pr. Pr.*, Prague 1966: 452–7); Bronze Age: 90–3, Monteoru; 97, Otomani; for Transylvania in general, see Popescu, D., as cited.

Driehaus, J. 1960. *Die Altheimer Gruppe und das Jungneolithikum in Mitteleuropa*. Mainz (Röm.-Germ. Zentral-Museum).

Ehrich, R. W., and Pleslová-Štiková, E. 1968. 'Homolka, an eneolithic site in Bohemia', Amer. School of Prehistoric Research, Peabody Mus., Harvard Univ., *Bulletin*, 24.

Filip, J. (ed.). 1966. *Investigations archéologiques en Tchécoslovaquie*, Prague, Académ. des Sciences. Here: 40 ff., 66, 72 ff., 83 ff., 122–6, 126–35, 270–7.

Foltiny, S. 1958 'Velemszentvid, ein urzeitliches Kulturzentrum in Mitteleuropa.' Vienna, *Veröff. d. Österreichischen Arbeitsgemeinschaft f. Ur- u. Frühgeschichte, III.*

Háyek, L. 1961. (On the fortified site of Barca, E. Slovakia) [Komm. für Aeneolithikum u. ält. Bronzezeit, Nitra (session of) 1958, 59 ff.

Kimmig, W. 1966. *Der Kirchberg von Reusten*. Stuttgart, Urkunden z. Vor- u. Frühgesch. Südwürttemberg-Hohenzollern Heft 2.

Lüning, J. 1968. 'Die Michelsberger Kultur.' 48. *Bericht der Röm.-Germanischen Kommission* (for 1967): 1–350, earthworks 113–19.

Mozsolics, A. 1957. (On Kosziderpadlás and other Middle Bronze Age sites' destruction), in *Acta Archaeologica Hungarica* 8: 131 ff., 141 ff., in course of a more widely-ranging study; hill-fort sites, as such, not yet dug in sufficient number to be treated here for Hungary in general.

Schmidt, R. R. 1945. *Die Burg Vučedol*. Zagreb, Croatian Archaeological National Museum.

France

Arnal, J. 1958. 'Die Struktur des französischen Neolithikums auf Grund neuester stratigraphischen Beobachtungen.' 37/8 *Bericht der Röm.-Germanischen Kommission* 1956–57, 1–90.

Bailloud, G. 1964. 'Le néolithique dans le bassin parisien', Paris, *Supplément II to Gallia Préhistoire*.

Bailloud, G. In preparation: full study of Fort-Harrouard (Eure-et-Loir).

Burnez, C., and Case, H. J. 1966. 'Les camps néolithiques des Matignons (Charente)', *Gallia Préhistoire* 9, 1; 131–245.

Giot, P. R. 1960. *Brittany*, London (Thames and Hudson). Here: 82–5, 209 n. 9, camp du Lizo and Croh-Collé.

Sandars, N. K. 1957. *Bronze Age Cultures in France*, Cambridge. Here: 24–36, 177, 244, Camp de Chassey; 33–7, 64–5 Fort-Harrouard.

Britain (*Neolithic and Beaker*)

(Smith, I. F.) 1965. *Windmill Hill and Avebury: Excavations by Alexander Keiller*, Oxford.

Bradley, R. 1970. 'The Excavation . . . at Belle Tout, East Sussex', *Proc. Prehist. Soc.*, 36, 312–79.

Comparative

Bellwood, P. 1970. 'Fortifications and Economy in Prehistoric New Zealand', *Proc. Prehist. Soc.*, 36, 56–95.

Shaw, C. T. 1970. 'Methods of Earthwork Building.' *Proc. Prehist. Soc.*, 36, 380–1.

PART 4. SETTLED FOLK AND CITADEL

Aegean: Middle to Latest Bronze Age

Blegen, C. W., Boulter, C. G., Caskey, J. L., and Rawson, M. 1954. *Troy*, vol. III; *Troy*, vol. IV, 1 and 2. Princeton (as here above, Part 3). See review by V. G. Childe 1954, *Antiquity*, 28–63, and review-article by (Sir) D. (L.) Page, 1959, 'The Historical Sack of Troy', *Antiquity*, 33, 25–31.

Blegen, C. W. 1964. *Troy and the Trojans*, London (Thames & Hudson).

Desborough, V. R. d'A. 1964. *The Last Mycenaeans and their Successors*, Oxford. See review-article, 'The Last Mycenaeans and the European Late Bronze Age', by N. (K.) Sandars, 1964, *Antiquity*, 38, 258–62.

Taylour, Lord W. 1964. *The Mycenaeans*, London (Thames & Hudson). Here: 89 ff., 139 ff., 166–78.

East-central European, Lausitz, Urnfield, Hallstatt

Berciu, D. 1967. *Romania*, London (Thames & Hudson). Here: 102 ff.

Bersu, G. 1945. *Das Wittnauer Horn im Kanton Aargau*. Basel: Monogr. Ur- u. Frühgeschichte der Schweiz IV.

Coblenz, W. 1958. 'Lausitz-cultyre forts in Middle Germany', *Ausgrabungen und Funde* (Berlin), 3, 227–8, figs. 45 (Lossow), 46.

Coblenz, W. 1970. 'Zur Frage der befestigten Siedlungen der Lausitzer Kultur.' *Act. VII. Congr. Internat. Sc. Pr. Pr.*, Prague 1966 (ed.) J. Filip, 1, 715–19. Illustrations here are from 717, *Abb.* 2, including Schafberg at Löbau and others.

Filip, J. (ed.). 1966. 'Investigations archéologiques en Tchécoslovaquie', Prague, Académ. des Sciences. Here: 137–68.

Piggott, S. 1965. *Ancient Europe*, Edinburgh. Here: 199, 199–207, 213, 14.

Spurný, V. 1954. 'Die Besiedlung von Hradisko bei Kroměříž. *Pamatky Archaeologicky* 45, 357 ff. (Pre-Lausitz primarily, Lausitz only afterwards).

Spurný, V. 1970. 'Zur Chronologie der frühen Phase der Lausitzer Kultur in Mähren', *Act. VII Congr. Internat. Sc. Pr. Pr.*, Prague 1966, (ed.) J. Filip, 1, 710–15.

PART 5. IRON AGE: CONTINENT AND BRITAIN

Germany, C., W., N.W.

Claus, M. 1958. 'Die Pipinsburg bei Osterode.' *Neue Ausgrabungen in Deutschland* (ed.) W. Krämer, 161–74, Berlin.

Dehn, W. 1939. 'Die Latènezeitliche Ringmauer von Preist, Kr. Bitburg,' *Germania*, 23, 23–6.

Neumann, G. 1961. 'Die Kelten in Thüringen,' *Bericht V. Internaz. Kongr. Vor- u. Frühgesch. Wissenschaften Hamburg 1958* (ed.) G. Bersu, 608–10, Berlin.

Peters, H. G. 1970. 'Ur- u. frühgeschichtliche Befestigungen zwischen Oberweser und Leine.' *Neue Ausgrabungen und Forschungen in Niedersachsen*, 5, 68–103.

Italy – S.W. Europe

Hencken, H. 1968. *Tarquinia and Etruscan Origins*, London (Thames & Hudson). Here: 20–1 with fig. 2.

Pallottino, M. 1970. 'L'Origine della Città di Roma', *Act. VII Congr. Internat. Sc. Pr. Pr.*, Prague 1966, (ed.), J. Filip, 2, 776–80.

Sandars, N. K. 1957. *Bronze Age Cultures in France*, Cambridge. Here: 283 ff., 337–41.

Savory, H. N. 1968. *Spain and Portugal*, London (Thames & Hudson). Here: 238–40, 248–59; and see below, Harbison, Hawkes 1971.

Middle Europe, France, Atlantic

Berciu, D. 1967. *Romania*, London (Thames & Hudson). Here: 125 ff., 136 ff.

Dehn, W. 1958. 'Die Heuneburg an der oberen Donau und ihre Wehranlagen.' *Neue Ausgrabungen in Deutschland* (ed.) W. Krämer, 127–45, Berlin.

Dehn, W. 1962. 'Aperçu sur les Oppida d'Allemagne à la fin de l'époque celtique', *Celticum III, Actes* 2. Colloque . . . Châteaumeillant 1961, *Supplt. Ogam*, 79–81, 329–86, Rennes.

Filip, J. (ed.). 1966. *Investigations archéologiques en Tchécoslavaquie*, Prague, Académ. des Sciences. Here: 176 ff., 182 ff., 189, 193–8.

Gallet de Santerre, H. 1965. 'Les civilisations classiques en Languedoc méditerranéen et Roussillon principalement d'après les fouilles d'Ensérune.' Le Rayonnement des civs. grecque et romaine sur les cultures périphériques, 8 *Congr. Internat. d'Archéologie Classique*, Paris, 1963, 625–8.

Giot, P. R., see pp. 155–160.

Harbison, P. 1971. Wooden and Stone, *Chevaux de frise* in Central and Western Europe, *Proc. Prehist. Soc.*, 37, 1, 195–225.

Hatt, J. J. 1970. *Celts and Gallo-Romans (Ancient Civilisations series)*, dir. J. Marcadé, Geneva. London: Barrie and Jenkins. Here: 82 ff., 101 ff., 126–31.

Hawkes, C. F. C. 1971. 'North-Western Castros: Excavation, Archaeology, and History', *Actas do II Congresso Nacional de Arqueologia*, 1970. Coimbra (Portugal): 283–6, pls. I–IV.

Hogg, A. H. A. 1969. 'A Sample of French Hill-forts', *Antiquity* 43, 260–73. See also *Gergovia* (Brogan and Desforges) above.

Joffroy, R. 1960. 'L'Oppidum de Vix et la civ. hallstattienne finale dans l'Est de la France', Paris, *Publs. de l'Univ. de Dijon* 20. Here: Mont-Lassois (Vix) hill-fort 15–35, others 161–8.

Kimmig, W. 1968. 'Die Heuneburg an der oberen Donau.' Führer (guide, of 128 pp.) zu vor- und frühgeschichtlichen Denkmälern in Württemberg und Hohenzollern: Heft 1.

Krämer, W. 1958. 'Manching, ein vindelikisches Oppidum an der Donau.' *Neue Ausgrabungen in Deutschland* (ed.) W. Krämer, 175–202, comparing others including Kelheim.

Krämer, W. 1960. 'The *Oppidum* of Manching', *Antiquity*, 34, 191–200.

Krämer, W. 1962. 'Manching II', *Germania* 40, 2, 297–317.

Müller-Beck, H., and Ettlinger, E. 1964. 'Die Besiedlung der Engehalbinsel in Bern . . .' 43–44 *Bericht der Römisch-Germanischen Kommission* 1962–63, 107–153.

Müller-Beck, H. 1965. 'Die Erforschung der Engehalbinsel in Bern bis zum Jahre 1965.' *Jahrbuch des Bernischen Historischen Museums* 43–4, 375–400, for 1961–2, see 41–2, 488–503.

O'Kelly, M. J. 1952. 'Three Promontory Forts in Co. Cork', *Proc. Royal Irish Acad.*, 55, C, 25–59.

Savory, H. N. 1968. As above.

Wheeler, R. E. M., and Richardson, K. M. 1957. *Hill-forts of Northern France*, London, *Research Rep. Soc. Antiq.* 19: includes gazetteer and bibliography 102–58, and Appendix on Muri Gallici by M. A. Cotton 159–225.

Britain: North, and Islands (selection only)

Feachem, R. W. 1966. 'The Hill-forts of Northern Britain', *The Iron Age in Northern Britain* (ed. A. L. F. Rivet), 59–88, Edinburgh, University Press.

Hamilton, J. R. C. 1966. 'Forts, Brochs and Wheel-houses in Northern Scotland,' same work as last, 111–20.

Hamilton, J. R. C. 1968a. 'Iron Age Forts and Epic Literature', *Antiquity*, 42, 103–8.

Hamilton, J. R. C. 1968b. *Excavations at Clickhimin, Shetland*, Edinburgh Ministry of Works Archaeo. Reports, 6. Here: 29 ff., 34 ff., 45–68, 97–112.

Hamilton, J. R. C. 1970. 'The Origin and Development of Iron Age Forts in Western Britain', *Act. VII Congr. Internat. Sc. Pr. Pr.*, Prague 1966 (ed.) J. Filip, 2, 846–9.

Jobey, G. 1966. 'A Field Survey in Northumberland.' Same work as Feachem above, 89–109.

MacKie, E. W. 1965. 'Brochs and the Hebridean Iron Age', *Antiquity*, 39, 266–78.

(MacKie, E. W.) 1969. 'Dun Lagaidh' (Argyllshire, Scotland), *Current Archaeology*, 2, 1 (no. 12, January), 2–13.

(Mackie, E.) 1967. 'Dun Ardtreck' (Isle of Skye), 'Dun Mor Vaul' (Tiree), *Current Archaeology*, 1, 2 (no. 2, May), 27–30.

Britain: Yorkshire (with Derbyshire)

Elgee, F. 1930. *Early Man in North-East Yorkshire*, Gloucester (John Bellows). Here: Eston Nab 152–6; Boltby Scar 157, and see below.

Elgee, F., and H. W. 1932. *Yorkshire*, London (Methuen's *County Archaeologies*). Here: 117–20 and gazetteers.

Macdonell (ed.). 1965. 'A History of the Helmsley and Rievaulx District', York (Stonegate Press), *Excavations at Boltby Scar* by G. F. Willmot (I owe the reference to Dr. I. H. Longworth).

Thompson, F. H. 1970. 'The Iron Age in the Southern Pennines of England', *Act. VII Congr. Internat. Sc. Pr. Pr.*, Prague 1966 (ed.) J. Filip, 2, 849–52 (for South Yorkshire and Derbyshire, with the Mam Tor hill-fort).

Varley, W. J. In preparation: report on his excavations (concluded 1971) at Castle Hill, Almondbury, near Huddersfield.

Wheeler, Sir (R. E.) M. 1954. 'The Stanwick Fortifications, Yorkshire', London, *Research Rep. Soc. Antiq.* 17.

Britain: England, various
(see otherwise Cunliffe, pp. 53–69)

Avery, M., and others. 1967. 'Rainsborough, Northants: Excavations 1961–5', *Proc. Prehist. Soc.*, 33, 207–306.

Cruso Hencken, T. 1938, 'The Excavation of the Iron Age Camp on Bredon Hill, Gloucestershire, 1935–37', *Arch. J.* 95, 1–111 (see Stanford, pp. 41–52).

Dixon, P. W., and Haldane, J. W. 1970. *Crickley Hill, Glos., Excavations*, 1969 (p. 10): 1–5, report, with full-page figs. 1–5; 1970 (p.14): 1–7, report with full-page figs. 1–7, 8–11 (Haldane) report on soil samples. Cheltenham (R. Savage, Gloucs. Coll. of Technology, Pittville).

(Harding, D. W.) 1967. 'Blewburton' (hill-fort in Berkshire). *Current Archaeology*, 1, 4 (no. 4, September), 83–5.

Hawkes, C. F. C. in Hawkes-Myres-Stevens: 1930. *Saint Catharine's Hill, Winchester*, part 1, the Early Iron Age: 11–66, excavation (of entrance 58–64; period B forms gap between A and C–D); 67–71, timber in Iron Age Fort-works generally; 72–84, development of hill-forts and their entrances, British and Continental, as known to that date.

Hermon, S. 1969. *Leckhampton Hill, Glos., Excavations*, 1969 (8), 1–6 report, 2 figs.

Richmond, Sir Ian, and others. 1968. *Hod Hill, II (Excavations . . . 1951–58 . . .)*, London, British Museum. On dump rampart (secondary, over primary wall) note flints restored by Richmond as parapet.

General

Hawkes, C. F. C., in Hawkes-Myres-Stevens. 1930. *Saint Catharine's Hill, Winchester*, part 1, the Early Iron Age: 140–61, 'The Earliest Iron Age Culture of Britain', surveyed in relation to the Continental evidence (to compare with the present volume, over the forty years between).

Hawkes, C. F. C. 1965. 'The Celts': Report on the study of their culture and their Mediterranean relations, 1942–1962. Le Rayonnement des civilisations grecque et romaine sur les cultures périphériques, 8. *Congr. Internat. d'Archéol. class.*, Paris, 1963, 61–76, bibliography 76–9.

UNFINISHED HILL-FORTS

By R. W. Feachem

The purpose of this paper is to summarize what can be discovered from studying some of the unfinished hill-forts which were abandoned before completion at a great many sites in Britain during the Iron Age. The examples cited vary very much in size and quite clearly in purpose, incidentally furnishing a reminder of the difficulties presented by nomenclature: for all except one which was discovered very recently have been published under the name of hill-fort.

The illustrations are reproduced from documents held by the Ordnance Survey with the sanction of the Controller of Her Majesty's Stationery Office, Crown copyright reserved.

INTRODUCTION

Twenty-one years ago Sir Mortimer carried out excavations at the fort on Bindon Hill, Dorset (Wheeler, 1953), where there are incomplete defences. The excavation report includes a reference to Piggott's account of Ladle Hill, Hampshire (Piggott, S., 1931) in which attention was first drawn to the nature and value of the information which can be derived from examining unfinished hill-forts and allied structures. Since Piggott's pioneering effort the study of native hill-forts in general has developed massively all over the country, both in the course of the broad surveys such as are carried out by the Ordnance Survey and the Royal Commissions and in the more minute investigations by excavators. The number of recorded unfinished works is now substantial – but as yet we know of nothing to exceed the spectacular incompleteness of Ladle Hill, although there are others which are equally informative.

Whether by surface observation or by excavation the study of unfinished works is of service in that it can extend our knowledge of methods of design and construction beyond the limits ascertainable from completed structures. In the first place the unfinished works may exhibit surviving examples of the devices used initially by the designers of forts when they marked out the lines they judged suitable for their purposes – devices which would in many cases have been destroyed had work progressed. In the second place the unfinished works provide sources of information about some of the constructional phases of which all traces would have been progressively destroyed had the work been completed. The main part of this study, therefore, comprises descriptions of the several kinds of markers which have been identified both on the surface and by excavation, and of accounts of selected unfinished works in which examples of passing constructional phases or techniques occur.

At the same time a study of unfinished hill-forts naturally gives rise to a certain amount of speculation about the reasons behind the cessation of work. And although there need be no doubt that the practical aspects of this subject overshadow the theoretical – although in general unfinished works are more valuable for adding to our knowledge of methods of design and construction than for contributing to the interpretation of the effects of historical events – it is nevertheless appropriate to consider briefly some of the possible causes of incompleteness in defences before proceeding to the material aspects of the matter.

Explanations of the state of incompleteness

One obvious category of possible causes is that of the pre- and proto-historic climacterics which affected Britain during the Iron Age. Conspicuous among these were the arrival of the Romans, the expansion of the Catuvellauni, the arrival of refugees from Caesar's campaigns in Gaul, the changes in society which were brought about from time to time in the earlier centuries of the Iron Age. Any or all of these and other disturbances could have resulted in programmes of construction work some of which remained incomplete when their originators were overtaken by events.

But the stresses due to such happenings as these need not have constituted the sole cause of incompleteness: hill-forts finished or unfinished were surely not abandoned only as a result of human aggressions. We should probably conclude that reasons such as epidemic diseases, the local malfunction of husbandry or actual famine, or a change in political or religious hegemony or in economic conditions should also be taken into consideration in this context. Comparison can be made with Deserted Medieval Villages. There are numerous reasons for the hundreds of examples of desertion which occur up and down the country, quite apart from violence. In the Iron Age as in later times stability of conditions of settlement may never have endured for very long.

In certain particular instances the incomplete state may have resulted from the inability of the work force to complete the amount of hewing of solid rock which the design of the hill-fort demanded. Limited examples of unquarried bosses of rock remaining in the ditches of what can be recognised as completed hill-forts are known, and it is reasonable to suppose that on occasion work had to be abandoned early on for this reason.

MARKERS

(a) The first constructional stage

There is plenty of evidence that designers of hill-forts indicated with markers the courses they thought the defences ought to take. The principal recognised forms of marker are a bank unaccompanied by a ditch, a ditch unaccompanied by a bank, and a bank and ditch together. The purpose of the marker was to enable construction workers to hold to the proper course without having to keep stopping to take stock. The marker is always of very much smaller proportions than the full-scale work, but is nevertheless often so robust and so well laid out that the question arises – in what way would making a marker along a desired line without the assistance of a guideline have been any less difficult than making a full-scale defence would have been under similar conditions – that is, in the absence of a marker? Once the work gangs got their heads down and began to dig they would find it in no degree easier to construct a marker along the right course than to construct full-scale works, unless some kind of indicator had been laid down beforehand.

It can therefore be suggested that the marker itself, when it was considered necessary, was a second stage in the work; that the first stage in constructing defences must have been marking them out rapidly and temporarily in the course of a visual appreciation of the ground by experts. As these experienced men went along deciding on the proper course to be followed, attendants would mark this by lightweight primary indicators such as sticks, stones, gravel or a woven strand. By this means the proposed course could be marked rapidly and efficiently as soon as decided.

Once the lines to be followed had been so marked the next stage could be either the construction of the full-scale defences themselves or the confirming and making permanent of the chosen line by a durable marker – a process which thus appears as an interim stage which was not obligatory, but depended upon the speed at which the available labour force could be expected to do the work. We can assume that where permanent markers do exist completion was not expected to be possible within the survival period of the lightweight primary indicators, and that where markers do not exist the work was expected to be done within that period.

In some unfinished forts the absence of a marker between the as yet unconnected stretches of rampart and ditch may be due to the presence of a natural feature acting as a guide, or to a formerly-existing marking having been ploughed away; but in other examples these explanations cannot be applied, and it can be concluded that there never was a permanent marker, that the defences were constructed on lines defined only by lightweight primary indicators. Traces of these are of course hard to find, but it is just possible that evidence of them may have been found at the hill-fort on Bredon Hill, Worcestershire. In the part of the excavation report devoted to the inner rampart (Hencken, 1938, 8) it is recorded that 'the line of the rampart may have been first marked out by a row of stakes, for traces of these markers were found in the front of two of the cuttings.' That thin stakes should have been driven in at intervals to mark the chosen line is clearly perfectly possible.

With regard to the supposed 'experts' concerned with laying out lines of defence, it is distinctly possible that in the earlier Iron Age as in the later and in early Medieval times professional designers of defensive works and of buildings occupied a place in society (Graham, 1950, 71; Ross, 1970, 87). Their advice was available to chiefs or groups wishing to build or extend defences in the most effective manner. The presence of such a professional class accounts for the existence over wide areas of defences or buildings constructed in one manner, or of features such as entrances being erected in accordance with one principle. Their influence can doubtless be seen in cases of elaborate planning, such as Maiden Castle, Dorset (Wheeler, 1943, 45), and in instances where subtleties appear in the lay-out of simpler works. At St. Catharine's Hill, Hampshire, for example, Hawkes has shown that the single line had been shrewdly drawn: 'the earthwork was evidently planned to take the line from which the contours allow most control of the ground beneath. Its builders clearly knew and guarded against the danger of 'dead ground' (Hawkes, 1930, 12). That, on occasion, it was nevertheless necessary to reconsider the positioning of defences is suggested in the plan of Casterley Camp, Wiltshire, which is discussed below.

Reference has been made to the relation between the speed at which construction work could be done and the nature of markers. The pace naturally depended on the labour force, the tools and the materials available. The speed at which a substantial earthen bank can be built with the vigorous use of simple tools by an enthusiastic work force has been recorded by Shaw (1970), and this can be compared with Caesar's account of the activities of the Nervii of Gallia Belgica during their seige of the winter quarters near Namur defended by Quintus T. Cicero:

> 'The Nervii encompassed the station with a rampart nine feet high and a trench 15 feet wide . . . but having no supply of tools suitable for the purpose they cut sods round with swords and lifted out earth with hands or cloaks. In less than three hours they completed an intrenchment 15 miles in circumference' (Edwards, 1966, 289).

It is remarkable that, while almost every other item pertaining to the everyday life of the pagan Celts is mentioned in the Classics hardly any reference to hill-forts and fort-building has been recorded. Caesar makes several general references to oppida in Gaul; in his account of the Celts of Galatia, on the Anatolian plain, Livy refers briefly to the fact that they fortify hill-tops (Rivet, 1962, 13); Tacitus includes such meagre observations as the use by the Iceni of a 'rustic embankment', and by Caratacus of 'stones composing a sort of rampart' (Jackson, 1963, 357, 363). These observations are of little value in the present context, and in the absence of information about the speed at which hill-forts were built it must only be assumed that the work was done as quickly as all the relevant factors permitted.

(b) Marker banks and ditches

The marker bank unaccompanied by a ditch has been recorded both on the surface and in the course of excavation, on the surface in cases where work on defences was stopped before completion, and during excavation in cases where the completed rampart submerged and so preserved the marker bank. Both circumstances occur at Bindon Hill (Wheeler, 1953), where the surface example, which survives as a low, turf-covered bank 2.0 m. wide, was originally laid down in preparation for the construction in the western part of the hill-fort of a linear bank and ditch defence system which was never completed. The submerged example at Bindon Hill was described as 'a small bank, not more than a foot high, of chalk rubble and turves. The feature was constant through our cuttings and presumably represents a setting-out bank.'

On Bindon Hill the banks marking out the fort and the linear work together cover a distance of 2.6 km., and would require several tons of aggregate. No quarrying or scraping was recorded near either bank, and it must be assumed that, as in the case of a wall or rampart unaccompanied by a quarry ditch, material for the banks must have been brought from convenient distant sources. The 'heaped line of large flints' found by Sir Mortimer at the forward foot of the innermost rampart at the Camp du Canada, Fécamp, Seine Maritime (Wheeler and Richardson, 1957, 62, pl. XXIX) was probably such a marker bank the material for which had been collected and brought to the site.

The position of the marker in relation to the proposed defences varies, as is demonstrated even by the two marker banks at Bindon Hill. The submerged bank was situated 3.0 m. in from the inner lip of the ditch immediately in front of and parallel to a line of posts which was originally intended to sustain the rear of the rampart but which, in the event, supported the front. In contrast, work had started on the linear defence with the ditch being dug as close as possible outside the marker bank, so that had the work been completed the marker bank would have been submerged beneath the front of the rampart.

The marker ditch unaccompanied by a bank is usually shallow, little more than 1.0 m. in width, with the spoil disposed on one or both sides so as to be barely recognisable if at all. While examples may survive in southern Britain the most numerous instances have been recorded in the permanent pastures of the north, such as Hamildean Hill, Peeblesshire (RCHM(Scot), 1967, 111, fig. 100).

The marker bank and ditch together are well illustrated at Ladle Hill, where bank and ditch survive to a width of 3.0 m., the ditch 0.3 m. in depth and the bank 0.3 m. in height. Work on digging the fort ditch had begun by quarrying away the marker ditch and the ground immediately outside it, so that had action not been suspended all traces of the marker ditch would have been removed and all evidence for its former existence would have disappeared. The bank would have survived submerged if the rampart had been of dump construction. Sir Mortimer found a marker bank of turf in this position beneath the forward foot of the innermost western rampart at Maiden Castle (Wheeler, 1943, pl. IX), and another, of clay, at the fort Le Châtellier at Duclair, Seine Maritime (Wheeler and Richardson, 1957, 77). It is of course impossible to tell now whether or not these had originally been accompanied by a ditch.

At Stanwick, in the north riding of Yorkshire, Sir Mortimer found that the defences of the second and third structural phases included ramparts of which the rear or inner feet were defined by marker banks with internal ditches (Wheeler, 1954, 9, 14). It was here, too, that the plan for a southern entrance was abandoned before completion, and an attempt was made to render the gateless gap in the rampart less vulnerable by the hasty removal of the causeway which had been left opposite to it in the ditch.

The effort of making permanent markers was evidently considerable, but as excavations have shown it was not wasted in the many cases in which the marker banks and ditches were eventually incorporated into their full-scale successors. Superficial observations might suggest that the kind of marker selected at any given site would depend on the nature of the subsoil, and indeed this may often have been the case. At Durn Hill, Banffshire, however, as described below, both marker ditch and marker bank are found on the same rocky hill where, *ceteris paribus*, only marker banks might have been expected.

(c) Existing natural or artificial features used as markers

Natural features such as the well-defined rims of summit plateaux or the clear-cut margins of ridges were on occasion used as markers, obviating the need for artificial markers. We should probably attribute some examples of unmarked gaps in incomplete defences to this cause rather than to the obliteration of a former marker or lightweight primary indicator.

Artificial features, too, could on occasion be used as markers. At Ladle Hill, for example, part of an existing linear earthwork was used to mark almost half the perimeter of the proposed hill-fort, the rest being defined by a marker bank and ditch. Palisade trenches, again, were often used as guidelines for the defences which were to supersede them as, for example, at Braidwood, Midlothian, described below. The surface appearance of a palisade trench is often by no means dissimilar to that of an unaccompanied marker ditch. At Castle Knowe, Midlothian, described below, an example of each survives on the surface and there is no doubt about which is which; but in some cases where only one appears excavation may be required to establish its identity.

CONSTRUCTIONAL PHASES

Unfinished forts are of two kinds – those in which the initial, the only structural, phase was never completed, and those in which attempts to provide additional strength for existing defences were abandoned unfinished. Three degrees of incompleteness can be distinguished. 1, the lines the projected defences were to take are marked out but little or no construction work has begun; 2, construction of defences has started but has not progressed very far, so that ephemeral constructional expedients and stages have survived which, had the work been completed, would have ceased to exist or have been hidden from sight; and 3, the defences are close to completion, and in their time-worn state now differ little in outward appearance from completed work of a similar age.

The earlier stages of construction of a hill-fort must have been accompanied by an apparent disorder comparable to that seen on road works or building sites today. But then, as now, as work progressed the foundations were hidden from sight, the material held in disorderly dumps was used, and by completion all was in good order. Where progress was arrested before completion, however, the unfinished work can now provide a view of some otherwise unrecorded aspects of what went on between marking out and completion.

Ladle Hill

Nowhere is this more strikingly demonstrated than at Ladle Hill (fig. 2). Piggott's account (1931) is so familiar that the briefest recapitulation of the more significant items will serve here. When work was abandoned the material from which the rampart was to have been constructed was being quarried from the ditch the inner lip of which was on the line of the marker ditch. First the turf, topsoil and chalk rubble were barrowed back into the interior and formed into dumps far enough away to leave the site of the proposed rampart clear. Then, as the ditch grew deeper, solid blocks of chalk suitable for forming the foundations, faces and core of the rampart were hewn out, and building was started on the berm left for the purpose between the inner lip of the ditch and the dumps. It was evidently the intention of the builders to construct the rampart and then cap it or back it with the soft material from the dumps. Had this task been completed all traces of the dumps would have been removed, and the marker ditch would have been entirely dug away, while the marker bank would have been submerged if the rampart was of dump construction or removed if there was to have been a berm. In the event, the dumps had hardly been disturbed when work was stopped.

Ladle Hill also exhibits evidence of gang work, showing how the labour force was divided to start work at several different points round the perimeter including the entrances. Gaps up to 24.0 m. wide still remained untouched when work stopped. Gang work is apparent in all unfinished hill-forts where construction of full-scale defences has actually started, and it may still be detectable in the uneven profiles of ditches and ramparts in forts which at first glance appear to be complete.

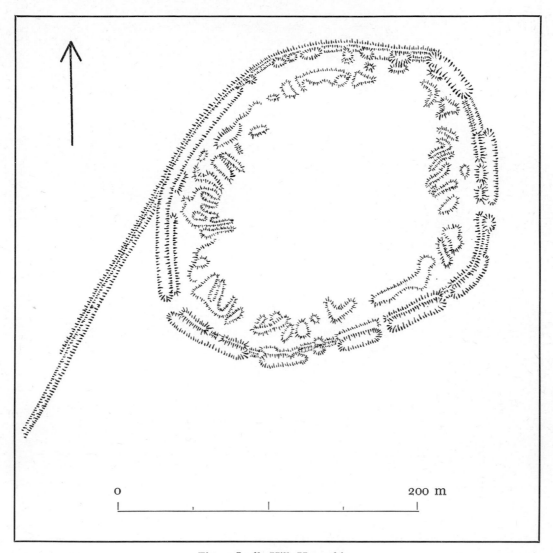

Fig. 2. Ladle Hill, Hampshire.

Elworthy Barrows

This unfinished fort (OS 1:2500, ST 0633/0733) reveals another method of reserving material before the time came for preparing the foundations of a rampart (fig. 3). On the north of the fort, where construction work was less advanced than elsewhere round the perimeter, material from the still rather slight quarry ditches is piled up well back from but parallel to the inner lip, leaving the site for the rampart clear. We

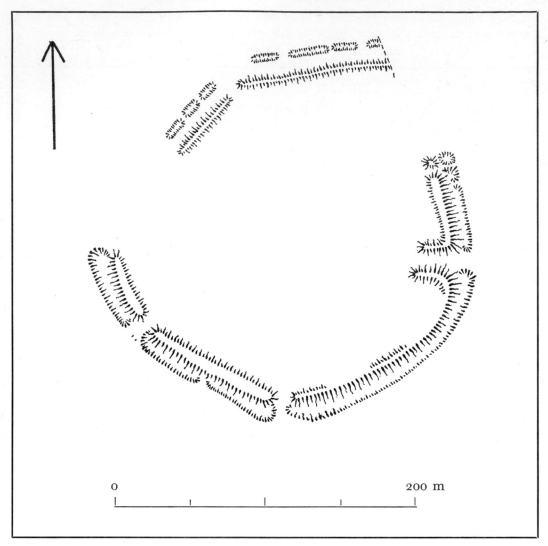

Fig. 3. Elworthy Barrows, Somerset.

could suppose that, as at Ladle Hill, the builders expected to reach more solid material as their ditch grew deeper, and had reserved for later use the softer material from on and near the surface. The difference would simply be that where the Ladle Hill gangs spread their dumps deep into the interior the Elworthy Barrows teams preferred to align them parallel to the ditch. But it may be considered more probable that at Elworthy Barrows the material was being dumped at the estimated rear of a proposed rampart of dump construction, with the intention of working forward from the growing pile as more material came from the ditch. This might indeed seem the obvious way to plan the construction of a dump rampart from a quarry ditch – and it was doubtless the method used in many cases. But that this was not necessarily the way, that an alternative method was practised too, was proved at St. Catharine's Hill, where one section through the rampart revealed that the first of seven recognisable successive component dumps was deposited immediately behind the inner lip of the quarry ditch (Hawkes, 1930, 15).

Evidence of gang work is plentiful at Elworthy Barrows. No traces of a marker appear in the spaces between the stretches of partly completed work, but as all the gaps have been ploughed there is no significance in their absence.

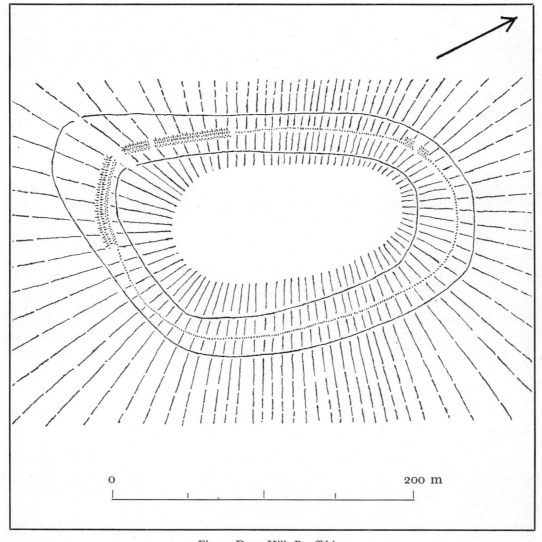

0   200 m

Fig. 4. Durn Hill, Banffshire.

27

Durn Hill

At each of the examples of markers so far cited only one kind of marker occurs at each site – the bank at Bindon Hill, the ditch at Hamildean Hill, the bank and ditch together at Ladle Hill. Where markers of different kinds occur together they usually indicate different periods of work. A striking example of an unfinished hill-fort exhibiting two kinds of markers occurs on Durn Hill, Banffshire (Yeats, 1884, 44–5), a gently rounded hill of white quartzite known as Durn Hill marble (Read, 1948, 21) clothed with sparse heather and shallow peat (fig. 4). The outermost and the innermost of three lines of markers are marker ditches with slight traces of spoil on their outer lips. The medial line, however, is a marker bank formed from gathered stones. Construction work, in which there is evidence of gangs, has started only on the medial line.

The occurrence here of the two marking techniques probably signifies the former existence of two separate constructional projects. First, the scheme which reached only the stage of marking out with ditches, and second the plan represented by the marker bank which is situated between, but not constantly equidistant from, the marker ditches. The latter project was barely begun before being abandoned.

In the course of the short stretches of work on the medial line it can be observed that the larger blocks of quartzite were thrown uphill as material from which a rampart would be built, while the moderate amount of small spoil was cast downhill to form a counterscarp bank.

Little Conval

At Durn Hill the embryo rampart was aligned on the marker bank. The relationship between the alignments of marker and proposed defence are seen again at the unfinished fort on Little Conval, Banffshire (Feachem, 1963, 110–111), where two lines of defence were marked out with ditches, as at the postulated earlier phases at Durn Hill (fig. 4). The marker ditches were hewn through the sparse topsoil into the uppermost layer of rock, the spoil being dispersed downhill.

Construction of permanent defences began on the inner line, on either side of an entrance. Stones probably gathered from the hill were heaped over the marker ditch, utterly obliterating it. In due course the stones would presumably have been formed into a rampart, but when work stopped no actual building had begun. Some idea of the manner in which the work would probably have progressed can, however, be seen at another unfinished fort not far away.

Cnoc an Duin

This unfinished fort occupies a promontory at the west end of a ridge of this name which overlooks the left bank of the Strathrory river, in Ross and Cromarty (Feachem, 1963, 149). The line to be followed by the proposed inner defence, a stone rampart, was clearly indicated by the well-defined margin of the promontory which forms a natural marker (fig. 5). When construction work ceased a bank of stones about 3.0 m. wide had been piled up along a little under half the perimeter of the proposed fort. On the west, where a start had been made on actually building the wall or rampart on either side of an entrance, there remains a continuous line of built outer face 53.4 m. in length, the lowest course of which runs across the entrance to form a doorstep. The

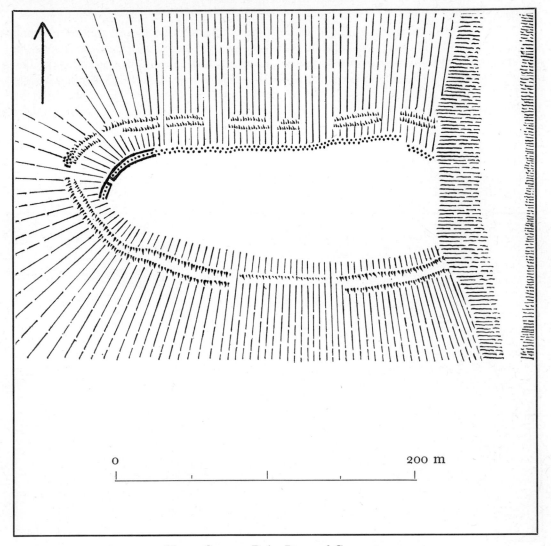

Fig. 5. Cnoc an Duin, Ross and Cromarty.

parallel inner face is interrupted at the entrance by a gap 1.8 m. wide. On the north side of the entrance the built faces of the wall, now collapsed inwards over the core, reach eight courses in height, but on the south side, as far as their termination, only two courses.

From these remains and those on Little Conval it would appear that walls of this kind were built by first gathering a certain amount of stones along the chosen line, then building the foundations of the wall-faces, and finally gathering or quarrying more stones to increase the height of the faces and the core to the desired limit.

29

Castle Knowe

An important example of the juxtaposition of marker ditch and palisade trench occurs on Castle Knowe, Midlothian (OS 1:2500, NT 2264/2364), an eminence on the Pentland Hills which overlooks Castle Law hill-fort (Feachem, 1965, 195). The first occupation of Castle Knowe comprised a settlement of several timber houses within a single palisade. Rig-and-furrow and modern ploughing have obscured or obliterated all but a short stretch of the palisade trench and all but three of the houses (fig. 6).

A second constructional and perhaps occupational phase is represented by a marker trench and several sections of an unfinished rampart with external quarry ditch, aligned some 5.0 m. outside the palisade. Castle Knowe thus furnishes a rare opportunity of seeing the surface traces of marker ditch and palisade trench together.

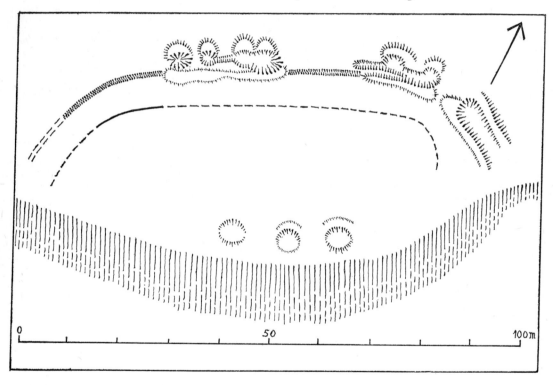

Fig. 6. Castle Knowe, Midlothian.

Castell Odo

While unfinished circuits of palisades are, of course, just as possible as unfinished markers or full-scale defences, surface traces alone are not reliable. Perhaps as good an example of this as any was experienced at Hayhope Knowe, Roxburghshire (Piggott, C. M., 1949), where twin palisades which appeared on the surface to be intermittent were shown in excavation to be continuous. What may, however, have been an example of a palisade which was abandoned before completion in favour of a more robust kind of defence was revealed in excavation at Castell Odo, Caernarvonshire (Alcock, 1960, 88–90, 109–12), beneath a later rampart.

Butser Hill

Promontory forts, too, include unfinished examples among their number. Several different kinds of structure are included in this classification. The first definition of the word which may spring to mind is the dictionary definition – a point of high land jutting out into the sea. As used in connection with Iron Age hill-forts, however, it is a commonplace that the promontory need not necessarily have any water other than a river, a stream or a lake at its foot if, indeed, it has any at all.

At one extreme of the class of promontory forts is the kind which has a complete defensive perimeter and is situated on the nose of a ridge or a promontory, usually an inland rather than a coastal feature. Although the circuit of the defences is complete and continuous the hill-fort can be approached with ease only from one direction, the spine of the ridge or the neck of the promontory, as for example at Eggardon Hill, Dorset (RCHM(Eng) 1952, 13).

At the other extreme are the coastal works known as cliff castles, such as Gurnard's Head, Cornwall (Gordon, 1940), which occur, amongst other places, along the south-western coasts of Britain and in Brittany. The single or multiple lines of defence run from cliff to cliff to isolate the promontory from approach from the land. Their effectiveness is witnessed by Caesar's comment on examples he encountered in Brittany:

'The positions of the strongholds were generally of one kind. They were set at the end of tongues and promontories, so as to allow no approach on foot, when the tide had rushed in from the sea – which regularly happens every 12 hours – nor in ships, because when the tide ebbed again the ships would be damaged in shoal water. Both circumstances, therefore, hindered the assault of the strongholds' (Edwards, 1966, 153).

The unfinished promontory forts discussed here fall between these two extremes, combining characteristics of both. For they comprise single or multiple lines of defence which cross from one side to the other of an inland promontory or the spine of a ridge to block the easiest line of approach. Now while these defences may be very strong, the whole of the rest of the perimeter of the summit plateau of the promontory or the margin of the ridge-top is apparently defenceless from approach from below. The question arises, what measures were taken to discourage access to the interior of the promontory fort from all directions except what might be termed the front gate? Such promontory and ridge forts, many with dwellings inside them, are commonplace, and clearly it is not enough to account for their largely defenceless state by proposing that 'the natural steep slope acted as a defence' unless the steepness is very real. Natural slopes may considerably protect, but are not enough by themselves. The problem remains to be solved.

The promontory fort on Butser Hill, Hampshire (Piggott, S., 1930) illustrates the point. The perimeter of the summit plateau measures about 3 kilometres in length. Although certain stretches of the flanks of the hill fall comparatively steeply, though by no means precipitously, the plateau can be approached with ease up gentle slopes from most directions. There are spur-dykes and cross-ridge roads at various points, but these

31

would all seem to belong to periods when the ground was farmed. The only recognisable Iron Age defensive work is the barrier to approach from the south-west.

This level approach from Hillhampton Down is blocked by a rampart and ditch some 300 m. in length which cross the neck between the heads of two steep coombs. The rampart and ditch are unfinished: they exhibit gang work in their irregular profiles and sinuous outlines, and they are separated over about half their length by a berm up to 5 m. wide which recalls the constructional method employed in the linear defence at Bindon Hill. There is one original gap through which an ancient ridgeway runs.

Chillerton Down

A comparable example, in a mutilated condition, survives on Chillerton Down, Isle of Wight (OS 1:2500, SZ 4783/4883). An incomplete defence comprising a straight rampart and ditch crosses part of the way between the opposite sides of a broad promontory, but no traces of any other artificial work can be detected round the rest of the spur, a distance of 1.6 kilometres.

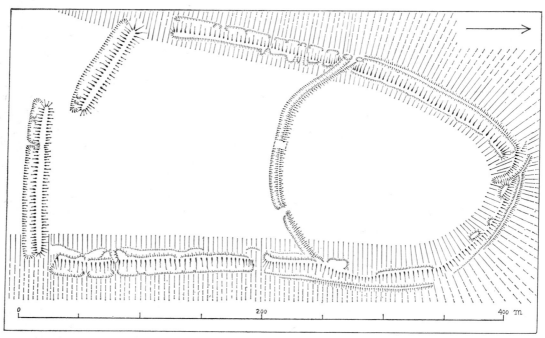

Fig. 7. Winklebury, Wiltshire.

Winklebury Hill

At Butser Hill the defence work forms an arc between the heads of two ravines, while at Chillerton Down the comparable rampart and ditch run straight across the saddle. The spectacular remains of unfinished earthworks on Winklebury Hill, Wiltshire (OS 1:2500, ST 9521; and fig. 7) appear to represent three unfinished structural phases or plans, the first a promontory work in the form of straight stretches of rampart and ditch crossing the broad neck of the promontory. The rampart is uniform in neither height nor profile, and the ditch exhibits traces of gang work, as if construction had ceased not very long before completion. The ends of rampart and ditch are set askew to each other at the entrance, but not so as to overlap.

In the second phase an attempt was made to incorporate the straight rampart and ditch into a hill-fort shaped like an elongated D – to create, that is, complete defences round the whole of the promontory in the manner already mentioned as being represented by Eggardon Hill. But this project, too, was abandoned before completion. The awkward joints at either end of the first-period defences were not tackled, and the new rampart had hardly reached half the height of the old when work stopped. Gaps in the new defences, evidence of gang work along its entire length, dumps of material lying untidily behind certain sectors of the rampart – all these testify to the incompleteness of phase two.

Lastly, an attempt was made to construct a much smaller, almost circular enclosure at the tip of the promontory, incorporating the north part of the second-phase work. The relationship between the work of the second and third periods is demonstrated most clearly on the west, where the later rampart overrides the earlier and the later ditch cuts through the earlier rampart to merge with the earlier ditch. North from this point of junction, and from the corresponding point on the east, the ditch is accompanied by a counterscarp bank. There are two entrances to the unfinished third-phase work; one, on the south-east, the other on the north. The defences are set slightly askew at the former which is situated in the entirely new sector of the phase three work. The northern entrance may well have been planned during the second phase, to give access to water in the valley below as in the case of certain Belgic hill-forts. This entrance is now occupied by a farm track which rises up a well-marked ascent from the north-west, runs through the interior of the third-period work and out over its defences at a point some 30 m. west of the south entrance.

Caster Cliff

In the examples cited so far the initial, the only structural, phase of any given period was abandoned before completion. Another important category of unfinished works is characterised by attempts to supersede or to reinforce existing defences by stronger works. At Caster Cliff, Lancashire (Forde-Johnston, 1962, 28), for example, what was probably originally a rubble-filled, stone-faced rampart (without a ditch) was to be superseded by ramparts and ditches. The rampart now appears as a very low, stony bank measuring about 7 m. in width and having a definite entrance on the west and a probable one on the east. Work on the new defences was begun outside the original rampart on either side of two opposing entrances, but was abandoned long before completion.

Earl's Hill

On Earl's Hill, Pontesbury, Shropshire (Forde-Johnston, 1964), two attempts, whether contemporary or not, were made to inhibit access to the existing hill-fort up a gentle incline from the north by reinforcing works. The attempt nearer the fort is represented by two stretches of quarry ditch with pronounced counterscarp bank and slight inner bank which were begun on the slope at a point some 70 m. north of the

33

hill-fort, but which appear to have been abandoned long before completion. The other attempt, 70 m. further down the slope again, is represented by an unfinished rampart without a ditch which runs for a distance of some 290 m. athwart the incline from one steepish flank to another. Where best preserved these remains measure 15 m. in width and stand to a height of 1.3 m. above the ground on the uphill side and to 2.6 m. on the lower side. Elsewhere, however, they degenerate to the condition of a mere scarp, and it would seem certain that this secondary work, too, was not completed.

Tor Hill

An interesting example of defences which were to be reinforced by what turned out to be an abortive effort is evident at Tor Hill, Peeblesshire (RCHM(Scot) 1967, 144–5, fig. 136), in the form of a marker ditch outside a weak sector of established defences. No construction work had begun on this new line when events overtook the designers. This, and certain other incomplete works in the vicinity, very probably represent one of the rare instances of the unfinished condition being referable to an historic event. Tor Hill is situated two kilometres from an Agricolan fort (RCMH(Scot) 1967, 169–71), and in the territory of the Selgovae, a tribe upon which the Romans leaned rather heavily (RCHM(Scot) 1956, 25–9). There are numerous unfinished works in this territory, as well as a marked scarcity of native occupation during the ensuing centuries of the Roman occupation. In direct contrast to this state of affairs the neighbouring territory of the Votadini, clients of the Romans, contains numerous hill-forts and settlements which testify to occupation throughout the whole period but few, if any, unfinished works. Indeed, field work in Northumberland, the southern part of that territory, has resulted in a recent authoritative statement that 'it is not possible to point to a series of unfinished forts in the county' (Jobey, 1965, 39). The cases of the Selgovae and the Votadini, then, probably furnish examples of cause and effect.

Charge Law

The Roman influence may appear again at Charge Law, Peeblesshire (RCHM (Scot) 1967, 107–8, fig. 85), where there is an example of a site occupied after an initial uncompleted phase, which comprised an attempt to construct a rampart from an external quarry ditch with a counterscarp bank. Two timber houses on levelled platforms had been established in the nascent enclosure before work stopped.

At a later time one of the comparatively few walled settlements with stone houses which occur in the region was completed on the same site.

Hammer Knowe

On Hammer Knowe, also in Peeblesshire (RCHM(Scot) 1967, 118, fig. 101), a similar sequence of events probably took place *before* the Roman period, for some other reason. In the first instance an oval area was defined by a marker ditch and a start was made on constructing a rampart of material derived from an external ditch on the line of the marker. This work was abandoned before completion, and at some later time a stone-walled settlement with timber houses was established on the site. As these houses would appear to have gone out of use after the beginning of the Roman period some purely local circumstance must have given rise to the abandonment of the first constructional phase.

Braidwood

An example of an earlier palisade being used as a marker for earthwork defences occurs at Braidwood, Midlothian (Feachem, 1965, 135). Excavations (Piggott, S., forthcoming) have shown that the site was first occupied by a settlement enclosed within two palisades which were joined on either side of the entrance passage.

The inner palisade was eventually removed altogether, and the foundation trenches of several timber houses were dug across its course. At some later time the decision was taken to substitute earthwork defences for the single remaining (original outer) palisade. Excavation revealed that the palisade was still standing when the construction of the new inner rampart from material derived from an internal ditch was begun. An outer rampart was also started, again from an internal quarry ditch.

The construction of the new inner rampart evidently began on either side of the entrance and at a point at the opposite end of the enclosure, but work was abandoned shortly before the gangs met. The palisade trench survives in the resulting lateral gaps.

Casterley Camp

This account of some of the evidence for constructional methods which can be derived from the study of unfinished hill-forts concludes with Casterley Camp, Wiltshire (OS 1:2500, SU 1153), a work which is not only incomplete but which appears to exemplify a change of plan decided upon during construction.

The remains (fig. 8) comprise an unfinished rampart and ditch enclosing an area of some 27.5 hectares (68 acres). The profile of the rampart is irregular, as if the gangs had been far from finishing their work when the place was abandoned, and it is higher, more advanced, on the east and south than elsewhere round the perimeter.

At first sight a most remarkable feature of the earthworks is a gap some 170 m. long across which excavation (Cunnington, 1913) has revealed that the ditch, and presumably the rampart, never existed. The gap, at the northern extremity of the east side, is covered externally by a rampart and ditch forming an arc or salient to the northeast. The salient rampart and ditch join those of the main defences smoothly at the north end of the gap, but at the south end the ditches join at a sharp angle at a point south of the termination of the main defences and the ramparts remain separate. Had the work been concluded the ramparts presumably would have been merged and the ditches dug to a uniform depth, and the short, ragged ends of the main defences which overlap the junction would have been obliterated (fig. 9).

The salient rampart, like the main rampart, is obviously unfinished; a majority of the score of depressions which interrupt its course can be put down to the effect of gang work rather than to later breaks.

Such an extraordinary arrangement challenges explanation. The first which springs to mind is, of course, that the original design embodying as regular an enclosure as the terrain would permit was found to be deficient in that the dead ground at the head of a coomb north-east of the site would allow intruders to approach in strength without being seen to within about 250 m. of the defences. In this case it would follow that the

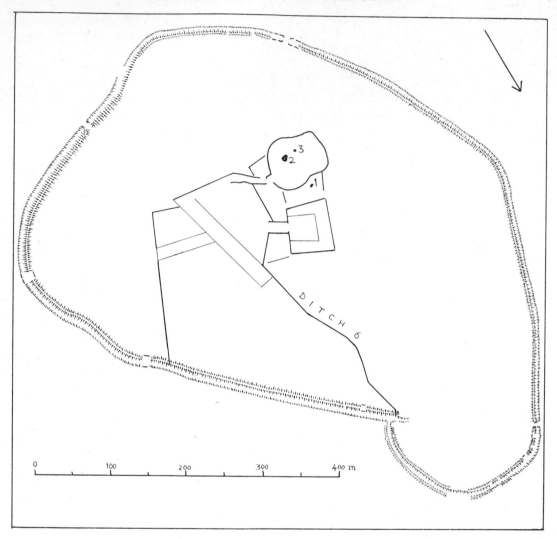

Fig. 8. Casterley Camp, Wiltshire.

construction of the north-east sector of the main defences would be cancelled and the salient substituted, in what in the event turned out to be an abortive effort to achieve increased security.

This proposition might of course involve the supposition that the earthworks were purely defensive in character. But the topographical situation, at the lower margin of a broad expanse of very gently falling ground, is not characteristic of most so-called hill-forts. However, the 1913 excavations revealed that the interior contains two en-closures, one subrectangular and formed by a ditch with an external bank, the other shaped like a broad pear. These are shown in fig. 8 reconstituted from the excavation report and from air photographs. The linear ditch numbered 6 by the excavators (fig.

36

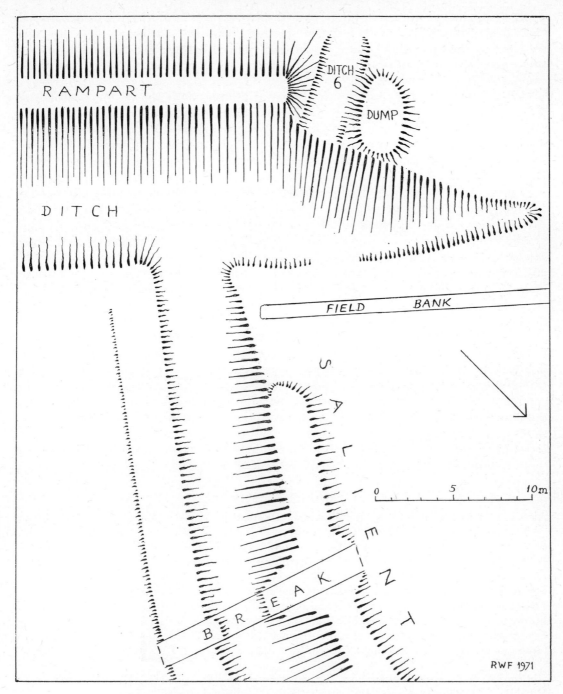

Fig. 9. Casterley Camp: junction of salient and original works.

9, which also includes what is assumed to be the excavator's dump, derived from material cleared out from the end of ditch 6), and another linear ditch farther to the south-east, were cut by the main ditch, and it would thus appear that these linear ditches, and so presumably one or both of the internal enclosures, were in existence before the main rampart and ditch were begun.

Within the pear-shaped enclosure there was a large pit (2 on fig. 8) which had a post nearly one metre in diameter rising from a hole in the pit floor and which contained four human skeletons and 14 antlers of the red deer. The connection of ritual pits with hill-forts and allied structures (as, for example, at Bossens, Cornwall; Cadbury Castle, Devonshire; Danebury, Hampshire; Dunstable, Bedfordshire; Maiden Castle, Dorset; Mount Caburn, Sussex (Ross, 1968, 261, 262, 263, 264, 267, 267 respectively)), may be compared with that of other Iron Age ritual or religious structures in similar situations (see Cunliffe, below), as, too, with pre-Iron Age works of like kind – among the many examples of which we should probably include Lyles Hill, Co. Antrim (Evans, 1953). If, then, as would seem very probable, the subrectangular and pear-shaped enclosures within Casterley Camp were shrines or temples (Piggott, S., 1968, 76), the dual character of the main earthworks – defence and precinct – which has so often been noted elsewhere might account for the rather exceptional choice of site.

Conclusion

This paper began with brief consideration of some possible explanations of why hill-forts were unfinished – through violent happenings, disease or famine, because of political, economic or religious pressures, for example, or – exceptionally – the intractability of rock. There followed observations on the designing of hill-forts, the conception of the lightweight primary indicator, the existence and nature of markers, both purpose-built and fortuitous; and descriptions of some unfinished works, both the initially unfinished and those at which reinforcements of existing defences were left incomplete. The purpose has been to indicate how the study of unfinished works can make a unique contribution to our knowledge of some aspects of Iron Age technology.

BIBLIOGRAPHY

Alcock, L. 1960. 'Castell Odo, an embanked settlement in Mynydd Ystum, near Aberdaron, Caernarvonshire', *Arch. Cam.*, CIX, 78–135.

Cunnington, B. H. 1913. 'Casterley Camp', *WAM*, XXXVIII, 53–105.

Edwards, J. 1966. (ed.) *Caesar, The Gallic War*, London, Heinemann.

Evans, E. E. 1953. *Lyles Hill*, Belfast, HMSO.

Feachem, R. W. 1963. *A Guide to Prehistoric Scotland*, London, Batsford.

Feachem, R. W. 1965. *The North Britons*, London, Hutchinson.

Forde-Johnston, J. 1962. 'The Hill-forts of Lancashire and Cheshire', *TLCAS*, 72, 9–46.

Forde-Johnston, J. 1964. 'Earl's Hill, Pontesbury', *Arch. J.*, CXIX, 66–91.

Graham, A. 1950. 'Archaeological Gleanings from Dark Age Records', *PSAS*, LXXXV, 64–91.

Gordon, A. S. R. 1940. 'Excavations at Gurnard's Head', *Arch. J.*, XCVII, 96 ff.

Hawkes, C. F. C. 1930. 'Saint Catharine's Hill, Winchester', *PHFC*, XI.

Hencken, T. C. 1938. 'The Excavation of the Iron Age Camp on Bredon Hill, Gloucestershire', *Arch. J.*, XCV, 1–111.

Jackson, J. 1963. (ed.) *Tacitus, The Annals*, London, Heinemann.

Jobey, G. 1965. 'Hill-forts and Settlements in Northumberland', *Arch. Ael.*, 4th series, XLIII, 21–64.

Piggott, C. M. 1949. 'The Iron Age Settlement at Hayhope Knowe, Roxburghshire', *PSAS*, LXXXIII, 45–67.

Piggott, S. 1930. 'Butser Hill', *Ant.*, IV, 187–200.

Piggott, S. 1931. 'Ladle Hill', *Ant.*, V, 474–85.

Piggott, S. 1968. *The Druids*, London, Thames and Hudson.

Piggott, S. Forthcoming *Proc. Soc. Ant. Scot.*

RCHM(Scot). 1956. *Inventory of Roxburghshire*, Edinburgh, HMSO.

RCHM(Scot). 1967. *Inventory of Peeblesshire*, Edinburgh, HMSO.

RCHM(Eng). 1952. *Inventory of Dorset, I, West*, London, HMSO.

Read, H. H. 1948. 'The Grampian Highlands', *British Regional Geology*, 2nd edition, Edinburgh, HMSO.

Rivet, A. L. F. 1962. Introduction to *Map of Southern Britain in the Iron Age*, Chessington, Ordance Survey.

Ross, A. 1968. 'Shafts, pits, wells – sanctuaries of the Belgic Britains?', in J. M. Coles and D. D. A. Simpson (eds.), *Studies in Ancient Europe*, Leicester, Leicester University Press.

Ross, A. 1970. *Everyday Life of the Pagan Celts*, London, Batsford.

Shaw, T. 1970. 'Methods of Earthwork Building', *PPS*, XXXVI, 380–1.

Wheeler, R. E. M. 1943. 'Maiden Castle, Dorset', *RCSA*, XII, Oxford, Oxford University Press.

Wheeler, R. E. M. 1953. 'An Early Iron Age "Beach-head" at Lulworth, Dorset', *Ant. J.*, XXXIII, 1–13.

Wheeler, R. E. M. 1954. 'The Stanwick Fortifications', *RCSA*, XVII, Oxford, Oxford University Press.

Wheeler, R. E. M., and Richardson, K. M. 1957. 'Hill-forts of Northern France', *RCSA*, XIX, Oxford, Oxford University Press.

Yeats, Mr. 1884. 'Camps', *TBFC*, 43–9.

LIST OF ABBREVIATIONS

Ant.	Antiquity
Ant. J.	Antiquaries Journal
Arch. Ael.	Archaeologia Aeliana
Arch. Cam.	Archaeologia Cambrensis
Arch. J.	Archaeological Journal
HMSO	Her (His) Majesty's Stationery Office
OS	Ordnance Survey
PHFC	Papers and Proceedings of the Hampshire Field Club and Archaeological Society
PPS	Proceedings of the Prehistoric Society
PSAS	Proceedings of the Society of Antiquaries of Scotland
RCSA	Reports of the Research Committee of the Society of Antiquaries of London
RCHM(Scot)	Royal Commission on the Ancient and Historial Monuments of Scotland
RCHM(Eng)	Royal Commission on Historical Monuments, England
TBFC	Transactions of the Banffshire Field Club
TLCAS	Transactions of the Lancashire and Cheshire Antiquarian Society
WAM	Wiltshire Archaeological and Natural History Magazine

INVENTION, ADOPTION AND IMPOSITION –

The Evidence of the Hill-forts

By S. C. STANFORD

THE hastily devised original title of this paper – *Invasion and Diffusion* – revealed a significant quirk of an old-fashioned mind by omitting 'Invention'. While the title is being amended it will be useful to bear in mind that by invasion we normally mean the evidence for the imposition of ideas from outside, and by diffusion the adoption of ideas and techniques freely within a recognisable cultural unity. The title might be changed to *Invention, Imposition and Adoption*. In seeking to define and understand these processes we have at our disposal evidence of four kinds: chronological, typological (including both structures and artefacts), sociological (where deducible from hill-fort plans) and demographic (stemming from the structural and sociological evidence). I shall review some of the recent evidence, but do not promise any dogmatic conclusions. I am very glad of the opportunity to be able to offer these thoughts to Sir Mortimer's pile of birthday presents.

THE CHRONOLOGICAL EVIDENCE

Dates whether absolute or relative must be the essence of any serious attempt to discern these processes. The invasion hypothesis requires the contemporary appearance of critical phenomena on either side of the frontier and if we are to distinguish between adoption and invention we need to be able to date, if only relatively, the appearance of similar phenomena in different areas. It follows that our energies should be directed especially towards the establishment of closely linked chronologies across our field of study, in which matter we are now aided immensely by the growing number of radiocarbon determinations for hill-forts resulting in the collapse of the former hypothetical hiatus between the use of timber in the Hallstatt ramparts of the Continent and in our own insular examples.

Timber ramparts

Although the timber-framed box-rampart has long been accepted as an early fossil in the British Iron Age the natural inclination to derive it from the Continent was until recently made difficult by the short chronology in vogue for British hill-forts and the confusion of our timber-laced ramparts with the Gallic walls of Caesar's Gaul (Cotton 1954). Professor Piggott's prescient objectivity in linking these ramparts with the Urnfield cultures of the Continent (1965, 203) was put to the test by Mr. MacKie and others (1969) with the disturbing result that Scotland became possessed of hill-fort dates earlier than any seriously argued for southern Britain. The conclusion that the Abernethy culture with timber-laced ramparts emerged as a result of immigration in the 7th or 8th centuries allowed a fresh look at the dating evidence from two English sites with timber ramparts – Grimthorpe (Stead 1968) and Ivinghoe (Cotton and Frere 1968). Bones from the Grimthorpe ditch had been dated 690 ± 130 B.C. and

970 ± 130 B.C., and the abundant bronze-work from Ivinghoe had been dated by Mr. Britton as from the later 8th century onwards. However cautious we may be about dates based on bones in ditch filling or tempted to invoke a cultural lag for metalwork, these assessments are broadly in accord with the Scottish dates. Most recently, as I am kindly informed by Dr. H. N. Savory, radiocarbon determinations for the hill-fort of Dinorben give 895 ± 95 B.C. and 765 ± 85 B.C. for the period I timber-framed rampart and 535 ± 85 B.C. and 420 ± 85 B.C. for the period II timber-laced rampart. Subject to refinements of the C14 determinations, these timber-framed and timber-laced ramparts are thus to be regarded as ranging from the 9th to the 5th century B.C.

From the middle of the Welsh Border comes supporting evidence for such early dating. An unstratified sherd from Caynham Camp (Gelling and Peacock 1966, C13 on fig. 21) has the same temper and rim form as a vessel from the cemetery at Bromfield with a radiocarbon date of 762 ± 75 B.C. (Stanford 1971A), and in an early stage Caynham Camp had timber incorporated in its rampart construction (Gelling 1959, 148). The value of this evidence becomes the more apparent when we consider the long history of the nearby hill-fort of Croft Ambrey (fig. 10). There a sequence of structures is dated

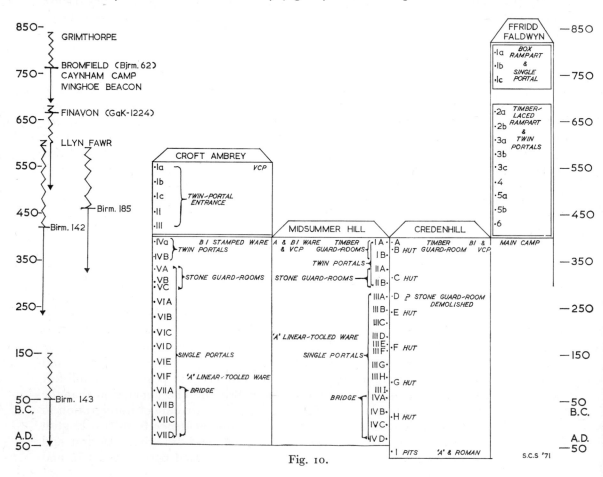

Fig. 10.

back to *c.* 550 B.C. with support from C14 determinations and parallel gateway constructions at Midsummer Hill; yet neither timber-framing nor timber-lacing was found on either site (Stanford 1967, 38). This absence of timber-work at Croft Ambrey supports the early date indicated for such structures elsewhere and we begin to see where the late Mr. O'Neil's Ffridd Faldwyn evidence stands in relation to the rest. The original defence of the Inner Camp was of the narrow box-rampart (or double palisade) type and was succeeded by a timber-laced rampart. In the absence of stratification it is not possible to be dogmatic about the gateway sequence, but one can argue that the two long forward post-holes (O'Neil 1942, postholes I and II on fig. 5) mark the box-rampart gateway and are of at least two, and probably three phases. The post-holes within the timber-laced rampart entrance may be grouped in threes to suggest nine successive twin-portal gates. This Inner Camp will have been succeeded by the Main Camp defences constructed outside a broad and irregular quarry-ditch. The most likely time for the Main Camp construction is *c.* 390 B.C., when Croft Ambrey was enlarged and Midsummer Hill founded and the Ffridd Faldwyn sequence may be calculated back from this horizon. Using the same post-life as for Croft Ambrey a date of *c.* 800 B.C. is indicated for the box-rampart. O'Neil's report makes it clear that there was a break between the use of this rampart and the construction of the timber-laced one; it could have been longer than the 50 years allowed for on our diagram, but the present position of the early Ffridd Faldwyn Camp contemporary with Grimthorpe, Caynham and Ivinghoe looks about right. Meanwhile Mr. C. Musson's interim comments about his current work on The Breiddin have prepared us for early hill-fort occupation there too (1970). The use of the more accurate half-life of C14 (5,730 ± 40 years instead of the Libby half-life of 5,570 ± 30 years) would not affect the date from which the Ffridd Faldwyn sequence is to be calculated since *c.* 390 B.C. remains the best all-round solution to the structural, chronological and historical requirements. Ivinghoe too would be unchanged but the Bromfield and consequently the Caynham dates would be increased by about 80 years, still remaining within the period envisaged for the Inner Camp occupation of Ffridd Faldwyn where the timber-laced rampart would remain *c.* 670 B.C. It may be noted, with satisfaction, that the central date for the timber-laced fort of Finavon on the new half-life would be 665 B.C. at which level the site is named on fig. 10, although the accompanying C14 range is based on the Libby half-life. Finavon and Ffridd Faldwyn thus agree in date and structure, whereas both look at least a century early compared with Dinorben.

Later gateway sequences

These dates create problems of new dimensions in retaining a proper perspective over a hill-fort period of 800 years or more. Unless we seek hard to detail events closely through these long centuries we may be in danger of falling into the 'straight track' confusion and linking together structures and finds as distant in time and remote in purpose as Norman mottes and World War II pill-boxes. While looking for opportunities to secure more radiocarbon dates it is more important than ever that we seek with the spade the evidence to fill in the intervening years. The Herefordshire sites summarised on fig. 10 show that such dirt archaeology can still be profitable and produce a relative chronology on the basis of post-hole replacements. The Credenhill report should shortly be available for criticism (Stanford 1970) and reports on the work at Croft Ambrey and Midsummer Hill are in preparation. For the time being the information given here provides an improved interim statement to replace those previously issued for Croft Ambrey (Stanford 1967) and Midsummer Hill (Stanford 1971A). The south-western entrance of the Main Camp of Croft Ambrey had 15 successive gates following the construction of the large rampart and these in number and plan match fairly closely the 17 gates of the southern entrance on Midsummer Hill Camp, 30 miles away. It becomes an unnecessary elaboration to suggest that these sequences are anything but parallel and the three radiocarbon determinations provided by the Birmingham Laboratory support this conclusion. Birm. 142 (420 ± 185 B.C. on the Libby half-life) was for thin branches of wood on the floor of the quarry scoops dug for the construction of the inturned rampart at Midsummer Hill and Birm. 143 (50 ± 100 B.C.) was obtained from carbonised grain associated with the destruction of the period III i gateway. The use of the historical date of *c.* 390 B.C. for the first of these gives the maximum utilisation of these determinations in the long gateway sequence at Midsummer; and if the resulting dates are applied to the Croft Ambrey sequence, period Vb there should be *c.* 300 B.C. The radiocarbon date, Birm. 185, obtained for the burnt timbers of the Vb guardroom, was 460 ± 135 B.C. The mean date of 460 would be met if the structural timbers concerned included the heart of trees 160 years old. Between these two sites we have sufficient structural information to provide a detailed chronology for the last 600 years of the pre-Roman hill-fort period, and it has already been shown that the Inner Camp sequence at Ffridd Faldwyn may be linked to this.

Of special importance in these sequences is the occurrence of certain forms of entrance in restricted periods, notably the use of stone guardrooms between *c.* 325 and 275 B.C. and bridges after *c.* 60 B.C. Unless it can be shown on independent evidence that similar structures elsewhere have their own date it must seem reasonable for the time being to suppose that they are to be related chronologically to these Herefordshire examples. The rectangular stone guardrooms have their parallels far to the north in the Welsh Border (Gardner and Savory 1964, 88–90) and I have elsewhere remarked on the parallel to be drawn between the timber guardroom of Midsummer Hill and one phase of the early Maiden Castle west entrance (1971A). On our present dating this parallel, if valid, would place that phase of Maiden Castle at *c.* 390 B.C.; and the original timber box-rampart there is even earlier. Some difficulty arises with the C-shaped guardrooms of Rainsborough Camp where there was a timber-laced rampart (Avery *et al.* 1967). By analogy with similar ramparts Rainsborough should be dated to the 7th or 8th century; and its guardrooms were thought to go with its original construction (Avery *et al.* 1967, 253). Before concluding that these semi-circular guardrooms are quite separate and earlier than the rectangular forms of the Welsh Border we must note that since the north guardroom floor extended beneath the guardroom wall (*ibid*, 235) there is a real possibility that the latter was not of the earliest defensive phase. The answer to this intriguing question should come in due course from the northern part of the Welsh Border where both C-shaped and rectangular guardrooms occur.

The direct chronological evidence has pointed to three main horizons in hill-fort construction. For the 7th and 8th centuries we have timber box-ramparts followed by timber-laced ones at a time when such work was common on the Continent and we have no need therefore to invoke local invention. Timber-framing looks on balance to be earlier than timber-lacing but we cannot yet afford to regard this succession as proven for all regions. A third horizon present at Croft Ambrey is placed at no great distance from the late Bronze Age/Iron Age hoard of Llyn Fawr and tentatively dated *c.* 550 B.C. In view of the nondescript nature of the small dump rampart and ditch that protected the Plateau Camp at Croft Ambrey at this stage this is a horizon which may well be very difficult to recognise without extensive excavation of a particular site; it may be no horizon at all but merely a local phenomenon, although it may be noted that a small dump rampart is associated with early pottery and square buildings at Balksbury, Hants (Wainwright 1969, 26–28). Finally, *c.* 390 B.C., the chronological data provides us with an important horizon involving the introduction of timber guardrooms just when historical and typological data would invite consideration of a major invasion. The distinctive timber guardroom plan of Midsummer Hill and conjecturally Maiden Castle should, if introduced from outside, be capable of verification on the French side of the Channel.

Within the limited evidence so far available there seems to be every indication that these horizons are roughly contemporary across the country and, whether the synchronism of events is the result of rapid adoption or quick imposition, it certainly provides no support for a culture-creep process extending over centuries. It shows that it was virtually impossible to remain isolated for long in prehistoric Britain.

SOME STRUCTURAL EVIDENCE

In defences

Hill-fort structures can provide parallels of similar plans and techniques used in different communities and the frequency of their repair can indicate the degree of local continuity and provide a measure of distant contemporaneity as already argued for Croft Ambrey and Midsummer Hill.

Although it may be valid to group together as early all ramparts with timber-work there are various types of such rampart as already emphasised by Avery *et al.* (1967, 247–251) and Stead (1968, 155–158). They include the narrow timber box-rampart or double palisade, about 7 ft. wide, as at Ranscombe Camp, Sussex (Burstow and Holleyman 1964, fig. 4), Grimthorpe, Yorkshire (Stead 1968, figs. 4 and 5), Hollingbury, Sussex (Curwen 1932) and Ffridd Faldwyn, Montgomeryshire (O'Neil 1942, fig. 5) where it preceded a timber-laced rampart. The parallel in plan between these and the palisaded sites of the Hownam Culture (MacKie 1969, 21) supports an early date, but raises the possibility that such structures developed locally from single palisades. In the absence of abundant imports the interpretation of the process involved is likely to rest upon personal preference.

A second type of rampart is the wider box form, about 12 ft. wide, as at Bindon Hill, Dorset (Wheeler 1953, pl. iiib), Wandlebury, Cambridgeshire (the outer rampart, Hartley 1956, fig. 4a) and Maiden Castle, Dorset (Wheeler 1943, pls. XI and XII), Even this width is almost paralleled by the widely spaced palisades of High Knowes,

Northumberland (Jobey 1962, fig. 10) and although the form is primary in a long sequence at Maiden Castle it is not independently dated. A third type has only a front timber revetment and includes Cissbury, Sussex (Curwen 1931). While acknowledging with respect the alternative 'box-rampart' interpretation given in the report, Hod Hill, Dorset (Richmond 1968, figs. 64–66) may also belong to this class. The inner rampart of Wandlebury Camp (Hartley 1956, fig. 4c) with posts 14 ft. apart is presumably similar.

Lastly, there are the timber-laced structures which themselves show some variety of form (Cotton 1954 and Avery et al. 1967). These four main types could represent either different traditions or different stages in the development of a local timber tradition, and will need to be studied with such possibilities in mind. At present it can only be reiterated that there is a rapid and widespread distribution of the timber tradition in general, which must either represent very large scale imposition or general adoption of a current idea within a cultural province extending from the Danube to the Clyde.

Sequences like those at Croft Ambrey and Midsummer Hill not only allow us to recognise the major building periods with which our earlier hill-fort studies were largely obsessed, but also show how structural phase plans developed upon and from existing plans and were widely adopted. We must imagine a common motive for these developments within the cultural province in question and when we see the rendering in stone and timber of a previously timber guardroom at Midsummer Hill it suggests that here at least we may invoke a measure of local invention. If Herefordshire were unique in its hill-fort gateway complexities this kind of study would have close limitations but there are ample signs that sites further afield will eventually provide detailed sequences allowing correlation with the Herefordshire forts. We have already made use of Ffridd Faldwyn and Maiden Castle, and mention may be made here of the current work of Mr. L. A. Probert on the Monmouthshire hill-fort of Twyn-y-Gaer where numerous phases of gateway construction have been observed. I understand from Professor Cunliffe that Danebury also, has many gateway phases. Elsewhere, if we pursue the hazardous game of reinterpreting old evidence, Dinorben must have seen something like the intensity of work found at Croft Ambrey; at least this seems the best explanation for the great depth of road metalling excavated by Willoughby Gardner in the south-east entrance (Gardner and Savory 1964, 18–26). Still in the west, a complex history was clearly involved in structures excavated at Pen Dinas (Forde et al. 1963, fig. 6) and a longer history than that deduced by the excavator could be postulated for Bredon Hill (Hencken 1939). There is evidence of at least nine successive gateways on this site showing that the Welsh Border complexities may in general be extended to the western front of the Cotswolds.

By contrast with Bredon Hill, Mrs. Champion and Mr. Dixon have recently been uncovering very different stories, apparently earlier in date and simpler in history at nearby Leckhampton Camp and Crickley Hill, collecting the timber-laced rampart horizon which was absent at Bredon. Their work has underlined an unconformity in the hill-fort record which prepares us for the recognition of distinct eastern and western British hill-fort provinces; for relatively simple defensive sequences seem to be characteristic of eastern sites, to judge by places like Grimthorpe, Ivinghoe and Rainsborough.

46

Internal structures

One of the fundamental changes in our approach to British Iron Age settlements in recent years has been the recognition that the dwelling huts were often small rectangular buildings no larger than about 10 ft. x 12 ft. (Stanford 1970). New support for this identification came in 1970 when four of the rectangular huts on Midsummer Hill Camp were found to contain hearth sites. Here, and at Croft Ambrey and Credenhill, buildings of this type are stratified with the early phases of the defences and on other sites like Rainsborough and Grimthorpe the absence of different structures must make it probable that the huts belong to the hill-fort occupation. In the absence of overwhelming examples safely dated to pre-Hill-fort Britain this evidence disposes of the main argument against the invasion hypothesis as an explanation of the hill-fort phenomenon. There is now widespread evidence of domestic building traditions that are paralleled in form on the Continent. Since the house-type must reflect common technical skills and social arrangements it may be regarded as better evidence than pottery or even rampart styles for the intrusion of new peoples. We may go further and distinguish between the more or less square houses at Rainsborough, Ivinghoe, Grimthorpe and Balksbury and the oblong ones of the three Herefordshire forts. It so happens that the former are known from sites with timber ramparts or other evidence for establishment before the 4th century whereas the latter are confined to sites or levels that post-date 400 B.C. The correspondence with separate hill-fort horizons suggests a chronological rather than regional explanation for the distribution, and although rectangular buildings are limited to the west, square buildings may also be discerned there. At Croft Ambrey they occur with the earliest Plateau Camp occupation of the 6th century and I have elsewhere indicated that if rectangular structures are to be seen at Dinorben they are of square form (Stanford 1970). The limited evidence points towards the introduction of the oblong form at our 390 B.C. horizon. For reasons of pottery discussed below it may be appropriate to point out that in size and shape the Midsummer buildings are matched at Castel Coz (le Men 1872).

SOCIOLOGICAL EVIDENCE

It has already been indicated that sociological reasons should lie behind the use of small rectangular dwellings which contrast with the large round huts that were inherited from the British Bronze Age. If from the plan of individual huts we turn to the overall hill-fort plan and compare the differences in hut arrangement and density we see once more that there are broad differences between east and west Britain. At Credenhill (Stanford 1970) and Ffridd Faldwyn (O'Neil 1942, fig. 5) rectangular structures occurred in lines on something approaching a grid-iron pattern and there was only about 15 ft. between individual huts. This arrangement has been seen also at Croft Ambrey and Midsummer Hill and must reflect a distinctive local Marches social organisation. In southern and eastern Britain extensive open spaces were left between individual or small groups of square buildings at Grimthorpe (Stead 1968, figs. 4 and 5), Ivinghoe (Cotton and Frere 1968, fig. 8) and Balksbury (Wainwright 1969, figs. 12 and 13). The sites with square huts may prove different in this respect as well from those with oblong huts. A difference in function, and perhaps in the success of imposed ideas,

47

is indicated in these areas where it is possible to interpret hill-forts as intrusive elements in an otherwise dispersed settlement pattern, established as tribal centres with buildings for retainers and open spaces for the gathering of the clans when military, social or religious needs dictated. By contrast the Welsh Border forts are literally packed to the rampart and it would be superfluous to imagine that there were many farmsteads lying outside the defences. In this area a new settlement pattern has been created and it is difficult, on the present evidence from the Herefordshire forts, to imagine this arising slowly and naturally from internal impulses. We do not necessarily have to bring the whole hill-fort population from abroad but a heavy lacing of new chieftains is surely needed to carry out this reorganisation.

A further important difference between these two hill-fort regions lies in the replacement of internal buildings. At Credenhill, a hut behind the rampart showed six phases of construction spanning the life of the quarry-ditch from c. 390 B.C. until c. A.D. 60 (Stanford 1970) while at Croft Ambrey a contemporary quarry-ditch had within it a hut of five phases covering approximately 400 years. At Midsummer Hill Camp in 1970 it was seen that comparable huts spanning the same period as Credenhill were of between four and six phases. Examples of this type show that these hill-forts were permanently occupied and that the internal social organisation must have been largely maintained throughout the period. They provide an independent check on our relative chronologies, and present formidable evidence of the permanence of hill-fort societies in the Welsh Border, societies whose stability for such long periods makes the Roman occupation appear but a short and untidy episode in the history of these islands.

By contrast with the Border hill-forts the internal building plans of Rainsborough, Grimthorpe, Ivinghoe and Balksbury are essentially simple and basically of a single, or at most double, period. On these sites it is possible to argue either that the huts moved around from time to time, or (preferably) that there were few huts and the life of the hill-fort was short, perhaps no more than a century. As with the defences, the internal structures of these eastern forts seem to point to an unsuccessful introduction of a settlement form in an alien environment.

The recovery of sufficient structural detail to allow us to even guess at differences in social organisation must be a slow process but the details indicated above show that it is not an entirely hopeless aspiration. Whatever might have been the family groupings and political hierarchies in our hill-forts it does appear from the house-types and density of buildings that these communities were in a different class from the Little Woodbury-type farmsteads; and a broad distinction is emerging between the hill-forts of eastern and western England. Whereas an artefactual similarity might be readily explained in terms of the copying of a prototype looted or traded from some distant source it seems less likely that the whole way of life and communal organisation would be changed without the presence on the ground of a number of influential teachers whom we would normally call invaders. Against the imprecise detail that we of necessity use for our time-scale it is idle to ask whether trade followed the flag or *vice versa*. It is more profitable to accept Dr. Peacock's conclusion from his study of pottery that invaders and traders do not need to be of the same group (Peacock 1969, 53) nor strictly contemporaries (Peacock 1968, 424). By demonstrating the presence of professional potters he has, however, pointed to a further sociological trait in the western hill-fort communities which were not locally self-sufficient in this matter. The professional manufacture of pottery may have been established in some areas before hill-forts were built and the apparently general use of dolerite from five miles away for pots in the Bronze Age cemetery at Bromfield, Salop, underlines the need for caution here. Nevertheless, the fine finish of the 'Western Third B' Iron Age Group B1 pots (Peacock 1968, 421) lends colour to the present impression that a commercial change coincides with an important hill-fort horizon.

DEMOGRAPHIC EVIDENCE

Recognition of the close cover of buildings within certain Welsh Border hill-forts allows the size of the enclosed area to be considered to be proportionate to the population within the ramparts, and on this assumption estimates of population of 70–100 persons per acre (180–240 per hectare) have been argued for the hill-forts of Herefordshire and Shropshire (Stanford 1971B). Long ago Sir Mortimer thought 100 per acre to be a reasonable density for Maiden Castle (1943, 68). Whatever the value attributed to such estimates it remains true that under these conditions an increase in the number or size of hill-forts will reflect changes in population. It may be that there were occasions when additional inhabitants were simply brought in from the surrounding area although it is unlikely that many scattered communities existed side by side with the hill-forts of the central Welsh Border. In that area at least any widespread establishment or enlargement of hill-forts may be conjectured to result from new arrivals from outside and this I believe to be the case certainly with the 390 B.C. horizon, for which the Herefordshire and Shropshire enlargements could reflect the arrival of 19,000 newcomers (1971B).

Artefacts

Although it is not proposed to deal at length with artefacts here some comment is appropriate on the Group B1 stamped wares associated with the conjectured invaders of *c.* 390 B.C. If in other areas we still hanker after the old equation of invaders with pottery types the position of this pottery may provide an alternative explanation and some solace for those who meet the same problem elsewhere. It is still difficult to derive this Western Third B pottery directly from Brittany and all that can be positively asserted is that there are similarities in the professional competence of the potters, the use of stamped decoration (although with a much more limited repertoire), and the presence of internal grooves on the rims. These perhaps are sufficient to indicate that someone with ceramic skills came from the French side of the Channel at about the time when the Herefordshire hill-forts were being reorganised *c.* 390 B.C., but it will be noted that I have already invoked some parallel architectural influence at Maiden Castle which was achieved without affecting the pottery record. The latest assessment of the Breton stamped pottery places its development between the end of the 6th century and the late 4th century so that our conjectured 390 B.C. horizon is well within this range (Schwappach 1969). The removal of the time lag formerly invoked for late Hallstatt-early La Tène pottery in Brittany emphasises the current preparedness to allow material and ideas to move quickly from central and south central Europe – even from northern Italy – through a Celtic province. At certain times the further movement of ideas and pottery across the English Channel may have been just as rapid. The Breton stamped pottery however is not likely to point precisely to the springboard whence came those who reorganised the Welsh Border forts in the early 4th century. Just as Sir Mortimer was unable to match the defences of Dorset slingers in northern France (Wheeler and Richardson 1957) so must we recognise that the small hill-forts of the Breton promontories and especially those of the southern coast where most of the pottery is found, are not a proper environment for the chiefs of our great Border hill-forts. The sociological and ceramic factors involved point in different directions. The pottery and metal-work found in our hill-forts should perhaps be regarded as the flotsam and jetsam that is tossed hither and thither by the turbulence of the breaking waves. They may decorate the beach but they give little clue to the forces that produced it. They may help us with dates but if we wish to identify the people concerned we may do better to put our faith in less exciting material like the field-oven VCP that is a feature of our Welsh Border cultures (Gelling and Stanford 1965). If such material were to come from future hill-fort excavations in northern France it would indeed be perverse to argue that it was traded.

Summary and Conclusions

Against the trend of much of our modern thinking this discussion has led to the suggestion of four horizons in our hill-forts when the observed phenomena might be most easily explained in terms of imposition from outside, i.e. invasion. They may be summarised as follows:

1. In the 8th century, with narrow timber-framed ramparts (or double palisades) and square buildings, occurring right across southern Britain from Grimthorpe in Yorkshire to Ffridd Faldwyn in Montgomeryshire.

2. In the 7th century timber-laced ramparts, again probably with square buildings are found throughout Britain from Finavon in Scotland to Crickley Hill in Gloucestershire, and from Dinorben in Flintshire to Rainsborough in Northamptonshire.

3. Wider timber-framed ramparts and timber revetments, not closely dated, but perhaps associated with square buildings, e.g. at Maiden Castle, Dorset.

4. In the early 6th century – exemplified by Croft Ambrey and perhaps Balksbury – small dump ramparts for hill-forts that again had small square buildings.

5. In the early 4th century an important horizon with large dump ramparts, timber guardrooms and oblong huts. This distribution is restricted to the west, perhaps from Maiden Castle, Dorset to Dinorben, Denbighshire, and in the southern and central Marches is associated with Groups A and B1 pottery. We have quickly listed five occasions for possible invasions without even reaching the old invasion horizon of 300 B.C. which will still be required to provide Maiden Castle with its extension to 45 acres; and after that there are still the local affairs that affected the south coast until Caesar's conquest of Gaul brought cross-Channel wanderings to an end (Thomas 1966, 75–82).

If we feel overwhelmed by the mass of invasion campaigns thus indicated our alternative would be to reject the analogy of waves of invaders breaking over the British beaches and invoke something like the deep sea motion of waves with the surface form being translated readily across wide oceans without movement of the mass of water itself. If this analogy seems helpful and provides a desirable contrast to the forced wave analogy which has normally been in our minds it may be worth considering the cultural and political implications if it were adopted for Iron Age Europe. For such motion to take place the area showing similar forms of defences or houses should be a unitary cultural province – unitary, that is, in terms of the sociological and economic foundations of society rather than metal styles and pottery fabrics. This manoeuvre would help us with the earliest impositions with their widespread repercussions but we would still run into a problem with the conjectured invasions of the early 4th century. Here is something which probably does not occur in the same form widely through Britain. The success of the hill-fort communities in the Welsh Border is in direct contrast to the poverty of the hill-fort experiment in eastern England. We cannot avoid asking why this should be so, and wondering whether the reason lies in geographical contrasts, in the culture of the Welsh Border aborigines, in the weight of invasion or imposition, or in the absence of subsequent counter-impositions which established their own pattern afresh in eastern Britain. Whatever the reason, such differences must account for the differences in emphasis on the hill-forts between those of us who work in their midst in the west and those whose schemes of the Iron Age have been based largely upon other criteria (e.g. Hawkes 1961 and Hodson 1964).

BIBLIOGRAPHY

Avery, M., Sutton, J. E. G., and Banks, J. W. 1967. 'Rainsborough, Northants.' *Proceedings Prehistoric Society*, 33, 207–306.

Burstow, G. P., and Holleyman, G. A. 1964. 'Excavations at Ranscombe.' *Sussex Archaeological Collections*, 102, 55–67.

Cotton, M. A. 1954. 'British Camps with Timber-laced Ramparts.' *Archaeological Journal*, 111, 26–105.

Cotton, M. A., and Frere, S. S. 1968. 'Ivinghoe Beacon Excavations, 1963–65.' *Records of Buckinghamshire*, 18.

Curwen, E. C. 1931. 'Excavations at Cissbury.' *Antiquaries Journal*, 11, 14–36.

Curwen, E. C. 1932. 'Excavations at Hollingbury.' *Antiquaries Journal*, 12, 1–16.

Forde, C. D., Griffiths, W. E., Hogg, A. H., and Houlder, C. H. 'Excavations at Pen Dinas, Aberystwyth.' *Archaeologia Cambrensis* (Cambrian Archaeological Association), 112, 125–153.

Gardner, Willoughby and Savory, H. N. 1964. *Dinorben*. Cardiff.

Gelling, P. S. 1959. 'Excavations at Caynham Camp, near Ludlow. First Interim Report.' *Transactions Shropshire Archaeological Society*, 56, 145–148.

Gelling, P. S., and Peacock, D. P. S. 1966. 'The pottery from Caynham Camp.' *Transactions Shropshire Archaeological Society*, 58, 96–100.

Gelling, P. S., and Stanford, S. C. 1965. 'Dark Age Pottery or Iron Age Ovens?' *Transactions and Proceedings Birmingham Archaeological Society*. 82, 77–91.

Hartley, B. R. 1956. 'Excavations at Wandlebury, 1955–6.' *Proceedings Cambridge Antiquarian Society*, 50, 1–28.

Hawkes, C. F. C. 1961. 'The ABC of the British Iron Age', in S. S. Frere (ed.) *Problems of the Iron Age in Southern Britain*, 1–16. London.

Hencken, T. C. 1939. 'The Excavation of the Iron Age Camp on Bredon Hill.' *Archaeological Journal*, 95, 1–111.

Hodson, F. R. 1964. 'Cultural Grouping within the British pre-Roman Iron Age.' *Proceedings Prehistoric Society*, 30, 99–110.

Jobey, G. 1962. 'An Iron Age homestead at West Brandon, Durham.' *Archaeologia Aeliana* (4th set), 40, 1–34.

MacKie, E. 1969. 'Radiocarbon Dates and the Scottish Iron Age.' *Antiquity*, 43, 15–26.

le Men, R. F. 1872. 'Gaulish fortresses on the coast of Brittany.' *Archaeological Journal*, 29, 314–30.

Musson, C. 1970. 'The Breiddin, 1969.' *Current Archaeology*, 2, 215–8.

O'Neil, B. St. J. 1942. 'Excavations at Ffridd Faldwyn Camp, Montgomery, 1937–39.' *Archaeologia Cambrensis* (Cambrian Archaeological Association), 97, 1–57.

Peacock, D. P. S. 1968. 'A Petrological Study of Certain Iron Age Pottery from Western England.' *Proceedings Prehistoric Society*, 34, 414–426.

Peacock, D. P. S. 1969. 'A Contribution to the Study of Glastonbury Ware from South-western Britain.' *Antiquaries Journal*, 49, 41–61.

Piggott, S. 1965. *Ancient Europe*. Edinburgh.

Richmond, I. A. 1968. *Hod Hill II*. London.

Schwappach, F. 1969. 'Stempelverzierte Keramik von Armorica.' *Fundberichte aus Hessen*, 1, 213–287.

Stanford, S. C. 1967. 'Croft Ambrey – Some Interim Conclusions.' *Transactions Woolhope Naturalists' Field Club*, 39, 31–39.

Stanford, S. C. 1970. 'Credenhill Camp – An Iron Age Hill-fort Capital.' *Archaeological Journal*, 127, 82–129.

Stanford, S. C. 1971A. 'Welsh Border Hill-forts,' in C. Thomas (ed.) *Problems of the Iron Age in the Irish Sea Province*. Forthcoming.

Stanford, S. C. 1971B. 'The Function and Population of Hill-forts in the Central Marches,' in C. Burgess and F. Lynch (ed.) *Prehistoric Man in Wales and the West*. Forthcoming.

Stead, I. M. 1968. 'The Iron Age Hill-fort at Grimthorpe, Yorkshire, England.' *Proceedings Prehistoric Society*, 34, 148–190.

Thomas, C. 1966. 'The Character and Origins of Roman Dumnonia,' in C. Thomas (ed.) *Rural Settlement in Roman Britain*. London.

Wainwright, G. J. 1969. 'The Excavation of Balksbury Camp, Andover, Hants.' *Proceedings Hampshire Field Club*, 26, 21–55.

Wheeler, R. E. M. 1943. *Maiden Castle, Dorset*. Oxford.

Wheeler, R. E. M. 1953. 'Excavations of the Earthwork on Bindon Hill, Dorset.' *Antiquaries Journal*, 33, 1–13.

Wheeler, R. E. M., and Richardson, K. M. 1957. *Hill-forts of Northern France*. Oxford.

SOME ASPECTS OF HILL-FORTS AND THEIR CULTURAL ENVIRONMENTS

By BARRY CUNLIFFE

I

IN THE past hill-forts have usually been considered as isolated structures related only to other hill-forts. Accordingly a policy of excavation has grown up concerned primarily to elicit details of structural development which, when linked to a local cultural sequence, could be compared over wide areas. Such an approach was, of course, a necessary precursor to more widely based studies and was developed to great effect by the Curwens in Sussex and by Professor Hawkes in Hampshire in the late 1920's and 1930's. Sir Mortimer Wheeler's work in Dorset took hill-fort studies a stage further with the careful examination of three geographically related forts, Maiden Castle (Wheeler, 1943), Poundbury (Richardson, 1940), and Chalbury (Whitley, 1943), the stripping of internal areas to examine the nature of the occupation and an attempt to study the relationship of the forts to historical events, which led to his campaigns of survey and excavation in Northern France (Wheeler and Richardson, 1957). This more widely conceived approach has not been followed up since the war and it is fair to say that hill-fort excavations have progressed relatively little beyond purely typological and chronological studies.

If, however, we regard a hill-fort as a structural manifestation of society's labour, created by the needs of the community, the development of a pattern of hill-forts can be seen to reflect social change. It follows that an analysis of hill-forts seen in relation to economic change and population growth will bring us closer to an understanding of the dynamics of social evolution. There are, of course, many difficulties in attempting such an approach, not the least being the severe limitations imposed by the evidence at present available, but if the attempt does nothing more than to force us to look at familiar material in a different way and to ask new questions of it, it will have served its purpose.

In the discussion to follow I have restricted myself to material from one environment, namely the chalklands of the south-east of Britain, and have considered the nature of the origins of hill-forts, the factors leading to the selection of certain sites for continued use and fortification and the emergence of recognisable political groupings.

II

THE ORIGINS OF HILL-FORTS

The enclosures which are normally classed together under the portmanteau heading of hill-forts often originate on sites which have previously been occupied or used in a variety of ways. These may be listed as follows:

E

53

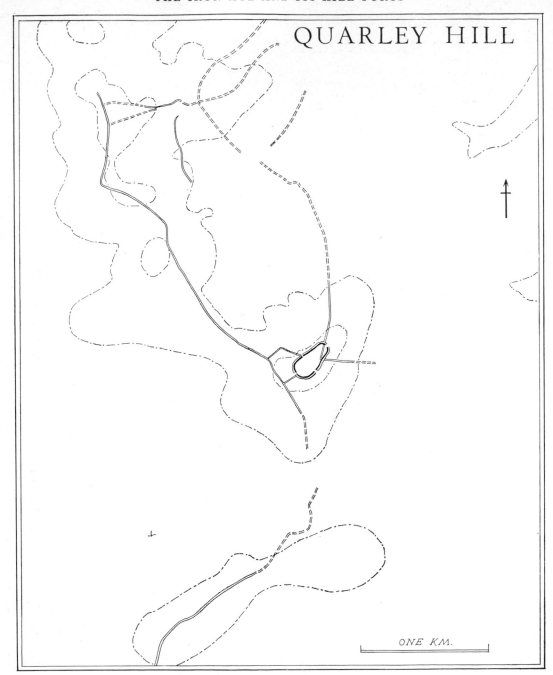

QUARLEY HILL

ONE KM.

Fig. 11. The 'ranch boundaries' and hill-fort on Quarley Hill, Hants.

1. *Settlement sites*

It is becoming increasingly clear that a number of hill-forts are built around sites which have a tradition of occupation stretching back to the beginning of the first millennium or even earlier. At South Cadbury, for example, a well defined and quite rich settlement existed on the summit of the hill sometime *c.* 1000 B.C. and continued in use possibly until the time that the defences were built. The 'Late Bronze Age' occupation at other sites like Mam Tor, Derbyshire, and Ivinghoe (Cotton and Frere, 1968) is also likely to have preceded the defences. Elsewhere the evidence for early occupation comes mainly in the form of stray finds like the collection of Late Bronze Age bronzes from Ham Hill, Somerset, or the gold lock rings from Harting Beacon, Sussex. At Highdown, Sussex, however, a continuous sequence can be traced from an open settlement probably of late second millennium date, through several phases of enclosure, to a reconstruction associated with pottery of about the fifth century B.C. (Wilson, 1940 and 1950).

2. *Religious foci*

At present Danebury is the only site which has produced evidence of a pre-hill-fort phase of apparently ritual use. The evidence takes the form of a series of ritual pits, which once contained upright timbers of considerable proportions, lying in an arc outside the line later taken by the hill-fort earthworks. Dating evidence suggests a date within the first half of the first millennium for the pits which would still have been visible by the time that the fort was built in the fifth–fourth century. Whether the area defined by the pits contained other ritual structures is at present unknown.

The fact that the pits were discovered by accident, outside the main enclosures, is a firm reminder that other forts may yet produce similar structures.

3. *Focal positions in relation to ranch boundaries*

The best known example of this type of siting is provided by Quarley Hill (Hawkes, 1939), where Professor Hawkes was able to demonstrate how the hill-fort had been constructed over a series of ranch boundaries which, by virtue of later additions relating to the defences of the fort, must still have served as significant boundaries (fig. 11). It is possible that some of the ditches radiating from Sidbury also pre-date the fort (but see p. 62).

4. *Pastoral enclosures*

Sometimes small pastoral enclosures originating in the Bronze Age were later incorporated into hill-forts. Rams Hill, Berks. (Piggott and Piggott, 1940), is a case in point. Here an irregular enclosure dating to the second millennium and showing signs of occupation into the beginning of the first millennium was later surrounded by a more considerable enclosure of hill-fort proportions dating to the sixth century. A similar situation, less closely dated, appears to have existed at Thundersbarrow Hill, Sussex (Curwen, 1933). The little rectangular enclosure on Harrow Hill, Sussex (Holleyman, 1937), which probably belongs to the early mid-first millennium, is a good example of a pastoral enclosure which was not later consumed by a hill-fort. Its position, on a hill-top surrounded by a number of open farming settlements sited on neighbouring

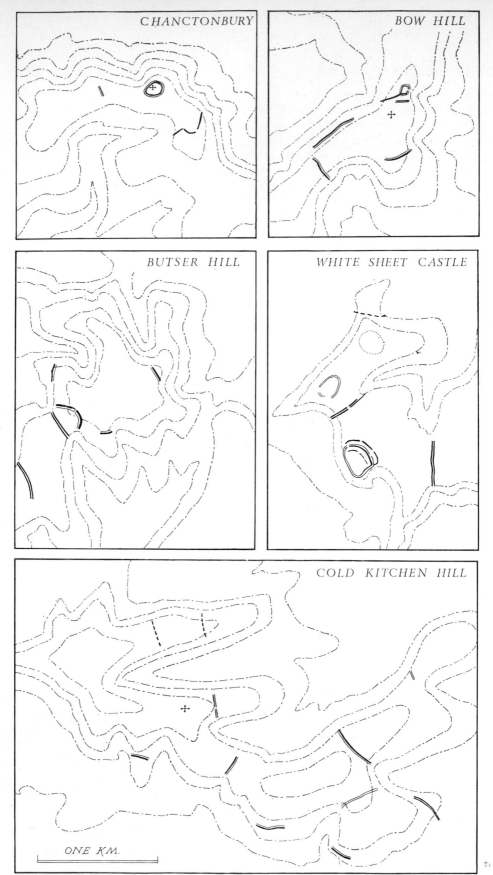

Fig. 12. Plateau enclosures in Southern Britain. Contours at 100 ft. intervals.
Romano-Celtic temples marked with a cross.

spurs, strongly suggests that it served as a collecting enclosure for the livestock of several local communities. The unusual number of cows' skulls found in the limited excavation indicates that the enclosure may have been used for periodic slaughter on a large scale.

5. *Plateau enclosures*

A number of the hill-tops along the chalk downs are partially enclosed by short lengths of banks and ditches which cut across necks of land and spurs, defining considerable tracts of flat or slightly undulating land. While most are undated, there is good reason for suggesting an early first millennium date. The function of these enclosures is uncertain but they would have been ideal for the collection of large herds of livestock or for tribal or religious meetings. A selection are illustrated in fig. 12 to demonstrate the range both of siting and complexity.

Having described the potential locations of hill-forts in typological terms, something must be said of the social significance of the various foci. The settlement sites differ noticeably from contemporary open farms in that the farms tend to be sited on spurs and hill-slopes rather than on hill-tops. Furthermore many of the hill-top settlements are rich, producing surprising quantities of bronzes and even occasional gold objects. It is difficult to resist the conclusion that a difference in status may have existed between the two types of settlement, those on the hill-tops belonging to the upper échelons of a developing class structure. The fact that some of the sites were enclosed by earthworks points to the existence of incipient coercive power in the hands of the occupants.

The small pastoral enclosures, on the other hand, must represent the communal activity of a group of families while the much larger plateau enclosures presumably reflect the effort of larger groupings, perhaps of tribal size. It is tempting to see the plateau enclosures as following in the tradition of the Neolithic causewayed camps, and serving as places of tribal assembly where periodic gatherings could be held, business transacted and the gods worshipped. Positive evidence is not, admittedly, forthcoming but the fact that many of the sites are later graced with small Romano-Celtic temples (e.g. Chanctonbury, Bow Hill, Cold Kitchen Hill etc.) might point to a continuity of religious tradition. Moreover the continued use of old hill-fort sites as *loci* for tribal meetings is dramatically borne out by the listing of a number of such sites in Northern Britain as tribal centres in the *Ravenna Cosmography*.

While there are, of course, underlying economic aspects behind the differences in the siting and the types of foci, it is the purpose of this contribution to emphasise the social aspects and leave the other matters for discussion elsewhere.

III

THE SELECTION OF CERTAIN FOCI FOR FURTHER ENCLOSURE AND DEFENCE

Having described the principal types of locations from which some hill-forts later develop, it is necessary to examine briefly the process of selection leading to the continued use of some sites and the abandonment of others.

The plateau enclosures sometimes develop into hill-forts. Butser Hill with its un-finished defensive earthwork would appear to provide a good example of the beginnings of such a process (Piggott, 1930). At Chanctonbury Ring a simple enclosure was completed in the centre of the defined plateau area, while at Whitesheet the history of enclosure and defence is evidently far more complicated leading, in its final stages, to the development of a hill-fort of substantial proportions. The smaller pastoral enclosures like Thundersbarrow, Rams Hill and probably Hollingbury, all developed into the sites of hill-forts built on a much larger scale than the original enclosures, while at Highdown the defensive circuit first constructed in the early first millennium was later refurbished on exactly the same lines. Many other enclosures of this kind were, however, abandoned.

Of the religious foci there is little at present to say. The one certain example, at Danebury, did continue in use as a conventional hill-fort but the possibility remains that many similar sites, at present unrecognised, were abandoned.

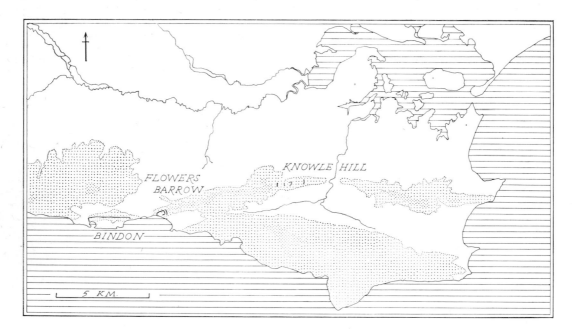

Fig. 13. Enclosures on the Purbeck Hills, Dorset. Land over 250 ft. is shaded.

The process of selection and abandonment is very clearly demonstrated by the sites on the chalk ridge of the Purbeck Hills in South Dorset (fig. 13). Here there are three potential locations for hill-forts: the early pre-Roman Iron Age settlement site at Church Knowle (*RCHM Dorset* II, 509) where the process of enclosure had begun; the vast hill-top of Bindon (Wheeler, 1953) with its extensive series of earthworks, some of them unfinished, dividing up large territories; and the ridge-end at Flowers Barrow (*RCHM Dorset* II, 490), where there are traces of cross-ridge dykes which probably pre-date the later earthworks. Of these, Flowers Barrow developed as a hill-fort in the conventional sense of the word, the others were abandoned or neglected. Whatever the reasons for the emergence to dominance of Flowers Barrow were, there can be little doubt that the defensive potential of the site will not have gone unnoticed. This is but one example, there are however many other areas where this early selection of one location at the expense of others can be seen to take place.

Since the construction of hill-fort defences would have entailed the organised labour of considerable numbers of people, it can be said that in the middle of the first millennium there began a polarisation of coercive power on certain centres. There is, as yet, too little evidence to be dogmatic as to the type of location commonly selected, but superficially it would appear that the occupation sites were more often chosen than the clan or tribal pastoral enclosures. If this observation eventually proves to be true, *one* interpretation would be that power was passing into the hands of individuals at the expense of communal organisation. Put another way, the process of enclosure in the period *c.* 600–400 is consistent with the emergence of a powerful aristocracy. A few hundred years later Caesar and Tacitus provide us with indisputable proof of the ultimate development and breakdown of this aspect of the social scene.

IV

THE RISE TO DOMINANCE OF SELECTED CENTRES

The process of selection which we have just outlined continued throughout the Iron Age – a few centres rose to dominance, others were abandoned.

Perhaps the clearest demonstration of this at present available is provided by the settlement pattern of the Sussex Downs, the evidence for which has been meticulously amassed by several generations of local archaeologists beginning with Pitt Rivers. The number of defended or enclosed sites occupied during the period *c.* 600–400 is considerable, covering the chalkland in an even scatter, but when those sites occupied in the second–first centuries B.C. are planned a totally different pattern emerges. There are many fewer and each clearly dominates a well defined territory of 25–40 square miles, usually bordered by river valleys which form the natural land divisions of the area. Much the same pattern appears to hold good for the chalkland of Wiltshire where natural boundaries are less evident, but by selecting those sites showing signs of occupation in the second–first centuries B.C., plotting them, and constructing their potential territories in terms of Theissen polygons, the probable spheres of influence of each fort emerge quite often closely related to river valleys (fig. 14). While it must be admitted that there is an element of subjectivity in this particular example, the overall impression is clear enough – that by the first century B.C. territories averaging 35 square miles were the normal socio-economic unit for a single large hill-fort on the southern chalkland.

Another, impressive, example of much the same point was made by Dyer in his plan of the Iron Age territorial divisions on the Chilterns (Dyer, 1961), where he was able to define a series of territories bounded partly by river valleys and partly by earthworks cutting across the chalk ridge. Within each of these land blocks there lay a

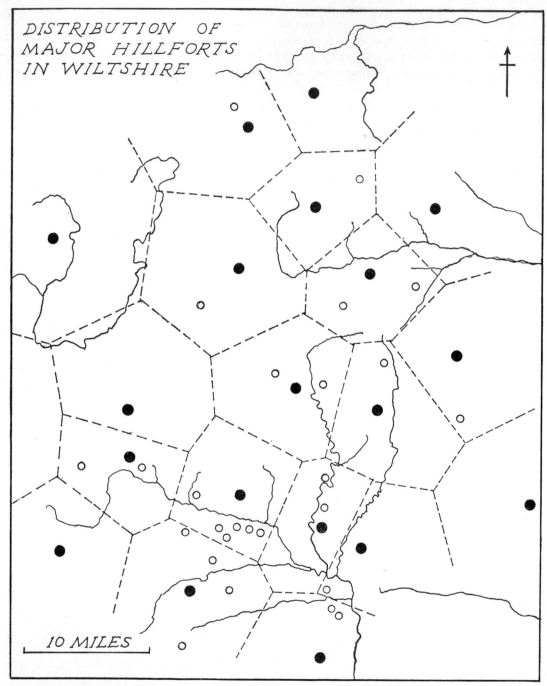

Fig. 14. Salisbury Plain showing hill-forts probably occupied in the first century B.C. (black circles) and their potential territories constructed as Theissen polygons. Other enclosures are shown as open circles.

hill-fort. Dyer's excavation of one of the dividing earthworks, Dray's Ditches, demonstrated dramatically both the antiquity and continuity of the land divisions.

We can assume then, that the emergence of strongly defended hill-forts dominating well defined territories was a late stage in a continuous process of social development. It is now necessary to examine some of the factors which may have affected this development (fig. 15).

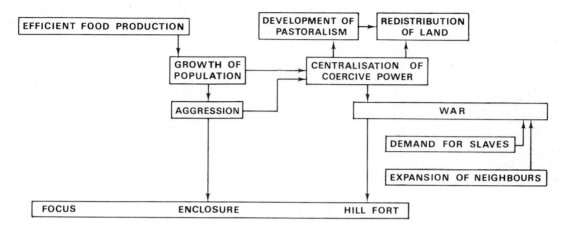

Fig. 15. Diagram to demonstrate factors affecting the process of enclosure.

The introduction of winter-sown barley and wheat early in the first millennium would have lengthened both the period of preparation and sowing and of harvest, making a fresh corn supply available earlier in the season. There can be little doubt that the added mastery over food supply, brought about by this development, would have tended to release productive forces in society. One possible consequence of such a change may well have been a gradual growth in population accompanied by a related expansion of the total acreage brought under the plough.

It is at present difficult to define population growth in archaeological terms, but one example may be quoted to give some support to the contention. On a typical stretch of chalk downland at Chalton, Hampshire, a detailed field and aerial survey has been carried out over a period of years in an attempt to discover the total settlement pattern of all dates. Such an aim has led to the discovery of a very large number of occupation sites, presumably approximating to a reasonably high percentage of the actual total. Now since it is permissible to assume that the sites of one period are generally likely to be no more difficult to discover than those of another, actual numbers may be compared. The number of late Bronze Age sites is six, the number belonging to the early part of the pre-Roman Iron Age is five, while of second to first century B.C. date there are 11 – a number which increases only a little in the Roman period. While we cannot argue in detail from these crude figures, the apparent increase in the number of settlements by the late pre-Roman Iron Age is surely meaningful. Unless special pleading is introduced it may reasonably be thought to imply an increase in population.

Increase in population and the colonisation of land consequent upon it would inevitably have led to conflict, the signs of which are not far to seek. The occupants of farmsteads like Little Woodbury and Meon Hill frequently adopted earthwork defences in place of fences; weapons, including slings, became relatively more common on occupation sites of the later Iron Age, and the universal adoption of the underground storage of food corn in the later period might also be interpreted, in part at least, as a protective measure. A situation in which there was stress and conflict would inevitably lead to the development of a warrior aristocracy. It is against this background that the emergence of strongly defended hill-forts must be seen.

There is a separate, less tangible, factor which is closely linked to social change (though whether as a cause or an effect is not immediately clear) that is the apparent increase in significance of herding in the later part of the Iron Age. It is not possible in this paper to parade all the evidence which may be thought to have a bearing on the matter, but merely to look at the problem in relation to hill-forts. We have already seen that the fort on Quarley Hill was built over a system of ranch boundaries, an observation which led to the general assumption that ranch boundaries were all early. But this is not so. At Sidbury, for example, one of the boundaries converging on the fort appears to join the earthworks of the fort entrance in its most evolved state and therefore must be late. Similarly the recent excavations at Danebury have shown that the boundary earthwork which straggles for a considerable distance across the countryside is part of the outer ditched enclosure dug around the fort, probably as late as the first century B.C. This outer enclosure delineates a considerable tract of pasture land, which lies between it and the main defences, dividing pasture from the surrounding arable. The first century enclosure was preceded by an earlier annex of smaller area, attached to the south side of the fort in the third or second century and rendered obsolete by the reconstruction of the main entrance in about 100 B.C. Simply stated the Danebury evidence shows an increase in the facilities for corralling livestock close to the fort as time passes. By the first century B.C. many thousands of beasts could be driven into the safety of the surrounding enclosure.

Before this line of approach can be pursued much further it is clearly necessary to examine in detail the relationship of hill-forts to the surrounding agricultural pattern. Danebury gives some idea of the potential of this approach with its field systems, areas of pasture and trackways developing in relation to the focus. The distinction between arable and pasture is even clearer in relation to the neighbouring hill-fort of Woolbury (fig. 16), while the recent work of the Royal Commission on Historic Monuments in the Sidbury region is holding out the possibility of being able to define periods during which linear ditches were being driven through field systems, suggesting the redistribution of land on a large scale.

The provision of enclosed pasture attached to hill-forts is by no means a feature restricted to the chalk areas. The multiple enclosure forts of the south-west are a specialised type of settlement employing exactly the same features, and forts like Almondbury and Old Oswestry (Varley, 1950) show much the same sequence as Danebury.

If, then, we are correct in assuming that livestock played an increasingly important part in the late Iron Age economy, we must briefly consider the social implications.

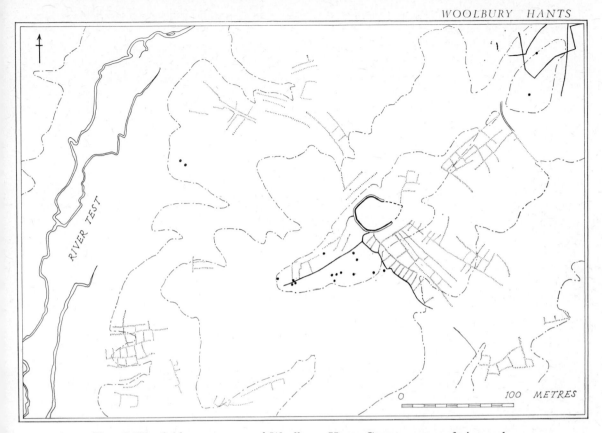

Fig. 16. The field systems around Woolbury, Hants. Contours at 100 ft. intervals.

Cattle were presumably now being regarded as a manifestation of wealth and it follows that the simplest way to demonstrate wealth, and indeed to accumulate it, was by the amassing of considerable herds. If the emerging warrior aristocracy of Britain compared with the heroic class society of the continental Celts, reflected in the classical literature, then one would expect there to be provision for herding on a large scale. While the evidence of corralling associated with the developing strongly defended hill-forts *proves* little, it is entirely consistent with the use of these places as the centres of the British aristocracy during the ultimate phase of their aggressive development. One further point must be made: the occurrence of large herds would encourage raiding thus adding to the active aggressive trends already present in society.

Finally, the increasing importance of external influences on social development must be stressed. The massive movements of population in Gaul in the first century B.C. and the threat, and actuality, of Roman attack in this country must have added to the growing turmoil. But a no less significant factor was the existence, after the mid-first century B.C., of an easily accessible Roman consumer market ready to absorb slaves in unlimited quantities. This is not the place to indulge in a detailed consideration of the matter except to stress that if a captive now had a cash value, raiding for the profit motive would undoubtedly have been encouraged.

Thus the direction in which society was developing during the latter part of the first millennium was towards active aggression and away from local self-protection. Social groups were polarising around individuals many of whom would have served principally as war leaders, not just as local kings. This situation was summarised by Tacitus when he wrote 'Once they owed obedience to kings, now they are distracted between the jarring factions of rival chiefs. Indeed nothing has helped us more in war with their strongest nations than this inability to co-operate. It is but seldom that two or three states unite to repel a common danger: fighting in detail they are conquered wholesale' (Tacitus, *Agricola* 12). The significance here is the distinction Tacitus draws between the early phase of kingship and the later phase in which active aggression was dominant. This is precisely the kind of social development which was occuring in Germany between the first century B.C. and the first century A.D. (Thompson, 1965).

V

THE FUNCTION OF THE FORTS IN THE FIRST CENTURY B.C.

It is not the purpose of this paper to discuss the vexed question of whether or not the late forts were permanently occupied. Sir Mortimer's work at Maiden Castle and his famous distribution map of 'hill towns' in Wessex leaves little doubt where his views lie – he considered the forts, in their late phases, to represent urban agglomerations. More recent work at Croft Ambrey, South Cadbury, Hod Hill and Danebury has gone a very long way to support this view. Indeed the social model which we have been considering, together with an assessment of the later social development into the Roman era, almost requires some form of nucleation to have come about by the first century B.C. Purists may argue that the use of the word 'town' to describe the larger late southern forts is incorrect, but the whole matter of urbanisation is in such a state of flux even in the minds of the geographers that dogmatic definition can no longer be accepted. At the very least it is true to say that large populations now inhabited the major hill-forts for much, if not all, of the year. In other words, a large labour pool was now concentrated on certain foci under the coercive power of individual leaders.

In such circumstances, with the coming together of population concentration, the emergence of a warrior aristocracy and the development of aggressive tendencies, it is hardly surprising that the structures of hill-forts should reflect the social situation. The famous east entrance at Maiden Castle provides a magnificent example with all its complex tactical planning and enormous expenditure of labour. Another example, smaller in scale but no less impressive, in concept, is Danebury where the east entrance can at last be understood (fig. 17). The focus of the plan is a command post, constructed on a hornwork in the centre of the complex, from which both gates, considerable lengths of the main fort ditches and the protecting outer hornworks can all be kept under strict supervision. Moreover all parts of the entrance complex lie within a 60–70 metre range: a distance within which any competent slinger could pick off an opponent with

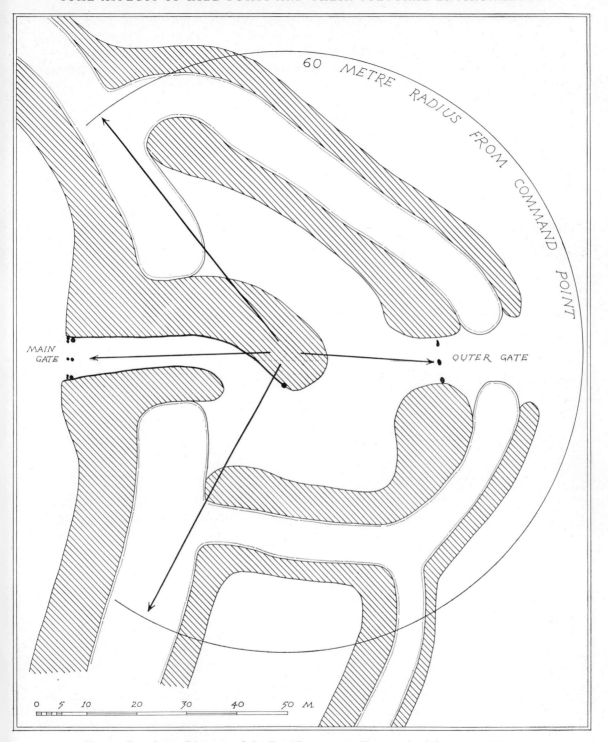

Fig. 17. Danebury. Diagram of the East Entrance to illustrate its defensive qualities.

deadly accuracy. There can be no doubt at all that the massive rebuilding of the gate *c.* 100 B.C., which resulted in its most developed form, came about in response to a deliberate and carefully prepared scheme in which defensive considerations were uppermost. However much the earlier gates owed their form to the desire to impress those who approached the forts, by the first century B.C. the structure of most fort gates was determined entirely by the need to withstand attack.

We have seen, then, that three trends emerge: the development of a single large focus within a territory, the nucleation of population at that focus and the growth of a strong defensive system. It must however be emphasised that hill-forts do not exist in isolation, they are part of a territory. One such territory, more clearly defined than most, is that lying between the rivers Arun and Adur in Sussex, centred upon the large and little understood fort of Cissbury (fig. 18). Cissbury became the dominant focus at the expense of Highdown, Harrow Hill and Chanctonbury, all of which originated as different types of potential *loci*. On this block of downland it stands unrivalled and must surely be the centre of local government, exercising control over the surrounding farming communities. Relatively few of the local settlements are known but if the density is anything like that of the Chalton region the size of the population must have

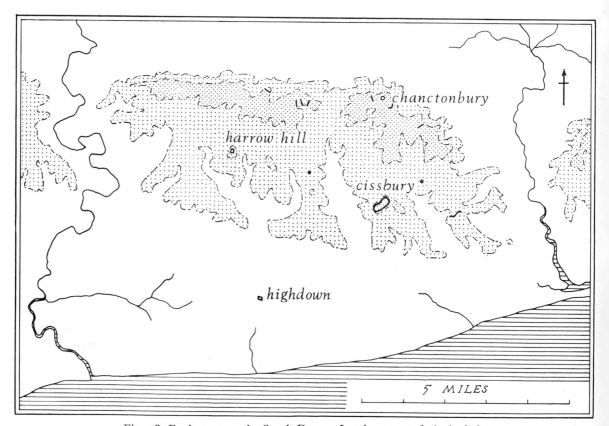

Fig. 18. Enclosures on the South Downs. Land over 250 ft. is shaded.

been in the order of 1,400. The changes taking place in the rural settlement in parallel with the development of centralised control are likely to be of considerable significance to the understanding of the social dynamics of the region but until an immense amount of fieldwork has been carried out together with a programme of selective excavation, the relationships between the dispersed and centralised communities must remain largely unknown.

VI

HILL-FORTS AND HISTORY

The work of Sir Mortimer at Maiden Castle and later at Stanwick demonstrated dramatically and convincingly the way in which hill-forts can, in their later periods, be linked directly to an historical framework built up primarily from literary sources. In much the same way, I believe, it is possible to isolate areas of diverse political affiliations.

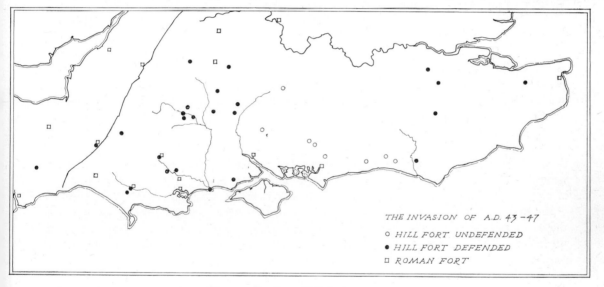

Fig. 19. Southern Britain in A.D. 43.

If, for south-eastern Britain, a map is drawn (fig. 19) plotting the hill-forts which show signs of defensive measures, or at the least intensive occupation, at the time of the Roman invasion of A.D. 43 in contrast to those forts where there is enough reasonable evidence to suggest abandonment by this time, a significant pattern is revealed. Between the Test and the Sussex Ouse there is no sign of hill-forts being brought into defensive readiness, whereas to the east, in Kent and East Sussex, and to the west, in Wessex, many of the forts produce evidence of mid-first century A.D. defences and some were actually attacked by the Roman army. On this evidence alone one might suggest that two different policies towards Rome were being pursued. Add to the plan the distribution of the coins of Verica, the last of the Atrebatic rulers, and they will be seen to concentrate in just the area of the undefended territory. Knowing, from the documentary sources, that this southern part of the Atrebatic kingdom was pro-Roman before the invasion and maintained an active Romanophile policy in the decades to follow, and the picture takes on a political form. The hill-fort evidence appears to reflect directly, as might reasonably be expected, the native political attitudes of A.D. 43. An alternative explanation is, however, possible. It could be argued that the abandonment of the Atrebatic hill-forts resulted from the growth of the oppidum at Selsey and the concentration of power on the single large urban agglomeration. Such an explanation lacks conviction, particularly when the situation is compared with East Sussex and Kent where both oppida and hill-forts continue in use side by side.

There is perhaps a further point to be made on the implications of the westerly part of the map, and that is the apparent difference between the treatment of the Salisbury Plain area and the region to the south of the Ebble-Nadder ridge extending into Dorset and Somerset. In this southern area, which represents the territory of the Durotriges, not only were hill-forts occupied in A.D. 43, they were also destroyed by Vespasian's troops and the territory garrisoned. This treatment appears to contrast with the northern area where the forts were indeed occupied and one at least was redefended, but there is no sign of Roman attack nor are any Roman garrisons known in the area. If, in the light of future work, this disparity still holds good, it will be tempting to explain it as a difference in political attitude towards the advancing army – at first both the Durotriges and then northern neighbours took up arms against the invaders, but only the Durotriges held out to the bitter end, the northern communities submitting without resistance.

Even without supporting documentary and numismatic evidence it would have been possible to work out something of the political pressures and reactions to the threat of invasion in A.D. 43. It is therefore not unreasonable to suppose that other widespread events may be fossilised in the structures of hill-forts. Could not the phase of massive refortifications which takes place in Wessex and Sussex about the beginning of the first century B.C. be in some way related to the incursion of Caesar's 'Belgae' and the dislocations which may have followed consequent upon them? Possibly, but such speculations, interesting though they may be, take us beyond the scope of the present paper.

VII

A hill-fort is an artifact. Sir Mortimer's early excavations taught us to study these artifacts thoroughly and he has shown us how to use them to build up a picture of people, their lives and the events which impinged upon them. In this paper I have attempted to extend the study by using hill-forts, together with other relevant evidence, to define the direction of social change and to attempt to elucidate some of its intricacies. If this has achieved no more than to stimulate discussion it will have served its purpose.

BIBLIOGRAPHY

Cotton, M. E., and Frere 1968. 'Ivinghoe Beacon, Excavations 1963–5', *Rec. of Bucks.*, XVIII, 187–260.

Curwen, E. C. 1933. 'Excavations on Thundersbarrow Hill, Sussex', *Antiq. Journ.*, XIII, 109–133.

Dyer, J. F. 1961. 'Dray's Ditches, Bedfordshire, and Early Iron Age Territorial Boundaries in the Eastern Chilterns', *Antiq. Journ.*, XLI, 32–43.

Hawkes, C. F. C. 1939. 'The Excavations at Quarley Hill, 1938', *PHFCAS*, XIV, 136–194.

Holleyman, G. A. 1937. 'Harrow Hill Excavations 1936', *SAC*, 78, 230–252.

Piggott, S. 1930. 'Butser Hill', *Antiquity*, 187–200.

Piggott, S and C. M. 1940. 'Excavations at Rams Hill, Uffington, Berks.', *Antiq. Journ.*, XX, 465–480.

Richardson, K. M. 1940. 'Excavations at Poundbury, Dorchester, Dorset, 1939', *Antiq. Journ.*, XX, 429–448.

RCHM(Eng), 1970. *Dorset* II, London.

Thompson, E. A. 1965. *The Early Germans*, Oxford.

Varley, W. J. 1950. 'The Hill-forts of the Welsh Marches', *Antiq. Journ.*, XXIII, CV, 41–66.

Wheeler, R. E. M. 1943. *Maiden Castle, Dorset*, Oxford.

Wheeler, R. E. M. 1953. 'An Early Iron Age Beach-head at Lulworth, Dorset.' *Antiq. Journ.*, XXXIII, 1–13.

Wheeler, R. E. M., and Richardson, K. M. 1957. *Hill-forts of Northern France*, Oxford.

Whitley, M. 1943. 'Excavations at Chalbury Camp, Dorset, 1939', *Antiq. Journ.*, XXIII, 98–121.

Wilson, A. E. 1940. 'Report on the Excavations at Highdown Hill, Sussex, August 1939', *SAC*, 81, 173–204.

Wilson, A. E. 1950. 'Excavations on Highdown Hill, 1947', *SAC*, 89, 163–178.

ECONOMIC CHANGE IN THE GROWTH OF EARLY HILL-FORTS

By Richard Bradley

SUMMARY

This paper is an attempt to consider the first hill-forts in central southern England in the light of the precursors from which they had developed. It is suggested that hill-forts growing up from preceding stock compounds or tracts of enclosed pasture are earlier in date than those developing from arable farms. An attempt is made to account for this pattern against a background of social change and arable intensification, both brought about by population increase and an attendant shortage of land. In this context changes in the nature and siting of hill-forts are explained mainly by changes in the basis of communal prosperity.

This contribution to the symposium is a personal attempt to start, though not to split, hares. Amidst its generalisations, some of these hares may prove to be lame, others may run the wrong way and others again make off so swiftly that this writer never catches them; but at least an essay devoted to future work provides the right opportunity to set speculation in place of dogma. This paper has two objectives: to relate the morphology and sequence of the earliest hill-forts in central southern England to the types of site from which they had developed, and to offer a general interpretation of the processes which governed their creation and their abandonment. In presenting so detailed a study of one phase and one region, I am proposing a change from a static to a dynamic conception of the Iron Age economy and its relationship to hill-fort building. In a paper in which the main emphasis falls upon continuity it is particularly pleasing that the discussion should again review the pairing of certain downland hill-forts highlighted more than 30 years ago (J. Hawkes, 1940: 345).

Within the chronological and regional limits already indicated it is possible to see hill-forts growing up upon four different types of site, though those enclosures constructed upon virgin land must fall outside this particular approach. Two of the remaining groups of site introduce the pastoral element in the economy of the early pre-Roman Iron Age and the third the arable contribution. This last group is by now so well known that little need be said of it in this short discussion. The hill-forts of this group grow out of open or palisaded arable farms, usually with storage pits and round houses, and seem to form only part of a continuum of earthwork enclosures that extends to the fortification of simple homesteads which have little claim to be considered as 'forts' at all (Bersu, 1940). As a settlement type these farms have their origin in the Bronze Age. The fort earthworks which take their places are frequently timber laced and normally follow the natural contours of the site. The gates are usually simple but strongly defended while the cleaning of the ditch silts frequently produces a counterscarp bank. Storage pits continue to be abundant within these new enclosures and so uniform have these earthworks seemed that they have at times been claimed as

71

a response to a single historical situation (C. Hawkes, 1940: 333). Examples are Mount Caburn (Wilson, 1938 and 1939), Blewburton (A. Collins, 1947 and 1952; A. and F. Collins, 1959; Harding, 1967) and the Trundle (E. C. Curwen, 1929 and 1931).

The second group of sites consists of hill-forts which develop from earthworks which had served principally as pastoral enclosures, though it would be wrong to assume automatically that they had never been occupied. The latter type develops directly from the feeble rectilinear enclosures found in Wessex in the Middle and Late Bronze Ages (C. Piggott, 1942) and now recognised in both Bronze and Iron Age contexts in Hampshire and Sussex. Here they frequently appear in direct association with linear boundary ditches (Bradley, 1971a). With the current emphasis on continuity it is worth remembering that their part in hill-fort development was first seen by Professor Hawkes 40 years ago (1931: 67). The earlier enclosures are up to one hectare in extent with simple entrances, dump ramparts and external ditches. The associated animal remains indicate an important connection with cattle farming (C. Piggott, 1942) and suggest that one use of the enclosures was for butchering (Bradley, 1967). The hill-forts which take their places normally enclose a larger area though the newer circuit is usually based upon the earlier enclosure. Sometimes, but not invariably, the newer earthworks retain something of the common subrectangular outline of their predecessors. With two important exceptions, Wolstonbury (E. C. Curwen, 1930a) and possibly Rybury[1] (E. C. Curwen, 1930b: 38), the ditches are external, while the fort ramparts are often timber revetted. Simple unelaborated gateways again occur but these sites are without traces either of internal storage pits or, frequently, of a counterscarp bank. Examples of this type are Hollingbury (E. C. Curwen, 1932), Thundersbarrow (E. C. Curwen, 1933) and Quarley Hill (C. Hawkes, 1939: 169).

The third group is the most important in this account but has not received attention until recently (Bradley, 1971a and b). It will therefore be necessary to outline this type in rather fuller detail. These sites grow out of a distinctive pattern of later Bronze Age and early Iron Age land use clearly recognised in Sussex and Hampshire and almost certainly represented in Wiltshire and Dorset. Here it seems that the spurs and valleys of the chalk downland were used for arable farming, though with intervals as grazing land in periods of fallow, while the open ridges above were divided by cross dykes into blocks of outfield pasture. On the more even plateau of central Wessex the same purpose was served by longer 'ranch boundaries' which, like cross dykes, seem to appear in the later Bronze Age. The hill-forts of this group develop in their different ways from the tracts of pasture defined by these earthworks.

These enclosures are unusually extensive in area and yet surprisingly slight in profile. They can cover as much as 35 hectares while in siting they tend to occupy high promontory positions. Their ramparts frequently present a greater obstacle than their slight surrounding ditches and may be partly derived from internal quarry scoops (Bradley, 1971b). The ditches are separated from their spoil by so wide a berm that a revetted rampart seems to have been intended rather than a continuous glacis. Partly as a result of these characteristics several members of this group have been described

---

[1] This argument assumes that the flattened inner enclosure concentric with the Iron Age fort rampart is its immediate precursor, as at Wolstonbury, and not the inner ditch of the Neolithic causewayed enclosure.

as unfinished. Not all of these earthworks can strictly be classified as promontory forts but on three sites where the circuit is continuous the rampart is partly or wholly external. In this group too, little emphasis is placed upon the gateway while domestic debris is often lacking from the interior of sites which are now under the plough. On undamaged sites there are no traces of pits. Examples where a hill-fort grows up directly from earlier land divisions are Butser Hill (S. Piggott, 1930), Ladle Hill[2] (S. Piggott, 1931), Walbury (Williams Freeman, 1915: 414), Chilcombe and Eggardon (RCHM, 1952: 97 and 13).

Other similar earthworks may, however, be admitted to this group. In Sussex possible examples are at Belle Tout, where the ditch of a 20 hectare promontory fort was barely one metre deep (Bradley, 1971b); Ranscombe Camp, where a timber laced promontory dyke develops from an earlier lynchet separating ploughed and unploughed land (Burstow and Holleyman, 1964: figs. 2, 5, 7 and 10); the Devils Dyke which develops from another promontory earthwork of uncertain nature (Clinch, 1905: 461); Rackham Bank, a greatly elaborated univallate cross ridge dyke, perhaps replacing a slighter bivallate ditch to its west (E. and E. C. Curwen, 1922: 45; E. Curwen, 1932); and Beacon Hill, Harting, where a large but feeble enclosure occupies a promontory position in between two spaced tracts of cross ridge dykes[3] (Keef, 1953). On the Isle of Wight Five Barrows may be an unfinished member of this group (Dunning, 1947), while on the Hampshire mainland the first 18 hectare enclosure at Balksbury calls for attention in view of its slight surrounding earthwork (Wainwright, 1969). In Wiltshire another possible site is Martinsell Hill which occupies an area of downland defined by a cross ridge dyke and is itself joined to a linear ditch (Meyrick, 1946: 256), while in Dorset the unfinished promontory fort at Nettlecombe Tout may similarly have developed from a complex of earlier cross dykes.[4] More generally, the 11 hectare enclosure at Hog Cliff Hill might be related to this group (Rahtz, 1960). Here only a limited area of an extensive earthwork enclosure seems to have been occupied by structures or pits while the site itself is surrounded by a ditch and external bank. It is now worth noticing how the sites of this group tend to occupy higher land than those developing from arable farms. Butser Hill is the highest point in Hampshire and Walbury that in Berkshire. In Wiltshire Martinsell Hill comes runner-up to Milk Hill by less than 5 metres.

There are perhaps three generalisations which may be taken without strain to link the sites of these different types. In the first place each of these groups of hill-fort is developing from a settlement or earthwork type which spans the division between Bronze and Iron Ages as normally defined. At the same time the close continuity between the boundaries of the earlier sites and the outlines of the succeeding hill-forts is too regular to suggest a major break in occupation. The palisade of the first farm may

---

[2] I have followed Piggott's suggestion that the earliest visible enclosure is a 'setting out bank' for the unfinished fort. An equally permissible interpretation would make it a pastoral enclosure comparable to that at Quarley Hill.

[3] One of the group of cross dykes on Harting Down to the west seems to be sealed by a round barrow and so these earthworks could possibly be much earlier than the fort. Compare the spaced cross dykes of Neolithic date flanking the approaches to the causewayed enclosure at Hambledon Hill.

[4] For a superb survey of this complex, with its possible concentric zones of pasture and arable, see new RCHM, Central Dorset (1971), 330–1.

be found beneath the rampart of the later fort, as at Blewburton, while the forts taking the place of pastoral enclosures may either remodel the existing earthwork, as at Quarley Hill, or base an enlarged circuit upon the line of the original, as happened at Thundersbarrow. Where a hill-fort took the place of two such enclosures at Ladle Hill it adopted not their own outline but probably that of the linear ditches defining the tract of associated pasture. The relationship of other hill-forts and land divisions created by cross ridge dykes is very similar and the existing earthwork might either be incorporated into the new design, as at Chilcombe, or used as the basis of the new enclosure as at Butser Hill. A mixture of either principle is apparently represented at Rockbourne Knoll (Williams Freeman, 1915: 400), while such a development in unfinished form may be seen about the pastoral settlement at Church Knowle (RCHM, 1970: 509).

The third feature is harder to treat with confidence in view of the imbalance in hill-fort studies towards the examination of defences. It does appear nonetheless that no major change of economy need be envisaged to accompany the transformation of these sites. The arable farms continue to contain storage pits and, presumably, houses, while the pastoral enclosures, though they may contain structures, do not seem to have included large pits. The same is true of the more extensive enclosures defined in the preceding section, which are not always accompanied by domestic refuse. Here the considerable areas of these sites, combined with their feeble defences, continue to be best suited for livestock. Certainly this observation applies to those sites of either pastoral group which have internal ditches. This is not of course to deny that grain can have been stored above ground on these sites nor that any may have been permanently occupied. What is suggested is that pastoralism continued to be sufficiently important on these sites that no attempt was made to assimilate them to the arable farms which seem to have existed in the same areas and at the same time. These arguments would be further strengthened if the excavators' suggestions that the timber structures inside the ramparts at Ivinghoe and Balksbury were not for grain storage could be substantiated (Cotton and Frere, 1968: 194; Wainwright, 1969: 32; cf. Tratman, 1970). At Ivinghoe it will be remembered that the evidence of pollen, animal bones and of the outline of the fort itself were felt to indicate a pastoral economy. It is worth noticing that the forts in the summer grazing areas of parts of Wales are also larger than the remaining examples and equally have a more upland distribution (Alcock, 1965: 188). About the south-western limit of the Jurassic Way another group of extensive univallate hill-forts have been interpreted in the light of a partly pastoral economy (Wainwright, 1967).

The chronology of these forts may be approached from two directions, though with the proviso throughout that any trends which emerge are probably only of local validity. No overall hill-fort 'horizons' are to be based upon this evidence, particularly in view of the regionalism shown by the distribution of the pastoral sites (fig. 20). In one sense the preceding arguments impose their own limitations on the possible date range for these sites since it appears that the dykes and enclosures from which they develop do not occur on the South Downs at least beyond the beginning of the Iron Age (Bradley, 1971a). More specifically it has been argued that the hill-forts developing from pastoral enclosures in Sussex belong to the early years of the Iron Age (Cunliffe,

1966: 118) while pottery in the relevant Caburn I style is associated beneath the rampart at Highdown with material in the local Bronze Age tradition (Wilson, 1940: 180). Of the sites suggested for this group only Rybury remains undated.

Rather similar considerations apply to both the forts developing from cross ridge dykes and their equivalents. Though the earthwork at Belle Tout has produced no stratified material, the interior of this site has included pottery in both Caburn I and later Bronze Age styles, while this site, like Highdown, has probably produced metalwork of the earlier period (Bradley, 1971b). Beacon Hill is associated with a foundation deposit of two penannular gold rings while the interior of this site too has produced a hoard of bronzes (Keef, 1953). Within Sussex again Ranscombe Camp has been partially excavated and, though the pottery is not fully published, this site also seems to predate the main Sussex hill-fort series and particularly the neighbouring fort of Mount Caburn which develops from an arable farm (Burstow and Holleyman, 1964: 64). Again an enclosure incorrectly described as a siege castle secondary to Rackham Bank seems better explained as an embanked farm in the later Bronze Age tradition (E. Curwen, 1932). In Hampshire recent excavation at Balksbury has suggested a date early in the sixth century B.C. (Wainwright, 1969: 53) and, although the pottery is entirely of coarse ware, it has been compared to the material from the further promontory dyke at Bindon in Dorset (Wheeler, 1953). Similar equations have been suggested

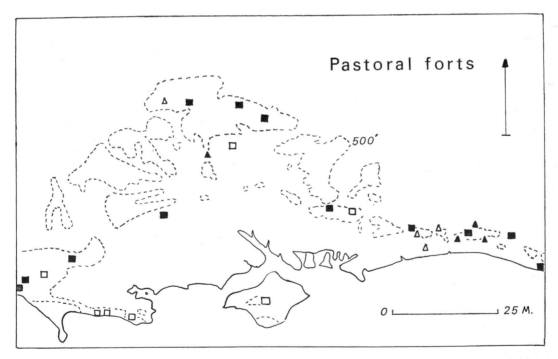

Fig. 20. Distribution of hill-forts developing from pastoral sites in Central Southern England. Black triangles: forts from pastoral enclosures; open triangles: possible sites; black squares: forts from enclosed pasture; open squares: possible or analogous sites.

75

by the excavator for the pottery from Hog Cliff Hill (Rahtz, 1960). The date of the earliest hill-fort at Chalbury is as difficult to assess as its economy. The earliest rampart on the site seals material of Bronze Age derivation in the Eldon Seat I tradition while pottery in the much later Eldon Seat II tradition fills the quarry for a controversial second phase of fort defences. The only structures and pit excavated inside the earthwork may belong to this second fort but, if this sequence is correct at all, much more extensive work would be needed before the nature of the earlier earthwork could be decided (Whitley, 1943; Cunliffe and Phillipson, 1968). Elsewhere in Dorset a date at the beginning of this period has been adopted for the settlement partially enclosed by cross dykes at Church Knowle (RCHM, 1970: 509), while one of the dykes facing the approach to Nettlecombe Tout has produced pottery attributed to the overlap of the Bronze and Iron Ages (Wacher, 1957).

The dating evidence for the main downland hill-fort series which finds its basis in arable farming is already well known and has often been discussed in the context of a possible invasion from the Continent. This problem is fortunately outside the scope of the present paper and it is merely necessary to repeat that a date in the fourth century B.C. would be generally appropriate for these sites. If the evidence for the sites deriving from pastoral enclosures and cross dykes is accepted a date in the sixth and fifth centuries B.C. might be more suitable for these. This sequence from excavation may now be strengthened by further evidence from the field.

It has long been noticed that pairs of hill-forts, one including grain storage pits and the other more suitable for containing livestock, are found in Sussex, Hampshire, Wiltshire and Dorset (J. Hawkes, 1940). While it might now appear that these morphological differences have been understood correctly, it is possible that these sites were not in use together and that one replaced the other. It is still uncertain whether this applies to the pairing of the forts of Balksbury and Bury Hill but if their excavators' datings are accepted this must have been the case (Wainwright, 1969; C. Hawkes, 1940). The same conclusion is demanded by the pairing of Ranscombe Camp with Mount Caburn which certainly began life as an arable farm (E. and E. C. Curwen, 1927). At this time a similar relationship could have existed between Rybury and the settlement of All Cannings Cross on the lower ground to its south. Another pair of sites where this contrast is well illustrated is Beacon Hill, Kingsclere, and the unfinished fort of Ladle Hill. Where the latter probably developed from two pastoral enclosures and two linear ditches, its neighbour little over a mile away includes the sites of pits and houses (Williams Freeman, 1915: 356). Other pairs of forts where this sequence may be represented are Beacon Hill, Harting, and Torberry (E. C. Curwen, 1954; Corcoran, 1959: 43); Butser Hill and Old Winchester Hill (Williams Freeman, 1915: 391); Martinsell Hill and Giant's Grave (Meyrick, 1946) and Chilcombe and Shipton Hill (RCHM, 1952: 97 and 222; Farrar, 1955). The likely sequence of forts at Eggardon may be possible support for this argument. Here it seems that an extensive univallate enclosure with an external bank took the place of two of a series of cross ridge dykes. This earthwork was subsequently replaced by a smaller and more massive hill-fort which was undergoing conversion into a bivallate earthwork when the site was abandoned. Fortunately the positions of the many pits on the site were visible until recently and could be seen to be entirely confined to the later univallate fort. However it must be added that for this argument to succeed the inturned east entrance of the earlier fort must be seen as secondary to its construction. Again less than 5 per cent of the pits have so far been excavated but these few have not proved to be for grain storage (Colley March, 1901).

In spite of such reservations it does seem that the earliest hill-forts in this region were mostly ones which developed from sites used for pastoral farming and that though arable farms were not lacking, these were only favoured as communal centres at a later date. The remainder of this paper must be devoted to an attempt to account for this paradox.

Though the main explanation to be offered here is economic, one aspect of the later Bronze Age background may be relevant. It has already been seen that within this period cross dykes seem to have divided up tracts of ridge-top pasture which may be associated with lynchet systems on the spurs below. In area, however, it is clear that these blocks of pasture must sometimes have greatly exceeded the extent of the arable fields, even under shifting cultivation. This disparity is even clearer with the blocks of upwards of 100 hectares of chalk downland enclosed by the earlier of the boundary ditches in Wessex (Hawkes, 1939: 141). At Chalton in Hampshire for example Cunliffe has suggested that a Middle Bronze Age farm may have had 6 hectares of fields (1970: 12) while the dykes on Butser Hill above, which may of course be rather later in date, enclose as much as 36 hectares. In other areas it is evident that the number of separate arable farms cannot always be equated with the number of areas of ridge-top divided up by these dykes, or indeed the number of associated pastoral enclosures. In fact it is possible that a community might be divided into several homesteads amidst their own fields and, whatever the accuracy of this assumption, it is inescapable that these areas of outfield must occasionally have been shared as common land. Their enclosure therefore is likely to have been the outcome of communal labour. It is likely that with expansion in this period a similar 'packing' of arable territories had been achieved by the early Iron Age (Fowler, 1964).

The possibility of earlier co-operation only provides a useful anticipation of the Iron Age pattern when it is linked to economic developments of far greater importance. In adopting this approach it is necessary to take notice of a background of population increase sufficient to bring about changes both in the size of individual communities and in the overall density of settlements. The evidence for these processes has already been presented in this conference and this must be accepted as a basic postulate of the discussion that now follows.

It is in fact possible that the period in which the earliest hill-forts in this region developed corresponds in time with two related thresholds created by the increase in numbers. These crises may be compared with the 'saturation' phenomena known to students of the social sciences (Feibleman and Friend, 1945). The first of these is represented archaeologically by the building of permanent land boundaries over much of the chalk downland and seems to represent a phase when the shortage of land for colonisation was giving rise to a more acute conception of territoriality, promoted no doubt by increased raiding between competing communities. In this context it is interesting to see that most cross dykes lack any entrances which would allow the ridges to be used as through routes from one area to another (Bradley, 1971a). It would be valuable to consider whether the more defensible univallate cross dykes of Wessex might sometimes be later in date than the bivallate ditches of Sussex (Fowler, 1964).

At the same time population increase might give rise to difficulties of a rather different nature, for it is clear that an unstratified community cannot easily increase in numbers beyond an optimum size as a result of internal tensions. 'The increase in numbers belonging to the same community is in itself sufficient to upset the balance between the personal bonds and the aggressive drive' (Lorenz, 1966: 217). It is usual in these circumstances for the group to divide and for one segment to colonise another area. Here, however, the scarcity of land seen earlier has its effects. Indeed, even though fresh areas may have remained to be settled towards the end of the Iron Age, these do not seem to have been perceived as potential territory at this stage. In any case the settlement of marginal land might bring little relief in view of its frequent inherent poverty and the resulting difficulties in achieving sufficient production. In a society in which importance was set upon stock raising this problem must have been especially acute since this requires only a limited labour force deployed over a wide area of land. This factor lay at the root of rural unrest following the Tudor enclosures and in the Iron Age must have added to the surplus population likely to turn to raiding.

Even so there is an alternative to fission in an enlarged unstratified community. In fact under conditions of external stress or threat this process is often suspended by the need to maintain the full group for mutual protection. On the other hand, there are obvious difficulties in preserving the unstratified group with an increase in numbers. Firstly it becomes increasingly difficult to maintain internal order unless some individual or body is empowered to adjudicate and make decisions. A mutual feeling of 'obligation' is too inefficient a response to so complex a situation (Hart, 1960). Secondly there appears to be a definite limit to the number of individual relationships that one member of a community is able to sustain with others without recourse to the inherent tendency to classify them together into groups (Forge, 1970). More important, however, is an economic argument. It is in fact apparent that the efficiency of an enlarged food producing group is impaired unless there exists some central direction of labour resources (Flannery, 1970). Indeed, unless work input is actually increased in these circumstances, production may even decline (Boserup, 1965). In a situation where an outside threat existed or was feared the most important or most vulnerable communal assets were probably those which would need protection. In this context cattle are especially susceptible to raiding but particularly easy to retain with even a relatively slight earthwork. It has already appeared that a basis for inter-communal co-operation may occasionally have existed here and for this reason stock compounds may also have formed a useful communal 'focus'. In other aspects the embellishment of existing earthworks in this way may have involved a display of wealth – indeed the choice of these sites rather than arable farms constitutes a statement of the basis of communal prosperity – and equally a visible symbol of organised resistance to aggression. Internally the building of these first forts with communal labour can have symbolised and even strengthened the recent development of central authority (Whittlesey, 1935). It is no surprise that it was in this volatile situation that so many of the forts were started but never completed.

78

However, the protection of one type of communal asset against predation in itself does nothing to ease the difficulties brought about by an enlarged population and a finite amount of land. These are problems that may only be approached by agricultural intensification. Some hint of a continuing emphasis upon pastoralism might be expected from the earlier part of this account but in fact it is evident that the existing areas set aside for livestock themselves had a limited carrying capacity. Pastoralism in any case employs only a limited labour force deployed over a wide area of land and would do little to provide work for the surplus rural population already likely to turn to raiding.

On the other hand, arable intensification might be better equipped to meet these difficulties and it might again be expected that this new approach would be evidenced by an extension of arable land at the expense of land set aside for other purposes. Even so, such an approach gives further difficulties. In the first place, the areas already adopted as permanent outfield pasture were only selected for this purpose because of their unsuitability as arable land. These areas are those which are exposed to the strongest winds and which have the thinnest soil cover. In some areas they include clay with flints or other strongly acid subsoils. Their conversion to arable fields therefore might be expected to involve an unusually great work input and a reduced crop yield. At the same time the symbiotic relationship of pasture and arable extends beyond the mere manuring of fallow land grazed as infield pasture in the winter. It has in fact been pointed out that the essentially limited and seasonal work of ploughing might mean that under short fallow cultivation each draught animal would need to graze an area far larger than it would be able to break in a year and under this system it might be necessary to leave at least two-thirds of the arable land fallow in order to provide enough grazing for these animals alone (Boserup, 1965: 35). A figure of 25 acres per ox has been quoted by Bowen (1969) and these figures do not of course include any allowance for those animals kept instead for their meat, hides, wool or milk. In fact, therefore, the conversion of the entire farm to arable fields and the provision of sufficient grazing land by fallowing might well sterilise higher quality arable land than the original, Bronze Age, pattern of exploitation. The spreading of the period of ploughing by the adoption of both spring and autumn cropping would bring only a marginal improvement in this situation. A better solution would of course be the provision of sufficient fodder but to do this would add greatly to the work input required from the members of the community and in comparable situations today it is usually preferred to set aside marginal land for grazing and to provide fodder for the shortest possible period of the year. In parts of India, for example, it has been found that the first course of action accounts for only 10 per cent of the total cost of producing a crop while the provision of fodder as an alternative covers more than 50 per cent of that cost (Boserup, 1965: 36). At present byres for the systematic winter stalling of cattle do not seem to have been recognised in the Lowland Zone of Britain.

From this it appears that any major change in the existing balance of arable and pasture creates more problems than it can solve and so it seems more likely that agricultural intensification must have depended upon the production of more food from the existing areas. Since more intensive stock raising would not provide a solution to these difficulties it is probably necessary to envisage more intensive exploitation of the existing arable fields. Normally it has been assumed, however, that arable intensification is merely the outcome of environmental change (Applebaum, 1954: 104) and the cause of population increase. Recently this view has been challenged by Boserup (1965) who has pointed out that each shortening of the fallow period in an attempt to achieve increased production in fact involves a great increase in the work input of every member of the community in relation to the resulting crop yield. She has been able to distinguish five stages of arable intensification ranging from long fallow cultivation to multicropping and has been able to show that a fivefold increase in individual work input is required between the extremes of this range. She has now been able to show from both recent and historical economic and ethnographic data that these changes will only come about with an increasing population. Quite simply communities are unlikely to work harder without any incentive and this position only changes when population increase and land shortage together precipitate a crisis.

For the Iron Age it may be argued that more intensive arable farming of this nature need only have come about in the period when the earliest hill-forts and boundary ditches give hints of overall strain and that such radical changes in the organisation, intensity and regularity of work could only come about under central direction. For example the shortening of the fallow period would restrict the rights of individual members of the community to pasture their livestock about the parent settlement, while comparable communities of the recent past have been extremely reluctant to give up a system of farming which demands short periods of intensive work at the annual ploughing and harvest and leaves the remainder of the cycle largely free for other activities. The prospect of less demanding but more regular work is one adopted with some reluctance.

It may be in a context of this type that the reference of Diodorus Siculus to two annual harvests in Britain in about 500 B.C. is to be understood. At the same time the appearance of spelt which may permit both spring and autumn cropping also deserves notice since this can lead to increased productivity by extending the period in which ploughing and harvesting are possible (Helbaek, 1952: 228). Though few grain impressions have been examined, this does at present seem roughly to correspond in time with the evidence for social stratification offered by the first hill-forts. Possibly as a further result of arable intensification made possible by central direction, an increase in the number and capacity of pits also becomes apparent. At Little Woodbury, for example, it is possible to correlate Bersu's pit classification and Brailsford's analysis of the pottery from the site to show that, as the proportion of the early haemetite ware falls and that of the later 'smooth dark ware' increases, the capacity of the pits steadily becomes greater. While making no assumption that any one type of pit is inherently more suitable for grain storage than any other, it is interesting to see that the earlier pits by this scheme, types A, B, and perhaps C, are ones which also occur on arable farms of the later Bronze Age (Bersu, 1940; Brailsford, 1948).

Changes such as these must, of course, modify the basis of communal prosperity, and it is possible that those communities in which the leadership was effective enough to bring about this change of balance might be those that would command support in times of crisis. Certainly it is with the emergence of forts based upon arable farms that the nucleation of settlement about clearly defined centres seems to commence. In this respect the economic basis of a site is a more valuable way of assessing differences of wealth than the survival of a few trinkets among the artefact remains. With modifications such as these it is equally clear that the earlier forts, deriving as they do from pastoral sites, would be of a reduced utility. They were sited on particularly high ground, often on the margin of the communal territory, and were merely designed to retain livestock against raiding. Neither their siting nor their defences would be suitable for protecting against the firing of the harvested crop and it is surely with the increasing emphasis upon the latter area of the economy that the newer hill-forts came into being. Like the arable farms of this date (Bonney, 1968: 33), these tended to occupy lower ground, and commonly they lie closer to the area of arable land, frequently straddling the apparent boundary of plough and pasture. Though Iron Age fields can rarely be distinguished from Roman examples, this is a problem which might profitably be approached by the techniques of site catchment analysis set out by Vita-Finzi and Higgs (1970). At the same time, the fact that the newer basis of communal prosperity also formed the staple diet of the population may explain the increased occupation of forts where grain for consumption was stored. This process may even have been accelerated by fresh economic change in the late Iron Age when increased pastoralism in Wessex seems to have created a further body of surplus labour which came to nucleate in the huge tribal oppida.

Such a relationship between economic change and the nature of field monuments can of course be seen only as an adjunct to the social hypotheses put forward by other contributors to this conference and in itself calls to mind the predicament of Alice Through the Looking Glass running as fast as she possibly can in order to remain in the same place. Such a conception of the changing balance of the Iron Age economy might best be approached by means of accurate practical experiment designed to quantify such essential factors in this account as work input, crop yield, fodder production and draught labour. With this as a basis it might then be possible to simulate the types of situation postulated in this paper and to analyse the likely responses in quantitative terms. Existing examples of this type of approach which might repay close study are an account of crop yield and environment in Ghana by Gould (1963) or a comparable study of labour productivity in Swedish agriculture by Wolpert (1964). Perhaps it is by isolating such processes as they are filtered through settlement patterns in this way that Iron Age studies may most usefully proceed. But here dogma threatens to take over from speculation and I must cease.

BIBLIOGRAPHY

Alcock, L. 1965. 'Hill-forts in Wales and the Marches', *Antiquity*, 39, 184–95.

Applebaum, S. 1954. 'The Agriculture of the British Early Iron Age as Exemplified by Figheldean Down, Wiltshire', *PPS*, 20, 103–14.

Bersu, G. 1940. 'Excavations at Little Woodbury, Wiltshire, Part I: The Settlement as Revealed by Excavation', *PPS*, 6, 30–111.

Bonney, D. J. 1968. 'Iron Age and Romano British Settlement Sites in Wiltshire: Some Geographical Considerations', *WAM*, 63, 27–38.

Boserup, E. 1965. *The Conditions of Agriculture Growth*, London.

Bowen, H. C. 1969. *The Celtic Background*: in *The Roman Villa in Britain*, ed. A. L. F. Rivet, 1–48, London.

Bradley, R. J. 1967. 'Excavations on Portsdown Hill 1963–5', *P. Hants FC*, 24, 42–58.

Bradley, R. J. 1971a. 'Stock Raising and the Origins of the Hill-fort on the South Downs', *Antiq. J.*, 51 forthcoming.

Bradley, R. J. 1971b. 'An Iron Age Promontory Fort at Belle Tout', *Sussex AC*, 109 forthcoming.

Brailsford, J. 1948. 'Excavations at Little Woodbury, Wiltshire 1938–9, Part II: The Pottery', *PPS*. 14, 1–18.

Burstow, G. P., and Holleyman, G. A. 1964. 'Excavations at Ranscombe Camp 1959–60', *Sussex AC*, 102, 55–67.

Clinch, G. 1905. 'Ancient Earthworks', in *VCH*, Sussex, I, 453–80, London.

Colley March, H. 1901. 'Report of Excavations on Eggardon 1900', *P. Soc. Ants.*, 18, 258–62.

Collins, A. E. P. 1947. 'Excavations on Blewburton Hill 1947', *Berks. AJ*, 50, 4–29.

Collins, A. E. P. 1952. 'Excavations on Blewburton Hill 1948 and 1949', *Berks. AJ*, 53, 21–64.

Collins, A. E. P. and F. J. 1959. 'Excavations on Blewburton Hill 1953', *Berks. AJ*, 57, 52–73.

Corcoran, J. X. W. P. 1959. 'European Iron Age Forts' – *Report on the Prehistoric Society Conference 1959*.

Cotton, M. A., and Frere, S. S. 1968. 'Ivinghoe Beacon Excavations 1963–5', *Rec. Bucks.*, 18, 187–260.

Cunliffe, B. W. 1966. 'Stoke Clump, Hollingbury, and the Early pre-Roman Iron Age in Sussex', *Sussex AC*, 104, 109–20.

Cunliffe, B. W. 1970. 'A Bronze Age Settlement at Chalton, Hampshire (Site 78)', *Antiq. J.*, 50, 1–13.

Cunliffe, B. W., and Phillipson, D. W. 1968. 'Excavations at Eldon's Seat, Encombe, Dorset', *PPS*, 34, 191–237.

Curwen, E. 1932. 'Rackham Bank and Earthwork', *Sussex AC*, 73, 169–86.

Curwen, E. and E. C. 1922. 'Notes on the Archaeology of Burpham and the Neighbouring Downs', *Sussex AC*, 63, 1–53.

Curwen, E. and E. C. 1927. 'Excavations in the Caburn, Near Lewes', *Sussex AC*, 68, 1–56.

Curwen, E. C. 1929. 'Excavations in the Trundle, Goodwood 1928', *Sussex AC*, 70, 33–85.

Curwen, E. C. 1930a. 'Wolstonbury', *Sussex AC*, 71, 237–45.

Curwen, E. C. 1930b. 'Neolithic Camps', *Antiquity*, 4, 22–54.

Curwen, E. C. 1931. 'Excavations in the Trundle', *Sussex AC*, 72, 100–150.

Curwen, E. C. 1932. 'Excavations at Hollingbury Camp, Sussex', *Antiq. J.*, 12, 1–16.

Curwen, E. C. 1933. 'Excavations at Thundersbarrow Hill', *Sussex Antiq. J*, 13, 119–33.

Curwen, E. C. 1954. *The Archaeology of Sussex*, 2nd ed., London.

Dunning, G. C. 1947. 'Chillerton Down Camp, Gatcombe, Isle of Wight', *P. Isle of Wight NHAS*, 4 (ii), 50–3.

Farrar, R. A. H. 1955. 'An Early Iron Age Fort on Shipton Hill, Shipton Gorge', *P. Dorset NHAS*, 77, 135–6.

Feibleman, J., and Friend, J. W. 1945. 'The Structure and Function of Organisation', *Philosophical Review*, 54, 19–44.

Flannery, K. V. 1970. 'The Origins of the Village as a Settlement Type in Meso-America and the Near East: a Comparative Study.' Paper to research seminar on Settlement Patterns and Urbanisation at the London Institute of Archaeology. Publication in proceedings forthcoming.

Forge, A. 1970. 'Normative Factors in the Settlement Size of Neolithic Cultivators (New Guinea).' Paper to research seminar on Settlement Patterns and Urbanisation at the London Institute of Archaeology. Publication in proceedings forthcoming.

Fowler, P. J. 1964. 'Cross Dykes on the Ebble-Nadder Ridge', *WAM*, 59, 46–67.

Gould, R. R. 1963. 'Man Against his Environment: a Game-theoretic Framework', *Annals of the Association of American Geographers*, 53, 290–7.

Harding, D. W. 1967. 'Blewburton', *Current Arch.*, 4, 83–5.

Hart, H. L. A. 1960. *The Concept of Law*, Oxford.

Hawkes, C. F. C. 1931. 'Hill-forts', *Antiquity*, 5, 60–97.

Hawkes, C. F. C. 1939. 'The Excavations at Quarley Hill 1938', *P. Hants. FC*, 14, 136–94.

Hawkes, C. F. C. 1940. 'The Excavations at Bury Hill 1939', *P. Hants FC*, 14, 291–337.

Hawkes, J. 1940. 'The Excavations at Balksbury 1939', *P. Hants. FC*, 14, 338–45.

Helbaek, H. 1952. 'Early Crops in Southern England', *PPS*, 18, 194–233.

Keef, P. A. M. 1953. 'Two Gold Penannular Ornaments from Harting Beacon, Sussex', *Antiq. J.*, 33, 204–6.

Lorenz, K. 1966. *On Aggression*, London.

Meyrick, O. 1946. 'Notes on Some Early Iron Age Sites in the Marlborough District', *WAM*, 51, 256–63.

Piggott, C. M. 1942. 'Five Late Bronze Age Enclosures in North Wiltshire', *PPS*, 8, 48–61.

Piggott, S. 1930. 'Butser Hill', *Antiquity*, 3, 187–200.

Piggott, S. 1931. 'Ladle Hill – An Unfinished Hill-fort', *Antiquity*, 4, 474–85.

Rahtz, P. 1960. 'Second Interim Report on Excavations at Hog Cliff Hill, Maiden Newton', *P. Dorset NHAS*, 82, 83.

Royal Commission on Historical Monuments (England) 1952, *West Dorset*, London.

Royal Commission on Historical Monuments (England) 1970, *Dorset*, II (iii), London.

Tratman, E. K. 1970. 'The Glastonbury Lake Village: a Reconsideration', *P. Univ. of Bristol Spelaeological Soc.*, 12, 143–68.

Vita-Finzi, C., and Higgs, E. S. 1970. 'Prehistoric Economy in the Mount Carmel area of Palestine: Site Catchment Analysis', *PPS*, 36, 1–37.

Wacher, J. S. 1957. 'Interim Report on Excavations at Bowden's Hill, Melcombe, Horsey', *P. Dorset NHAS*, 79, 115.

Wainwright, G. J. 1967. 'The Excavation of an Iron Age Hill-fort on Bathampton Down, Somerset', *T. Bristol and Gloucs. AS*, 86, 42–59.

Wainwright, G. J. 1969. 'The Excavation of Balksbury Camp, Andover, Hants', *P. Hants. FC*, 26, 21–55.

Wheeler, R. E. M. 1953. 'An Early Iron Age "Beach-head" at Lulworth, Dorset', *Antiq. J.* 33, 1–13.

Whitley, M. 1943. 'Excavations at Chalbury Camp, Dorset 1939', *Antiq. J.* 23, 98–121.

Whittlesey, D. 1935. 'The Impress of Effective Central Authority upon the Landscape', *Annals of the Association of American Geographers*, 25, 85–98.

Williams Freeman, J. P. 1915. 'Field Archaeology' as illustrated by Hampshire, London.

Wilson, A. E. 1938. 'Excavations in the Ramparts and Gateway of the Caburn, August–October 1937', *Sussex AC*, 79, 169–94.

Wilson, A. E. 1939. 'Excavations at the Caburn 1938', *Sussex AC*, 80, 193–213.

Wilson, A. E. 1940. 'Report on the Excavations on Highdown Hill, Sussex, August 1939', *Sussex AC*, 81, 173–203.

Wolpert, J. 1964. 'The Decision Process in Spatial Context', *Annals of the Association of American Geographers*, 54, 537–58.

SETTLEMENT PATTERNS AND EXCAVATION METHODS IN IRON AGE HILL-FORTS

By C. R. Musson

It is natural that archaeologists concerned with hill-forts should want to know more about patterns of settlement within their enclosing defences. Surface field-work can offer something in such enquiries, but realistic information can only come from large-scale excavations in the interior, using horizontal or vertical stratigraphy to unravel the inevitable palimpsest of structures. In planning such excavations it would be wise to think in terms of consolidated 'random' areas, rather than more widely distributed areas selected specifically because they show obvious signs of structural remains – in the study of settlement patterns the spaces between the buildings can be at least as informative as the buildings themselves.

For this reason a particular importance attaches to large-scale hill-fort excavations like those at Balksbury in Hampshire (Wainwright 1969) and South Cadbury in Somerset (Alcock 1967–1971).

At Balksbury a wide strip, both of the defences and the interior, was extensively sampled. The structural remains were few – a large group of hearths and a number of four-post structures (whether houses or granaries), most of them lying a few metres behind the line of the enclosing rampart.

At South Cadbury, as a deliberate matter of policy, more than half the total effort over five seasons of excavation was devoted to the interior as against the defences and entrances. There were two main areas of excavation in the interior, totalling 4,400 sq. m. in all. One covered the greater part of the summit plateau; the other sampled the more sheltered north-eastern slopes of the hill. Even though this area represents little more than 6 per cent of the interior it included (in addition to a number of rectangular Iron Age structures up to 6 m. x 4 m.) at least seven timber-built round-houses, ranging from 8 m. to 14 m. in diameter and frequently showing signs of repeated repair or rebuilding on the same spot.

The structure of these houses varied considerably, the more substantial showing clear evidence for solid walls of contiguous posts, split logs or planks up to 15 cm. thick, set in a relatively narrow ring-gully about 30 cm. wide and cut about 40 cm. into the bedrock. There were no detectable internal posts, despite diameters of between 10 and 14 metres. In some cases it was possible to see how repeated rebuilding of such houses on the same spot (at intervals of 10, 20 or even 50 years?) had resulted in the ring-gullies becoming wide and diffuse 'ring-ditches', up to a metre deep and a metre and a half in width.

Not all the structures, however, were as substantial as this, nor so easily detectable. In several cases narrow curving gullies could be traced in the bedrock, no more than a few centimetres deep. One of these, on excavation, produced a series of apparent stake-holes about 5 cm. in diameter, which gave rise to much argument over whether it was possible to 'create' evidence simply by trying too hard not to miss anything.

These doubts were allayed by the detection of similar patterns on other parts of the hill-top, and finally dismissed by the discovery of a finely preserved house about 8 metres in diameter on a levelled platform on the north-eastern slopes of the hill. Once again there were clear signs of rebuilding, the shallow gullies and individual stake-holes of the wattle and daub wall having been protected from subsequent erosion by the accumulation of hillwash on the house-platform after the house itself had gone out of use.

The experience of these houses at South Cadbury was an important, perhaps decisive, element in the detection of almost identical structures at the Breiddin hill-fort, Montgomeryshire (Musson 1970). Once again the walls were represented by very shallow gullies or lines of individual stake-holes, and once more there were clear signs of repeated rebuilding on the same spot. The lesson is not simply that many Iron Age buildings are less substantial (in terms of archaeological traces) than has often been supposed, but also that experience of their discovery on one site was in this instance an essential factor in their detection on another – not so much a case of the excavator finding what he expected to find, but rather of sharpening his powers of observation and interpretation so that he could detect what he (and others) might formerly have missed.

This difficulty of detection and interpretation is directly relevant to the question of settlement patterns within hill-forts, and in particular to the methods used to uncover them. Most excavation work in Britain is carried out by relatively large bands of 'volunteer' diggers, under professional direction, in fairly short periods in the summer, when the soil, in general, is fairly dry. This may be acceptable for the more or less unstratified areas in the centres of hill-forts, but these open spaces are by no means the only ones likely to produce evidence of settlement. A great many hill-forts have areas of deeper stratification preserved immediately in the lee of the ramparts, in conditions which, potentially at least, provide the chronological controls which are so frequently lacking in the heavily ploughed or eroded interiors. In these deeper deposits, however, the problems of excavation and interpretation are greatly intensified, not only because earlier structures are severely damaged by later ones, but also because the deposits themselves frequently consist largely of successive layers of black 'occupation soil', scarcely distinguishable from one another. In these conditions traditional methods of excavation may produce results which are so incomplete as to be misleading or virtually uninterpretable.

The danger, so far as settlement patterns is concerned, is that by using inappropriate methods of organisation and excavation, the archaeologist may fail to detect domestic and other structures in the lee of the rampart, and assume the pattern of settlement to be the one which he sees in the wider interior, where excavation is technically less difficult. In doing so he may grossly misrepresent the true character of settlement, because there is a distinct, though unproven, possibility that the structures which lie close to the ramparts may be different not only in size and construction from those in the interior, but also in function and perhaps in the social status of the people who lived or worked in them.

Assuming, for the purposes of discussion, that many buildings in the lee of the ramparts may have been insubstantial wattle and daub structures, it is legitimate to ask whether these would have been detected at Balksbury, where the work was carried out largely by mechanical excavation, on a clay-with-flints subsoil, in a summer which produced either continuous rain or unbroken sunshine, but never a moderate combination of the two. On balance, one would think not. The same might be said of South Cadbury, where the main area behind the rampart was dug before wider experience elsewhere on the site had shown the excavators how to detect these fugitive lines of stake-holes. At the Breiddin, with the benefit of experience and using different methods of excavation, it has now been possible to identify wattle and daub structures in practically all of the major trenches. In two cases the buildings, about 6 metres in diameter, occupy positions immediately in the lee of the rampart, with their outer walls almost touching the stones of the rear revetment (excavations still in progress at the time of writing).

At this site, then, and by extension at many others also, such houses might have stretched in close array or in ownership or functional groupings along the full circuit of the defences, giving quite different occupation statistics from those derived from the interior alone. It is possible – one can say no more – that *some* British hill-forts at *some* stages of their occupation may have looked like defended versions of a type of settlement found frequently in central and southern Africa today, with the houses of the chief and his retinue grouped in the interior and the homes, workshops and foodstores of the common people forming a tight circle round the periphery. (For an excellent example of such a settlement see Light 1941, pls. 110, 111.)

It is a matter of speculation whether such patterns existed in Britain also. But if they did, they will certainly not be revealed by small-scale selective excavation, however skilfully conducted. It will be necessary to dig not only extensive areas in the interior but also considerable stretches of these difficult but potentially informative occupation deposits in the lee of the ramparts. If the aim is to find out what these deposits *mean* in terms of the distribution of functions and the development of building patterns, the excavator will have to abandon the idea of trenches 3 or even 10 metres wide behind the ramparts, and think instead of stretches 30 or even 100 metres long.

One can also argue that in these difficult deposits, where a major investment of time and money is being made, the work can only be carried out to the necessary standard by the most skilled of excavators, able to cope with problems of interpretation and reconstruction at the actual time of the excavation. Moreover, if interpretation is to keep pace with excavation, as it surely must, the digging should be done in a way which allows adequate time for unhurried thought and observation – in a short summer dig, with a couple of dozen 'volunteers' waiting to get on with the work, the director simply cannot stop and look at a trench for a week if he doesn't understand it – the economics of the exercise will not allow it. Nor, in the majority of cases, will summer digging provide satisfactory soil conditions for the excavation of only faintly differentiated black occupation deposits. The hot sun and dry conditions of high summer spread a haze of grey dust over these friable soils almost as soon as they are uncovered, so that archaeological features which are only seen with difficulty in damp conditions become to all intents and purposes undetectable. In such deposits the summer is emphatically *not* the time to dig if the intention is to recover any kind of archaeological detail.

Nor are traditional British methods of stratigraphical excavation necessarily the best in such conditions. Stratified levels can only rarely be detected with any certainty, and attempts to 'follow the stratification' all too often become impossible or self-defeating. Certainly the idea of 'emptying' structural features on the principle of 'last in, first out' must go by the board in most cases – when the filling, sides and bottom of a post-hole all consist of virtually identical black occupation soils this kind of procedure is simply too difficult and too vulnerable to error to be worth attempting.

In such deposits a more profitable method may be to work entirely by plan, taking out successive 'spits' between 5 and 10 centimetres deep and planning each spit meticulously, stone by stone, soil change by soil change, with accurate levels at all key points. The spits need not be horizontal, nor of consistent thickness throughout; more probably they should reflect the natural slopes of the ground. Nor need they ignore stratification as they sometimes do on the Continent. Finds from obviously different layers, and from pits, post-holes or gullies can easily be kept separately, and the levels of identified surfaces can be recorded, wherever they occur within the depth of a spit. If this kind of recording is carried out with sufficient care, perfectly adequate 'notional' sections can be reconstructed from the plans on any desired line, without the need to subdivide the excavated area with potentially confusing standing baulks. Ideally, the position of every find should be recorded on its appropriate spit-plan, so that all can be related back, if necessary, to features not detected at the time of excavation. Post-holes cut through stone rubble, for instance, often remain undetected until excavation reaches the deeper levels where soil predominates over stone. But if planning has been carried out with sufficient care and accuracy, such post-holes can often be traced back upwards through successive plans until the true level from which they were cut can be identified. Meticulous planning thus introduces a valuable element of retrospective interpretation into the archaeological process.

Such techniques are not new, of course, but they demand a sophistication of survey and recording methods and a skill of excavation which it is difficult to reconcile with the pressures of a large-scale volunteer-based summer dig. In these deep occupation deposits in particular, on a proportion of our Iron Age sites we might achieve better results by thinking of digging with far fewer people, of greater individual skill, working on a larger scale over very much longer periods in the autumn, winter and spring, not in the summer.

Such a pattern, with smallish teams of archaeologists working on site virtually throughout the year, perhaps for two or three years at a stretch, could offer considerable advantages over traditional methods on some of the available hill-fort sites. The work of people like T. C. M. Brewster, Brian Philp and Mrs. M. U. Jones over the past few years, and of the Rescue Archaeology Group throughout the winter of 1970–71 at the Breiddin, have shown that winter digging is both possible and profitable. On many sites the soil is in far better condition for digging at this time of year, and there is little need in practice to fear loss of efficiency in winter digging. The use of plastic rain-covers, insulating frost-blankets and shelters to create 'indoor' digging conditions can reduce time-loss to negligible proportions – less than 5 per cent of the available time in six months at the Breiddin, for instance, as against 10 per cent over a similar period of summer digging at South Cadbury. Increased individual productivity also means that costs can be comparable with traditional volunteer-based digs, even when all the excavators are being paid proper professional salaries of between £1,000 and £2,000 a year.

There is every chance that such methods will be used increasingly over the coming years, and it would be unfortunate if the main academic arm of archaeology – the universities – were to fall behind in such developments. But they may well do so unless more of them accept that major excavations are a proper subject for postgraduate research, or that some of their staff, in a subject which draws its source material largely from excavation, should be appointed specifically to carry out field-work on a more or less full-time basis.

If, over the years, these methods (and improvements of them) are applied to carefully chosen Iron Age sites, preferably the less complex and more modestly sized ones on promising subsoils, it may be possible in 20 or 30 years' time to talk with more authority about building forms, settlement patterns and even social organisation within our Iron Age hill-forts.

BIBLIOGRAPHY

Alcock, L. 1967–71. Interim reports on excavations at South Cadbury, Somerset, *Antiquaries Journal*, vol. 47, 1967 – vol. 50, 1970; and *Antiquity*, vol. 41, 1967 – vol. 45, 1971.

Light, R. U. 1941. *Focus on Africa*, American Geographical Society Special Publication no. 25, New York.

Musson, C. R. 1970. 'The Breiddin, 1969', *Current Archaeology*, no. 19, March 1970, 215–218.

Wainwright, G. J. 1969. 'The Excavation of Balksbury Camp, Andover, Hants', *Proceedings of the Hampshire Field Club*, 26, 21–55.

SETTLEMENT ARCHAEOLOGY –
METHODS AND PROBLEMS

By ANNA RITCHIE

TAYLOR has argued recently that it is impossible to establish any true patterns of settlement in pre-Saxon Britain (1970); not only is the surviving material evidence too incomplete, but in many areas we lack the means of estimating what proportion of the original total of sites remains. Taylor was using the concept of settlement pattern in the geographer's sense of analysing the physical location of sites. If it is impossible to establish geographical and topographical patterns of settlement because of lack of information, it is certainly quite impossible to attempt a settlement pattern in the anthropologist's sense of socio-cultural systems (Clarke 1968, 102–4; *cf.* Finley 1971, 171–4).

If we accept that we cannot hope to establish any real *pattern* of settlement, the alternative is to examine the *types* of individual settlements. On the grounds that, in this context, it is better to proceed from the general to the particular, some idea of the nature and development of settlement types throughout Britain will provide a background for the understanding of settlement types on a regional basis.

The study of non-defensive Iron Age settlements in lowland Britain, on which this discussion is based, adopted a classification founded primarily upon the methods of construction employed and secondarily upon the social units represented (Ritchie 1969). It is thus a mixture of factual and interpretative information and the latter, because it is even more subjective than the material evidence upon which it is founded, is the weakest aspect of the classification. Nevertheless, the implications of the social unit are sufficiently vital to the study of prehistoric communities to justify an attempt to estimate its development. Sites consisting of up to three houses were taken to represent the homesteads of single family units, while those consisting of more than three houses were taken to represent communities, ranging from small hamlets to full-scale villages.

Of the two basic types of settlement, open and enclosed, little can be said about open sites except that they occur south of a line drawn from north Wales to Norfolk, with a concentration in central southern England, and that the type existed throughout the middle and later first millennium B.C. The fact that most open sites owe their discovery to the presence of large pits limits the usefulness of their apparent distribution.

Methods of enclosure are essentially the use either of timber palisades or of earthworks. Palisaded sites are concentrated on the uplands of southern Scotland and northern England with a scattered distribution further south, while earthwork-enclosed settlements show a reversed distribution with a concentration in southern Britain. Palisades belong to the period from the seventh to the second centuries B.C., but earthen sites are common throughout the middle and later first millennium. In terms of the social unit represented, there is a marked tendency among enclosed sites for the larger units to date from the seventh to the fourth centuries B.C., with homesteads predominating during subsequent centuries until villages reappear as a major unit in the first century

B.C. Many individual sites show a chronological succession of settlement types, and the sequence provided can be summarised in broad terms as open, palisaded and finally earthworks.

All these basic settlement types occur in a wide variety of topographical contexts which can have only local implications, though there is a marked preference for the lighter soils. Economic practice is related primarily to environment rather than to settlement type, but the decision to enclose can be linked with an increasingly stable economy and, of course, with the necessity to keep out marauding animals and raiders. The appearance of fine pottery supports the impression of a generally stable economy.

Archaeology seems to have entered a phase influenced to a potentially unhealthy extent by anthropology, from the level of concepts down to that of detailed interpretation of material remains. General observations drawn from the study of modern primitive societies can, of course, be useful to the archaeologist. For example, current work is showing that unstratified societies are usually under-productive, because production is limited more by the *organisation* of labour than by the tools available for labour. In the light of this observation, we can appreciate that the development of agriculture in Britain in the first millennium B.C. may have been linked more with social conditions than with the technological development of the plough.

It is when we come to the more specific ethnographic observations that the danger really appears. The work of Robbins on house-types and settlement patterns resulted in the observation that circular dwellings tend to correlate with nomadic or semi-nomadic societies, while rectangular dwellings tend to correlate with fully sedentary societies (Robbins 1966). He stressed that these are general tendencies rather than rules, an important point for any archaeologist attempting to derive similar information from archaeological material. The obvious example in the archaeological record is the tradition of circular houses in later British prehistory, for one would hesitate to assume that these imply an overall pattern of nomadism or even semi-nomadism.

Our assumption of an essentially sedentary society in southern Britain in the later first millennium B.C. is based to some extent on the presence of storage pits. Agriculture alone need not prevent a semi-nomadic life, but food storage must imply permanent occupation by the majority of the inhabitants of a site.

Ethnographic parallels have played an important part in the interpretation of internal features of settlements such as pits and post-structures. Pitt-Rivers was fortunate in having his ethnographic material on his doorstep, for he was able to compare the settings of four post-holes which he excavated at Rotherley with existing timber granaries built on stilts in the modern villages around him (1888, 55). In the last few years, there has been a delayed reaction against the predominant Little Woodbury-based interpretation by which all pits functioned for grain storage, all square settings of four post-holes represented granaries, and all pairs of post-holes held racks for drying corn in the ear. Alternative interpretations have been sought in ethnological data on the use of similar pits and structures among primitive communities, and we are now in danger of over-emphasising the value of such parallels. Ethnography can be no substitute for the sort of detailed analysis of surviving archaeological evidence that Bowen has been carrying out on pits (1969, 16–18). Even in early accounts of excavations, information can be found to indicate the function of pits; deliberately laid floors are a relatively common feature, and none more extraordinary than that excavated at Worlebury in the 1880's, where there was found 'a flat board under the grain, and strips of wood to separate the kinds' (Dymond and Tomkins 1886, 77). Wooden, stone or clay floors, linings of clay or stone, traces of wicker-work or textile containers, evidence of deliberate burning, the presence of significant quantities of grain, these are all among the categories of surviving evidence that can be used in the interpretation of individual pits. Detailed analysis of pit dimensions and locations, both in terms of subsoils and location within settlements, is now very necessary and might include the information from unpublished records in local museums.

Post-settings are less readily to be associated with features helpful to interpretation. Grain found in the post-holes of such a setting need not be evidence of its use as a granary. Occasionally, the association of a four-post setting with a hearth, as at Marnhull (Williams 1950, 31), allows interpretation as a frame for drying and smoking meat or drying corn, or, as Piggott has recently suggested, as shrines (Piggott 1968, 61–2). Again, location within the settlement is an important factor, but one which requires more total excavations of sites such as was achieved at Berwick Down South (Wainwright 1968).

Ideally, total excavation is also necessary in attempting to estimate the ratio of pits to houses. It is not unreasonable, however, to assume that the pits belonging to any one house are likely to have been situated close to that house; if this assumption is accepted, some estimation is possible from the evidence already available. For example, 66 pits and three houses were assigned to the first period of occupation at Marnhull (Williams 1950, 23–9), and one might therefore take an approximate figure of 20–22 pits in use during the lifetime of each house. This figure compares well with that from Berwick Down South, where approximately 17 pits belonged to one house, for a drop in the ratio of pits to houses must be expected towards the end of the first millennium (Radford 1954, 12).

It is doubtful whether, in the absence of major intrusive cultural factors, one should expect to find regional variations of non-defensive settlement types that can be correlated with cultural divisions indicated by portable artefacts, particularly pottery styles. Variations of settlement type are more likely to be founded on topographic and economic factors, such as readily available building materials and the nature of the subsistence economy, whether agricultural, pastoral or mixed.

There is one type of settlement showing a restricted geographical and chronological distribution which I have called the complex ditch settlement; this is a clumsy term but it is at least descriptive, for the type is characterised by a complex of ditches forming a series of enclosures of irregular area and shape. It is probable that the material derived from the ditches was piled up alongside as banks, but these have normally been ploughed away. Seven of these complex ditch settlements are known, all lying on the chalk plateaux of Wiltshire and Hampshire at heights of between 300 and 800 ft. OD. These are, in Wiltshire, the sites at Grovely Earthworks, Hanging Langford Camp, Huish Hill, Rotherley and Stockton Earthworks, and, in Hampshire, the sites at Worthy Down and Owslebury. Rotherley is the smallest example at 4 acres, and Stockton and Grovely Earthworks the largest at something like 62 and 100 acres respectively, while the other four are between about 10 and 20 acres in overall extent. Three sites are situated only half a mile from hill-forts, at least one and probably all of which were in occupation contemporary with the settlements.

Only three of these sites have been extensively excavated: those at Rotherley (Pitt-Rivers 1888, 51–231; Hawkes 1947, 36–42), Worthy Down (Hooley 1929) and Owslebury (Collis 1968). The ditches measure no more than $6\frac{1}{2}$ ft. in width and $4\frac{1}{2}$ ft. in depth, and must have functioned primarily as delineation of areas used for different purposes – for habitation, stock-penning, agricultural activities such as threshing and so on.

The artefacts associated with this class of site indicate a main period of occupation in the first centuries B.C. and A.D.; in a few cases, there is some evidence for earlier occupation but this cannot certainly be attributed to the settlement in its final form. Occupation continued into the Roman period at Stockton, Rotherley and Owslebury.

These complex ditch settlements can be linked with a specific type of earthwork enclosure recognised and named by Perry as 'banjo enclosures' (1966; 1969, 37), and to the related 'spectacles enclosures' recognised by Crawford and Keiller (1928, 224). The settlement complexes at Owslebury and Huish Hill include banjo and spectacles enclosures respectively, while Hanging Langford Camp complex ditch settlement is linked by a linear earthwork to the banjo of Church End Ring. The banjo at Gussage Cowdown contains traces of occupation (Hoare 1821, pt. 2, opp. 30), but that at Church End Ring almost certainly functioned as the cattle-pen belonging to Hanging Langford Camp. The same dual use can be seen among spectacles enclosures, for traces of occupation have been found in one of each pair of enclosures at Pewsey Down (Hoare 1812, 191), South Tarrant Hinton Down (Sumner 1913, 41) and Huish Hill (Hoare 1821, pl. III).

A notable feature associated with several of these complex ditch settlements and banjo and spectacles enclosures, is the use of large multivallate earthworks. These survive as lengths of earthwork with their ends 'in the air', not now serving to encircle the settlements, but it is clear that originally they functioned in conjunction with dense woodland which completed the protective barrier. Such earthworks are associated with the sites at Hanging Langford Camp, Gussage Cowdown, Hamshill and Huish Hill. This use of massive earthworks in conjunction with dense woodland recalls Caesar's description of the British custom of fortifying 'a thickset woodland with rampart and trench' (*De Bello Gallico*, V). The use of massive earthworks together with woodland has been noted by Wheeler at the Belgic stronghold of Wheathampstead (1936, 13–16).

This group of settlement types in Wessex would thus seem, by reason of lay-out and associated artefacts, to form a close-knit horizon of construction which may legitimately be linked with Belgic influence. This influence is more likely to be embodied in the large social unit and economic practice represented by this group of sites rather than in the physical form that arose from those conditions.

The future of Iron Age studies of non-defensive settlement lies in detailed regional surveys in which sites are related to those elsewhere and to observable widespread traditions, and in refraining from the sort of excavation that merely samples a site in favour of selected total excavations.

BIBLIOGRAPHY

Bowen, H. C. 1969. 'The Celtic Background', in Rivet 1969, 1–48.

Clarke, D. L. 1968. *Analytical Archaeology*, London.

Collis, J. R. 1968. 'Excavations at Owslebury, Hants: an interim report', *Antiquaries J.*, 48, 18–31.

Crawford, O. G. S., and Keiller, A. 1928. *Wessex from the Air*, Oxford.

Dymond, C. W., and Tomkins, H. G. 1886. *Worlebury: an ancient stronghold in the county of Somerset*, Bristol.

Finley, M. I. 1971. 'Archaeology and History', *Daedalus*, Winter 1971, 168–86.

Hawkes, C. F. C. 1947. 'Britons, Romans and Saxons round Salisbury and in Cranborne Chase', *Archaeol. J.*, 104, 27–78.

Hoare, R. C. 1812. *Ancient Wiltshire*, I, London.

Hoare, R. C. 1821. *Ancient Wiltshire*, II, London.

Hooley, R. W. 1929. 'The excavations at Worthy Down, Winchester', *Proc. Hants Field Club*, 10, 178–92.

Perry, B. T. 1966. 'Some recent discoveries in Hampshire', in Thomas 1966, 39–42.

Perry, B. T. 1969. 'Iron Age enclosures and settlements on the Hampshire Chalklands', *Archaeol. J.*, 126, 29–43.

Piggott, S. 1968. *The Druids*, London.

Pitt-Rivers, A. 1888. *Excavations in Cranborne Chase*, II, London.

Radford, C. A. R. 1954. 'The tribes of southern Britain', *Proc. Prehist. Soc.*, 20, 1–26.

Ritchie, A. 1969. *Settlements and Economy in Britain during the first millennium* B.C. Unpublished PHD thesis, University of Edinburgh.

Rivet, A. L. F. 1969. *The Roman Villa in Britain*, London.

Robbins, M. C. 1966. 'House types and settlement patterns: an application of ethnology to archaeological interpretation', *Minnesota Archaeologist*, 28(1), 3–26.

Sumner, H. 1913. *The Ancient Earthworks of Cranborne Chase*, London.

Taylor, C. C. 1970. 'The study of settlement patterns in pre-Saxon Britain', paper given to the Research Seminar on Settlement Patterns and Urbanisation, University of London, 1970.

Thomas, C. 1966. *Rural Settlement in Roman Britain*, London.

Wainwright, G. J. 1968. 'The excavation of a Durotrigian farmstead near Tollard Royal in Cranborne Chase, England', *Proc. Prehist. Soc.*, 34, 102–47.

Wheeler, R. E. M. and T. V. 1936. *Verulamium, a Belgic and two Roman Cities*, Oxford.

Williams, A. 1950. 'Excavations at Allard's Quarry, Marnhull, Dorset', *Proc. Dorset Nat. Hist. Ant. Soc.*, 72, 20–75.

MARKETS AND MONEY

By John Collis

The Iron Age has been approached primarily from two points of view. The historian armed with meagre contemporary or ambiguous later sources has attempted to interpret the material in historical or political terms, while the prehistorian with his concept of culture has attempted to define discrete groups in terms of their artefacts. Usually the two are combined, whereby cultures such as the Aylesford-Swarling group are given historical significance by correlating them with the Belgae of Caesar. Both methods have had their successes, but the earliest material is not susceptible to historical interpretation, and in the later phases at least we are dealing with a society as complex as that of medieval times, which is impossible to interpret in purely cultural terms. The work of Peacock (1968 and 1969) has further undermined the cultural concept, and though patterning does emerge, it must be interpreted in economic, or more likely social terms, rather than culturally. However, other approaches have been tried in the past with considerable success especially from an economic or geographical standpoint (Fox 1943) and in our present state of chaos these seem to offer a more hopeful approach to the Iron Age, in studying both simple and complex societies (Harriss 1971).

I have elsewhere discussed interpretations of the coinage in social and economic terms (Collis 1971) and here I shall follow up one aspect from that paper the appearance of a market economy based on money. Greek coinage had appeared in Gaul by the fifth century B.C. and was soon imitated by Gaulish tribes, but the market economy was only developing in Greece in the fourth century (Polanyi 1957) with the use of low value coins for minor financial transactions and the appearance of the profit motive. The appearance of the market in Gaul is not documented, but it presumably developed through the Greek colonies in the south, notably Massalia. By the middle of the first century B.C. major settlements had appeared in central Gaul. They are major production centres, engaged in active trade with one another and with the Mediterranean, and possessed market economies to judge by the wealth of low value bronze and small silver coinage they produce.

Classic examples in Gaul include Mont Beuvray, Alesia, and other 'oppida' familiar to us from the writings of Caesar. Archaeologically they produce evidence of bronze and iron industries, and glass working, and of trade with the Roman world, especially in the form of wine amphorae. Similar sites exist in central Europe, such as Manching, Stradonice and Staré Hradisko. An extreme example is the Magdalensberg in southern Austria where there is evidence of foreign merchants resident in the town. Inscriptions on walls tell us not only of Italians but also of an individual from Morocco (Egger 1961). We hear in Caesar of resident colonies of Roman merchants and a foreign population must have been usual in many of these oppida.

Most, though not all, of these sites produce coins in relative profusion. Exceptions include several of the Czech oppida, such as Třísov, and Hrazany (Jansova 1965) which despite extensive excavation and intensive occupation have produced only a handful

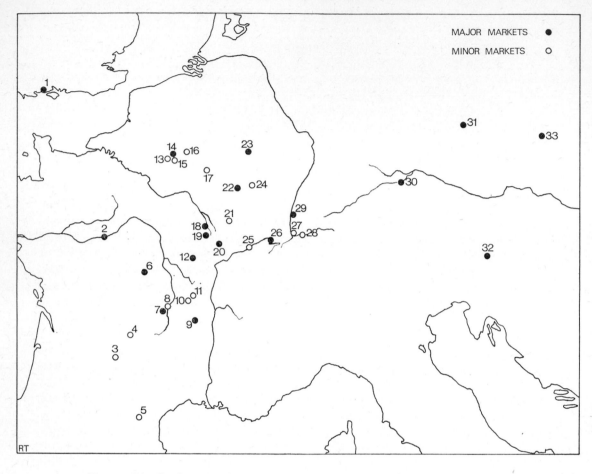

Fig. 21. Distribution of major and minor market centres in the first century B.C.

1. Hengistbury Head	18. Vertault
2. Amboise	19. Alesia
3. Murcens	20. Mont Afrique
4. Puy du Tour	21. Langres
5. La Lagaste	22. Boviolles
6. Chateaumeillant	23. Titelberg
7. Gergovia	24. St. Geneviève
8. Aulnat	25. Besançon
9. Palais d'Essalois	26. Mandeure
10. Joevres	27. Basel
11. Roanne	28. Altenberg-Rheinau
12. Mont Beuvray	29. Breisach-Hochstetten
13. Montigny l'Engrain	30. Manching
14. Pommiers	31. Stradonice
15. Ambleny	32. Magdalensberg
16. St. Thomas	33. Staré Hradisko
17. La Cheppe	

98

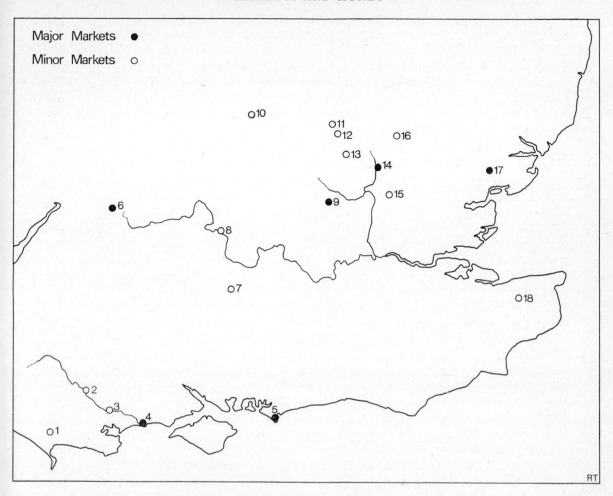

Fig. 22. Distribution of major and minor market centres in Southern Britain, first century B.C. and first century A.D.

1. Maiden Castle
2. Hod Hill
3. Badbury Rings
4. Hengistbury Head
5. Selsey
6. Bagendon
7. Silchester
8. Dorchester on Thames
9. St. Albans
10. Duston
11. Sandy
12. Biggleswade
13. Baldock
14. Braughing
15. Harlow
16. Great Chesterford
17. Colchester
18. Canterbury

99

of specimens, whereas Stradonice and Staré Hradisko which form part of the same trading system have yielded numerous examples, and clearly played some special role. Not all the sites referred to by Caesar as oppida produce numerous coins, and there is a marked lack of sites in Brittany and Normandy, though a couple have produced hoards. Of the sites that produce coins a rough division into minor and major sites can be made both in terms of size and number of coins – thus the contrast between the *chef lieu* of the Suessiones at Pommiers and the lesser sites at Ambleny and Montigny l'Engrain (Vauville 1886).

This set up is mainly post-Caesarean in Gaul, and it is difficult to point to any evidence of pre-Caesarean occupation on sites like Bibracte, Alesia, and the Titelberg. Nauheim brooches are generally absent (Thill 1969) and imported pottery tends to be late. Only minor settlements like Fort Harrouard and St. Geneviève near Nancy seem to be already in existence, and both have produced several examples each of potin coins. Another site is Aulnat, near Clermond Ferrand – the predecessor of Gergovia, though here coins only appear in the latest levels. Thus in Gaul, though the nucleated sites with coins appear prior to the conquest, the main development takes place in the third quarter of the first century B.C. It has however yet to be demonstrated whether the appearance of low denomination coins is directly correlated with the rise of nucleated settlements and oppida. In Britain at least the earliest potin coinage appears in an area where no nucleated settlements developed, but the earliest bronze coinages all turn up regularly in the oppida.

Another feature of the large nucleated settlements is their relative isolation from one another, and yet their obvious close trading contacts across occupied territories which seem to take no part in the trade network. Thus the close relationship between Stradonice and Mont Beuvray. Trade objects such as amphorae or mass-produced bronze trinkets show the same disjointed distribution. Pommiers and Hengistbury Head (Bushe-Fox 1915) fall into this category, and in the case of Hengistbury the plentiful occurrence of Roman amphorae and late La Tène bronzes implies direct contact with central France. Dressel 1 amphorae are virtually unknown in Normandy and Brittany, and the only site with metalwork of Beuvray type is Vernonnet (Gadeau de Kerville and Poulaine 1925, Wheeler and Richardson 1957, p. 121).

Hengistbury follows the pattern of Pommiers with a cluster of minor bronze coin-using settlements clustered around it – Maiden Castle, Hod Hill and Badbury, and as I have previously demonstrated, other hill-forts, if they produce any coins at all have, only gold or silver. The bronze coin-using is restricted to a limited number of sites, and they rarely if ever turn up on minor farming settlements. They were then primarily for use on the oppidum itself and its surrounding satellites.

Outside this nuclear set-up was a more extensive trade route, along which goods, gold and silver coins travelled, but not the bronze. This outer periphery of trade included, in the case of Hengistbury, south-west England, Somerset, Hampshire and Normandy. The contacts can be documented in pottery types like Glastonbury ware or the graphite-coated wares (i.e. trade with manufacturing centres), or in imported goods or in silver coins (fig. 23).

The appearance of these sites with their international trade contacts must have had a direct impact on nearby settlements. Thus at Owslebury (Collis 1968 and 1970) at

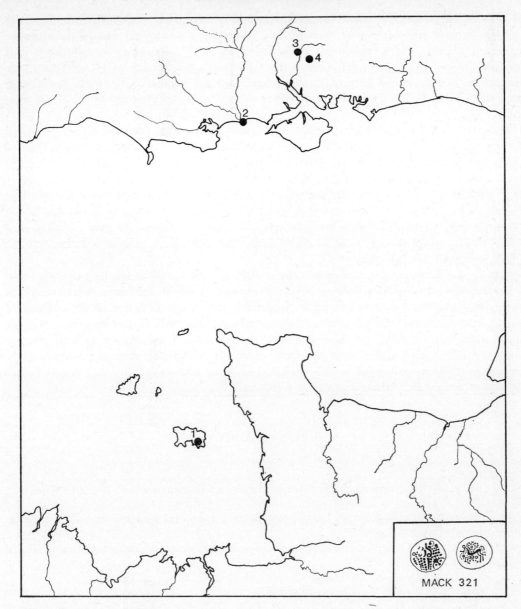

Fig.23. Distribution of the thin silver coin Mack 321, showing the peripheral trade contacts of Hengistbury Head.

1. Le Catillon
2. Hengistbury Head

3. Winchester
4. Owslebury

the time of initial contact with Hengistbury there is a total change in the layout of the ditch system on the settlement, presumably marking a profound economic change. A Dressel 1 amphora, a Mack 321 silver coin (fig. 23), a continental belt hook and Hengistbury class G wares mark this contact, but with the decline of Hengistbury, the orientation of the trade pattern changes and contact seems to be with Essex and Hertfordshire to judge from the occurrence of pedestal jars, tazzae and gallo-belgic wares.

In south-east England it was not until the end of the first century B.C. that the bronze coinage started to appear on the large nucleated sites. Again the basic set-up is that of a large nucleated settlement (St. Albans or Braughing) with a series of satellite settlements using bronze coinage (Baldock, Great Chesterford etc.) and an outer periphery using gold coinage, and presumably supplying mainly raw materials and agricultural produce. Colchester is a little exceptional in lacking the satellites, perhaps due to its pre-eminent position. The same may be true of Selsey, but it is less easy to judge due to bias of chance of discovery of small minims, and also silver minims can be used as bullion or small change alike.

Thus in the first century B.C. we see the sudden rise of major marketing centres each with a network of satellite sites or sub-centres, and a peripheral zone from which it draws its supplies. There is extensive 'international' trade between these individual centres, and perhaps foreign traders resident controlling this trade. Bronze, potin or minim coins are common on these sites and their satellites, but the peripheral area is primarily using high value gold or silver coins for wealth storage. In Britain only Hengistbury Head belonged to this earliest network, and only later did centres such as Colchester and St. Albans appear in south-east England.

BIBLIOGRAPHY

Bushe-Fox, J. P. 1915. 'Excavations at Hengistbury Head.' 3, *Research Rep. Soc. Antiqs.* III, London.

Collis, J. R. 1968. 'Excavations at Owslebury, Hants: an interim report', *Antiquaries Journal*, 48, 18.

Collis, J. R. 1970. 'Excavations at Owslebury, Hants: a second interim report', *Antiquaries Journal*, 50 (forthcoming).

Collis, J. R. 1971. 'Functional and theoretical interpretations of British coinage', *World Archaeology*, 3–71.

Egger, R. 1961. *Die stadt auf dem Magdalensberg: ein Grosshandelsplatz*, Vienna.

Fox, C. 1943. *The Personality of Britain*, Cardiff.

Gadeau de Kerville, H., and Poulain, A. G. 1925. 'Resultat des fouilles Gallo-Romaines effectuées au camp de Vernennet', *Bulletin de la Société Normaindes d'Études Prehistoriques*, 26–107.

Harriss, J. C. 1971. 'Explanation in Prehistory', *Proceedings of the Prehistoric Society*, 37–38.

Jansova, L. 1965. *Hrazany*.

Peacock, D. P. S. 1968. 'A Petrological study of certain Iron Age Pottery from Western England', *Proceedings of the Prehistoric Society*, 34–414.

Peacock, D. P. S. 1969. 'A contribution to the study of Glastonbury Ware from South-Western Britain', *Antiquaries Journal*, 49, 41.

Polanyi, K. and others. 1957. *Trade and Market in the Early Empires*, Glencoe, Ill.

Thill, G. 1969. 'Fibeln vom Titelberg aus den Bestanden des Luxemburger Museums', *Trierer Zeitschrift*, 32–133.

Vauville, O. 1886–99. 'Monnaies gauloises trouvees dans le Department de l'Aisne', *Revue Numismatique*, 3–193, 3–305, 4–257.

Wheeler, R. E. M., and Richardson, K. 1957. 'Hill-forts of Northern France', *Research Rep. Soc. Antiqs.*, London.

SOME APPLICATIONS OF SURFACE FIELDWORK

By A. H. A. HOGG

THERE are two main techniques for the investigation of field monuments: excavation and surface fieldwork. They are complementary, and the restriction of this discussion to one of them must not be taken as minimising the importance of the other. Surface fieldwork, though, is relatively neglected, and the object of this paper is to suggest ways in which further progress may be made. As a result it is necessarily less satisfactory than the other contributions to this conference, for they all arrive at fairly definite conclusions, whereas this is concerned with potential methods of investigation; but a few results are obtained which seem of some interest.

Fieldwork in its strict sense ought perhaps to be confined to recording the character and location of structures, but it seems reasonable to extend the meaning to cover the analysis of evidence collected in this way. The discussion which follows therefore falls into two main parts: the collection of data, for which the techniques are well known, and all that is needed is greater accuracy and objectivity in their application; and methods of interpretation. This second part can again be subdivided, into what may for convenience be called conventional methods, which are essentially intuitive, and more rigid treatment, usually numerical. It is this latter approach which offers the greatest prospect of future advance.

Intuitive interpretation has yielded very stimulating results – Crawford and Fox were perhaps its leading exponents – but it is open to the objection that intuition applied by two different people will not necessarily lead to the same conclusions. Moreover, the ability to weave material into a flowing coherent narrative is all too often taken as proof that the narrative is a true representation of events, and that evidence which conflicts with it should therefore be explained away or ignored.

The advantage of the more rigid approach is that the results obtained, even by different investigators in different areas, are directly comparable; subjective interpretation is eliminated. This point can perhaps be brought out most clearly by considering a different branch of archaeology, the study of pottery. By examination of thin slices, Dr. Peacock has demonstrated concisely and beyond all doubt the origins of various types of 'Glastonbury' ware; intuitive studies of style and distribution were quite inconclusive.

The development of these more rigid methods of analysing the results of fieldwork are primarily due to geographers. Haggett (1965) and Cole and King (1968) provide very useful compendia; the latter perhaps provides the more solid foundation for anyone who wishes to use the methods in practice. D. L. Clarke (1968) has produced a most stimulating, though in places rather uncritical, collection of potential applications to archaeology. It is worth noting here that a diagram, an arrangement of figures in a matrix, or even the use of a computer, are not necessarily guarantees that the results attained have any validity. Just as with the intuitive approach, the final conclusions may have been reached by means of a concealed fallacy in the reasoning. Numerical or other analytical methods, though, have the great advantage that the data and the steps in the analysis are all open to critical examination, so that any fallacy which exists can be demonstrated.

The references given above offer a great many lines of investigation which would be applicable to various kinds of archaeological material. In the latter part of this paper, two or three more are suggested. So far as the writer is aware, these have not been used before; but they are all rather obvious and elementary, and it may well be that although they have not come to his attention they have in fact been applied in this way. If so, apologies are offered for the oversight.

Before proceeding to detailed discussion, it is necessary to consider what material is available for investigation.

The Ordnance Survey Map of Southern Britain in the Iron Age shows 1,394 'Hill-forts and similar Defended Enclosures'; on the mainland of the northern half 1,056 more have been mapped. So Britain contains at least 2,450 recognised hill-forts. If excavation is regarded as the only way in which they can be investigated, this is a discouraging figure, for clearly it will be a long time before any adequate sample can be properly examined.

Another point of view is possible. Here is a class comprising some 2,500 artifacts, probably 80 per cent or more of all those made; more than half are well-preserved and accessible for study; and unlike museum objects the question of whether they were made locally or imported does not arise.

Potentially, then, there is a great mass of material available for investigation, and it is reasonable to suppose that much more information can be extracted from it than has yet been obtained. It is important to repeat, though, that excavation and surface fieldwork supplement each other. For example, some results can only be obtained by digging, such as the date of a site, but these can sometimes be extended to unexcavated hill-forts in the same region; and logically any programme of excavation ought to be preceded by a detailed and accurate field survey, for it is obviously more informative to study a typical structure rather than an exceptional one.

This argument assumes a fairly uniform improvement in technique over the whole field of archaeology, but that is a theoretical ideal which has not been realised in practice. The 1920s may be taken as a convenient datum, for it was during the latter part of that decade that the basic ideas of modern archaeology began to be fairly widely disseminated. Since then, excavation technique has made striking progress, even when the help obtained from other sciences is left out of account. In surface fieldwork and its interpretation, on the other hand, with a few rare exceptions there has been hardly any advance beyond the pioneering work of Crawford and Fox.

There seem to be two main reasons for this. The first is the low repute enjoyed by survey work: a young research-worker will add very little to his reputation by devoting several weeks to a careful survey of a large hill-fort. Standards, also, are low. Outside the three Ancient Monuments Commissions, very few people indeed are concerned to prepare really accurate surveys. Indeed, all too many archaeologists do not even recognise the need for accuracy in such work. Happily this situation is beginning slowly to improve.

That concerns the collection of the basic raw information. The second point relates to processing this material after it has been collected. As indicated earlier, if there is to be any advance in this field, some improved numerical or diagrammatic treatment is almost essential. Unfortunately, again with a few honourable exceptions, most archaeologists react emotionally to such an approach. A seductive diagram or an ingenious array of numbers is either accepted with quite uncritical enthusiasm as 'scientific' or rejected with equally uncritical horror as 'inhuman'. Certainly such methods need to be examined with great care; but if each step of the reasoning is sound it is no more inhuman to subject the sizes of hill-forts to statistical analysis, say, than it is to slice a fragment of pottery to determine its place of manufacture. Both approaches can add to our knowledge of life during the Iron Age; and both give more reliable results than unfettered intuition.

Although the major advances will probably be made in methods of interpretation, these depend on the preliminary collection of material to interpret. In theory, the primary sources are the sites themselves; but no one can really hope to visit all the hill-forts of Britain, so in practice the primary material for any site is a report by someone who has examined the place. In practice, also, such a report cannot always attain the ideal of complete objective accuracy, and a rough plan 'improved' from the 1/2500 map, or even based simply on pacing and a prismatic compass can be useful, always provided that the method used is stated. Unfortunately, even now it is not universally accepted that a plan should either be accurate, so far as the scale allows, or should have some indication of the degree to which it can be trusted.

It is equally important that the actual survey and description should be objective, with the interpretation kept separate so far as possible. An interesting and instructive example of the dangers of incorporating a subjective interpretation in a survey exists in the files of the Welsh Ancient Monuments Commission; as the incident occurred 30 years ago, it can do no harm to describe it.

A very distinguished continental archaeologist was invited to visit the hill-forts of Caernarvonshire, and to advise on their interpretation. In many parts of Europe, 'citadels' are accepted as a fairly common element in hill-fort planning; and four of them were discovered in the Caernarvonshire forts, thus apparently indicating a link with the social organisation of the European Iron Age. In fact, all four sites differ. At Carn Fadrun, the citadel certainly looks early, though its walls are better preserved than those of the main fort, and seem to differ in design by having a parapet walk; but there can be very little doubt that it is the castle built by the sons of Owain in the 12th century, as recorded by Giraldus Cambrensis (Caerns., III, no. 1650). At Garn Boduan, the masonry of the 'citadel' is of quite different character from that of the main fort; excavation has shown that it is not pre-Roman, but on surface evidence alone it would seem unreasonable to claim it as necessarily contemporary with the main fort (Hogg, 1960). At Tre'r Ceiri the 'citadel' is an ordinary hill-top cairn; its presence within the hill-fort is fortuitous (Hogg, 1960). Only at Conway Mountain is the small enclosure contemporary with the main fort (Hogg, 1956); whether 'citadel' is the right description is discussed below. The point here is that descriptions of these forts were drafted (though never printed) saying that they contained citadels. Anyone wishing to use those reports would have been presented with that, and all the associated implications, as an objective fact.

Returning to Conway Mountain, the small enclosure there is contemporary with the main hill-fort, as stated above; but whether it should be described as a 'citadel' is questionable. It is defensible against attack from the main enclosure, but has no entrance directly from it; and the actual interior is lower than the adjacent part of the main fort. So if 'citadel' implies a sort of acropolis to which the inhabitants can rush as a last defence, the term seems misleading. This is an example where an objective description is essential.

It also serves to illustrate two other points. Conway Mountain is a site where contouring is very desirable; for on the uncontoured plan the small enclosure really does give the impression of an acropolis. Further, it is a site where a very distinctive layout of the defences was used in the first period, and this should ultimately help to date the remains. Unfortunately no parallel is known as yet; but excavation has been very unproductive, so a proper understanding of this fort may well depend on the accuracy of the plan.

Actual planning may need to be supplemented for some sites by a study of the location; it is always desirable. Neglect of this has led to very mistaken ideas about promontory forts, for example. There are a lot of these in Brittany, Cornwall, and Pembrokeshire. The Veneti, noted sailors, lived in Brittany until they were heavily defeated by Caesar. The interpretation seems obvious; they moved in to south-west Britain and settled there, their maritime interests being implied by the coastal situation of their forts.

No doubt there is some connection between the three areas, but it cannot be quite so simple as that theory suggests. Many of the British forts are quite inaccessible from the sea; the only possible maritime interest of their inhabitants would be to wave to the ships as they went by. Others overlook rocky inlets where in calm weather one small boat might be drawn up, with some risk. Places of that kind cannot be compared with fortresses such as the enormous enclosure at Bindon Hill (Wheeler, 1953), with the excellent natural harbour of Lulworth Cove. That is too early to belong to the Veneti, but it is the right sort of location.

There is similar contrast further east, between Beltout (V.C.H. Sussex) on Beachy Head, which can never have been accessible from the sea, and East Hill, Hastings (V.C.H. Sussex), which overlooks a natural harbour and has very close parallels indeed among the 'barred spurs' of Northern France. Fieldwork alone, of course, cannot attempt to decide whether hill-forts like Bindon Hill and East Hill are 'invasion bases' or 'trading centres'.

The accurate description of a single hill-fort is valuable, and is equivalent to adding to museum collections; it increases the amount of raw material available, but does not enlarge our understanding of the period much otherwise. For that, classification and the study of distributions are needed.

Unfinished hill-forts, dealt with by Mr. Feachem, provide an excellent example of the value of surface fieldwork. Starting with Ladle Hill (Piggott, 1931) almost all have been identified in that way. and it is even possible to extract a little more information without digging. At Ladle Hill the work was evidently under some central control; there has been fairly uniform progress all round the circuit. At Hardings Down East, in Gower (Glam. I, no. 688), by contrast, about half the circuit was completed, together with a short isolated stretch, while in the intervening spaces nothing has been done at all. This must surely imply an arrangement whereby different families volunteered to undertake sections of the work, but with no overall control.

If completed, Hardings Down East would have been a good typical South-Western Multivallate Fort. The recognition of this class by Lady Fox is probably the most successful application of fieldwork yet made, and demonstrates what can be done using quite rough small-scale plans (Fox, 1958). Even here, though, detailed and accurate surveys can yield more information. At Y Bwlwarcau on Margam Mountain, for example, a detailed survey provides strong evidence for two periods of construction (Glam. I, no. 693), both retaining the same essential arrangement. This indicates a long continuation of the system of farming implied by these enclosures.

To identify a type and to establish its distribution is almost the full extent of what can be done reliably by 'conventional' fieldwork. It is tempting to go further, and to relate hill-fort types or other items with restricted distributions to the tribes recorded in classical sources. Success for such an attempt can be guaranteed, for the tribal boundaries have an uncertainty of 40 or 50 miles, and if the fort types cannot be persuaded to fit even with this wide allowance, some can always be written off as outliers. Some more precise way of defining the boundaries is essential if attempts of this kind are to carry any conviction; the distribution of coins suggests itself as a possible method. This requires to be investigated.

The coins of Cunobelin seem to offer a very clear example of a distribution pattern defining tribal territory (I.A. map, fig. 5; Allen, 1958, 225), and this may therefore be taken as a hypothesis to be tested, even though hill-forts are rare in that region.

Coins differ from most other artifacts in that they are normally made at a single centre, and are likely to spread from there by passing at random from hand to hand until they are lost. This mechanism of distribution corresponds quite closely to that assumed in the simplest case of the Theory of Random Flights (Pearson and Blakeman, 1906). From the formula (fig. 24) it will be seen that given a scatter of objects which are distributed according to that theory, then if we consider a ring of radius R with the source as its centre, the logarithm of the number of objects outside the ring plotted against the square of R gives a straight line. Also, if we consider a straight line at distance R from the source, and the proportion of the objects on one side of it is plotted against R on 'Probability Paper', this also gives a straight line. So there are two simple methods of testing whether a given distribution pattern corresponds to one which would be derived from Random Flights starting from a single source. Conveniently, also, the Standard Deviation for the second plot is almost exactly the radius of the ring outside which 40 per cent of the objects lie; one can refer to the '40 per cent Radius' or the Standard Deviation interchangeably.

Assuming a single mint, remote from any natural features which might affect the spread of coins, a Random Flights distribution might be expected. If some boundary such as a tribal frontier impedes the movement of coins, then the actual distribution will differ from theoretical. *Unless some such difference exists, no coin distribution can be claimed as providing evidence for a frontier, however strong may be the subjective impression of a boundary.*

In considering this actual example, three difficulties arise: there are two mints; part of the relevant area is water; and hoards present a problem. In this case, the easiest

RANDOM FLIGHTS

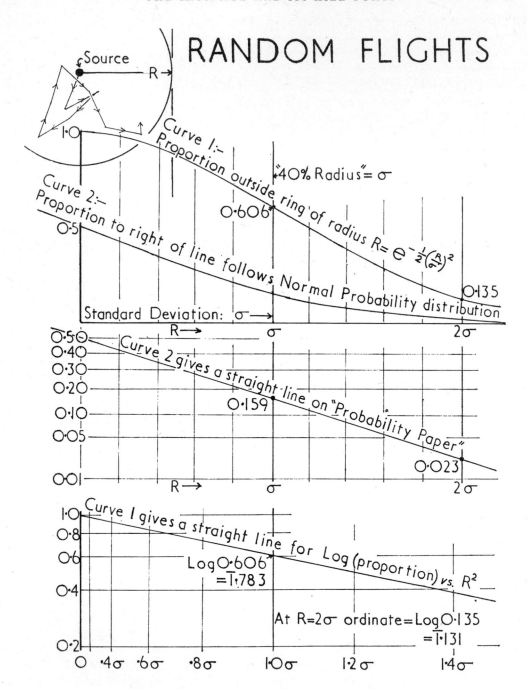

Source

R →

Curve 1:—
Proportion outside ring of radius $R = e^{-\frac{1}{2}\left(\frac{R}{\sigma}\right)^2}$

"40% Radius" = σ

0·606

0·135

Curve 2:—
Proportion to right of line follows Normal Probability distribution

0·5

Standard Deviation: σ →

R → σ 2σ

0·50
0·40
0·30
0·20
0·10
0·05

0·01

Curve 2 gives a straight line on "Probability Paper"

0·159

0·023

R → σ 2σ

1·0
0·8
0·6

0·4

0·2

Curve 1 gives a straight line for Log (proportion) vs. R^2

Log 0·606
= $\overline{1}$·783

At R = 2σ ordinate = Log 0·135
= $\overline{1}$·131

O   ·4σ ·6σ ·8σ 1·0σ 1·2σ 1·4σ

Fig. 24. Theory of Random Flights, General Diagram.

way of dealing with the water areas is to imagine a mirror image of the distribution pattern reflected about the St. Albans – Colchester line, and to see how many coins fall in the sea or the Thames Estuary. The number is in fact very small, and does not alter the pattern at all significantly. The two mints present some difficulty. At Colchester, the ground has been turned over much more than at St. Albans, and has thus yielded a disproportionately large number of coins, relative both to the other mint and to the countryside in general. It thus seems reasonable to leave out of account the immediate neighbourhoods of both mints, especially as the numbers to be plotted are those *outside* the ring centred on St. Albans. Further, there is the problem of how many coins should be attributed to the Colchester mint. An estimate can be made either by finding where the centre of gravity of all the coins lies, or by counting the number of coins on the Colchester side of a line through St. Albans as against those on the other side. These give consistent and surprisingly small results of only about 20 coins or 10 find-spots arising from Colchester. Once this number is decided, it is simple though rather laborious to allow for the proportion likely to have come from Colchester at any given distance from St. Albans. The question whether to plot all individual coins or only find-spots is not easy to resolve; in this case the conclusions are unaffected (fig. 25). In fact, the correction for the coins derived from Colchester makes no difference either. In every case, the relevant plot of coins (or find-spots) against radius from St. Albans gives a good straight line. That for find-spots is particularly close to theory. It seems more reasonable to accept this as the appropriate criterion rather than to count all coins, for each find-spot corresponds to a deposit made by a single individual, whether by accidentally dropping one coin or deliberately concealing a hoard. In any case, this coin-distribution seems quite unaffected by the possible presence of a frontier.

There is no other tribal mint very near St. Albans, so the apparently unhindered spread of these coins is not very surprising. It seems worth while to examine another case. The distribution of the coins of the Dobunni and Durotriges (I.A. Map, map 6; Allen, 1958, 239, 247) gives a strong subjective impression of a 'frontier' about half way between their mints at Bagendon and Hengistbury Head. This is evidently a case for considering the plot, on probability paper, of the percentages to north or south of a straight line as it is moved across the region. For the reason given earlier, find-spots are used. The very large hoards in this region would have caused difficulty in interpretation anyway.

The results obtained are curious (fig. 26). For the Dobunni, there are exactly 100 find-spots, and if the proportions north or south of the line are plotted without any adjustment they mostly lie on a very good straight line. This extends to the south coast, 120 km. from Bagendon, and cuts the 50 per cent mark only 10 km. south of that mint. Good agreement continues as far as 60 or 70 km. to the north, where the actual numbers fall off below the 'theoretical' line. The numerical difference is in fact quite small, so the validity of the following reasoning is questionable; but it is arguable that this deviation justifies calculating the proportions against an assumed total of 113 find-spots, instead of 100, so as to bring the 50 per cent mark exactly to Bagendon. The divergence then commences 40 or 50 km. to the north. There is no very obvious northern 'frontier' in that region, but hill-forts do seem to thin out at about 30 to 40 km., on the general line through Herefordshire Beacon, Bredon Hill, and Meon Hill. To the south,

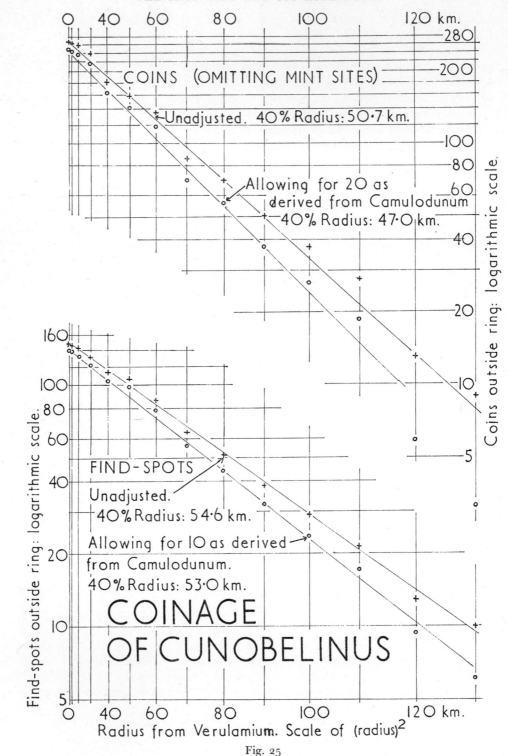

COINS (OMITTING MINT SITES)

Unadjusted. 40% Radius: 50·7 km.

Allowing for 20 as derived from Camulodunum 40% Radius: 47·0 km.

Coins outside ring: logarithmic scale.

FIND-SPOTS

Unadjusted. 40% Radius: 54·6 km.

Allowing for 10 as derived from Camulodunum. 40% Radius: 53·0 km.

COINAGE OF CUNOBELINUS

Find-spots outside ring: logarithmic scale.

Radius from Verulamium. Scale of (radius)²

Fig. 25

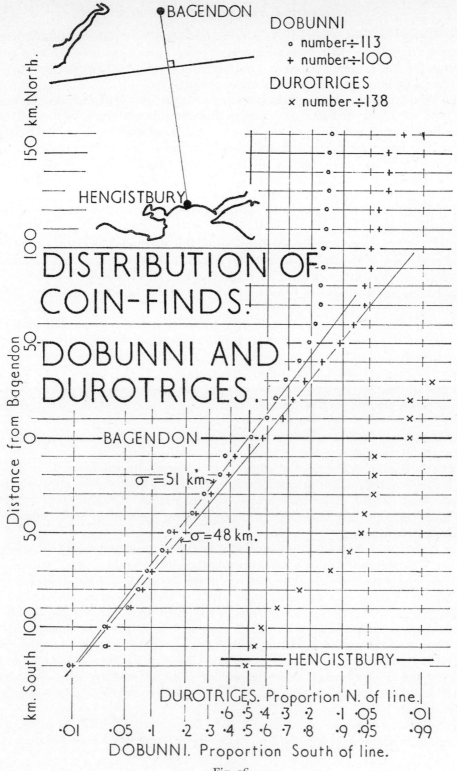

Fig. 26

though, whichever plot is used, there is no sign at all of any restraint on the use of the Dobunnic coins. It is interesting to note the close agreement between the Standard Deviation for this example (48 to 51 km.) and the 40 per cent Radius for Cunobelin's coins (47 to 55 km., according to the assumptions made).

The Durotriges give a very different result. A difficulty arises because Hengistbury Head is on the coast; does the sea act as an absorbent boundary or as a reflector? The distribution plotted assumes that the 50 per cent point should occur at Hengistbury, but several others have been tried, and all give a similar curve; more coins than would be expected near the coast, falling off rapidly about 60 km. to the north. A 'frontier' there does show some sort of agreement with the northern edge of the Wiltshire downs. Whatever conclusion may be reached about frontiers, though, there seems to be no doubt that the coins of the Dobunni circulated freely among the Durotriges, but that the converse was not true.

More work is needed on the applications of this method, especially to devise some way of making a numerical estimate of significance when dealing with relatively few items. Even at this rather elementary stage, though, there does seem to be a prospect of eliminating some subjective frontiers and of establishing some real ones with more precision than has so far been possible.

At best, distribution patterns can only indicate major regions. By analogy with later periods it seems likely that each hill-fort exercised control over some defined territory, primarily to feed its inhabitants. For a long time to come, most information relating to this must come from surface fieldwork.

There are four major questions concerning any given fort, besides that of date:
How many people lived in it?
Did they live there permanently?
What territory was associated with the fort?
Did all the inhabitants of that territory live in the fort?

As yet, excavation has hardly begun to deal even with the first two questions; at most, a rough answer might be possible for half a dozen hill-forts. So at present, surface evidence must be the major source of such information. In attempting to obtain it, there is also a hope that some way of distinguishing 'typical' from 'exceptional' forts may be devised.

The question of the total population in a fort is one to which fieldwork can make a valuable contribution. Quite a large number of forts retain surface traces of their dwellings. Those such as Garn Boduan, where the houses had stone walls, are particularly helpful. Taking that site as an example, 157 houses remain identifiable. Unfortunately, there are certainly two periods of building there, so it is impossible to say whether there were 80 occupied in each period, or 137, which is the largest total which could have been in use at one time (Alcock, 1965, 194); but this is really quite unimportant. In this sort of calculation, figures which differ by a factor of less than 2 can be regarded as in almost exact agreement. The general size of the settlement is clear. It was a small town of some 400 to 800 people, like medieval Conway or modern Montgomery.

Garn Boduan turns out to be fairly typical for southern Britain. Depending on the assumptions made, something like 8 to 12 dwellings per hectare seems normal in north

Wales. The surviving part of Hod Hill has 15 per hectare; Hambledon Hill, 12.5; Charlbury, with two periods, 14.5. So a reasonable figure would seem to be about a dozen dwellings, or say 60 persons, per hectare of enclosed area. It is important to realise, though, that these are all forts where the dwellings were predominantly round. It will be extremely interesting to see what the comparable figures are for settlements such as Croft Ambrey or Midsummer Hill.

The second question, did the inhabitants live permanently in the fort, is very difficult to answer by any means, but surface fieldwork can sometimes provide a clue. Taking Garn Boduan again as an example, there must have been at least 80 substantial houses in use within it. On the assumption that the place was only lived in during the summer, when raiding was easy, there ought to be at least 80 equally substantial winter houses outside, but intensive fieldwork has not been able to find any evidence at all for more than about half a dozen. Until several of these theoretical winter houses have been found in circumstances which would explain why most of them should have vanished, the hypothesis of seasonal occupation of this hill-fort must be considered unproven.

The question of associated territory can be examined from several points of view. The information which matters is not so much the actual area controlled, but how many people that area could support. Unfortunately, no data about this became available until more than a thousand years later. Despite the long interval, this information is useful as a guide to conditions during the Iron Age, except perhaps in the claylands; for it is reasonable to assume that the productivity of medieval agriculture, and thus the population which it could support, was rather greater than in pre-Roman times, and that the proportional improvement is of the same order throughout the country.

J. C. Russell has worked out the probable populations for each English county at the time of Domesday; for Wales he gives a lump total. If these figures are plotted (fig. 27, the reference is cited there) in terms of the average population per square kilometre they show a reasonable and consistent trend. This is true even for Wales, where it has been necessary to assume the same relative fertility for each county in 1100 as in 1700. This trend can be generalised, roughly, into a series of 'contours', showing a transition from about 2 per square kilometre in the north and 4 or 5 in the mountainous west to 10 in the South Downs and 15 or more in East Anglia. Obviously, these figures are subject to great uncertainty, so although it is convenient to refer to them as population per square kilometre they ought really to be regarded as arbitrary index numbers. It is probably much less inaccurate to say that the average population density in Sussex during the Iron Age was about 2.3 times that in Caernarvonshire, than to claim that the actual density was 9 or 10 per square kilometre.

This map, then, gives a background against which the areas of hill-forts can be considered. Reasons have already been given for regarding 60 persons per hectare as a representative figure for the population density in hill-forts. Again, this is not an exact figure. It may well be, for example, that the average in North Wales should be 40, and in Sussex 90, so one may imagine a *regional* correction-factor to be necessary; but this factor is likely to change fairly smoothly as one moves from one part of the country to another. Similarly, the population-density may require *regional* correction. The consequence of this argument can best be understood in relation to an actual example.

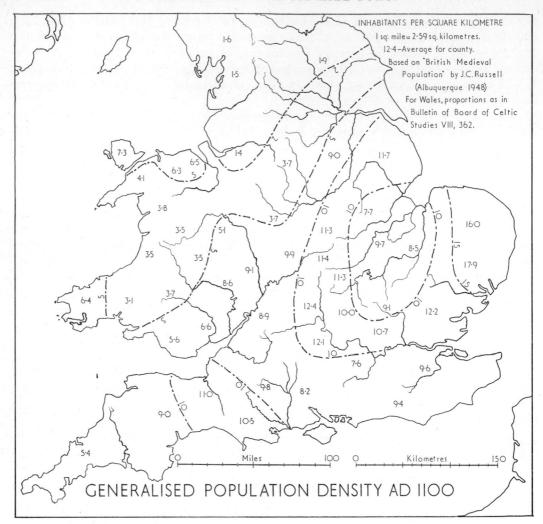

INHABITANTS PER SQUARE KILOMETRE
1 sq. mile = 2·59 sq. kilometres.
12·4 – Average for county.
Based on "British Medieval
Population" by J.C. Russell
(Albuquerque 1948)
For Wales, proportions as in
Bulletin of Board of Celtic
Studies VIII, 362.

GENERALISED POPULATION DENSITY AD 1100

Fig. 27.

One application of these figures is to provide an objective way of comparing hill-fort sizes. A 6 hectare fort in Caernarvonshire, say, is obviously more important relative to its background than one in Wessex; or considering only one region, some hill-forts stand out as exceptionally large. These are subjective qualitative judgments, and it is useful to be able to replace them by index numbers.

Using these figures, and making the artificial assumption that the inhabitants of the fort drew their subsistence from a circular area of radius r, then $r^2 \times$ density of population = 60 $\times$ area of fort. Again, the radius r can be regarded either as an index figure or as an approximation to a real quantity. If this calculation is applied to Maiden Castle, area 18 hectares in a region with population density 10.8, r comes out as 5.8 km.; for Hod Hill, in the same region, area 22.4 hectares, r = 6.4 km.; but Charlbury (4 km.) or Poundbury (6 ha.) only require r = 2.7 or 3.3 km. respectively. If r is taken as a real quantity, then at Charlbury and Poundbury the inhabitants could get to their fields and return daily, without much difficulty; at Maiden Castle and Hod Hill the distances are becoming inconveniently large. For Bindon Hill, of 114 ha., and on the coast so that it could only draw on a semicircle of land, r exceeds 20 km. Clearly, from this index, it stands out as exceptional, as indeed it does simply from a consideration of its area. It must be emphasised that the calculation merely picks out the fort as having an exceptionally high index figure; it does not explain why it is so large. Possible explanations would be that it was thinly inhabited; that it drew subsistence from a large subject territory; or that it was a trading centre. These are points which could be investigated by excavation.

All these forts are in the same region, so in effect the index r is merely another way of expressing the enclosed areas. It is of some interest to examine how forts in different regions compare on this basis. Listing some, in order of the index r, gives Markland Grips (4.8 ha., 3.7 km.^{2}) r = 5.0 km.; Foel Fenlli (8.4 ha., 6.4 per km.^{2}) 5.0 km.; Bathampton (32 ha., 11 per km.^{2}) 7.5 km.; Ingleborough (6 ha., 1.9 per km.^{2}) 7.8 km.; Dyke Hills (40 ha., 12.4 per km.^{2}) 7.9 km. So relative to its background, Ingleborough, which is not even 'large' in the O.S. map classification, is as important as the huge forts of Bathampton and Dyke Hills. As it is in a different region, the possible effect of a regional correction factor needs to be considered. For example, the population index figures used were 1.9 per km.^{2} at Ingleborough, 11 at Bathampton, 10.5 at Maiden Castle. If the medieval population was, say, twice that during the Iron Age, the real densities would be half these figures; but the density at Bathampton will still bear about the same ratio to that near Maiden Castle, not far away, and even at the more distant Ingleborough, the relative figures are not likely to be more than about 50 per cent out either way. Similar reasoning applies to the intensity of occupation within the forts, assuming that they are normal for their respective regions. Taking the Bathampton and Maiden Castle region as standard for comparison, then, the radius at Ingleborough, treated as an index figure, may be anything from 5.2 to 11.7 km. (7.8 ÷ 1.5 or × 1.5) but seems unlikely to be outside that range; so the place still falls into the Maiden Castle class, according to this criterion.

It is important to emphasise that this calculation has been given primarily as an example. Such a long-range comparison is not really justifiable on the basis of a single index figure; other data need to be taken into account at the same time. This reservation would apply even more strongly, though, to crude comparison of areas without taking background conditions into account.

This arbitrary assumption of circular territories provides a convenient way of expressing, as a single index, the area which the occupants of a hill-fort might be expected to need; but it is not very helpful in determining how much they actually had. Sometimes, though very seldom, a reasonably convincing estimate can be made from the evidence of the topography.

One such region is the Lleyn peninsula. It falls naturally into three zones, two of which are dominated by Garn Boduan and Carn Fadrun. The number of dwellings associated with each of these forts is known, though unfortunately they are both two-period sites. The remaining forts in the area are so small that they can be neglected.

For all three zones taken together, the area is 256 square kilometres, and according to what assumptions are made about how many dwellings were in use at once there were either 148 or 237. At 5 persons per house, this gives 2.9 or 4.6 persons per square kilometre. Omitting the zone with no large hill-fort, the other two total 171 km.[2], giving 4.3 or 6.9 per sq. km.; or taken separately, Carn Fadrun dominates 100 sq. km., with 68 or 100 houses, corresponding to 3.4 or 5.0 persons per sq. km., while for Garn Boduan the figures are 71 sq. km., 80 or 137 houses, and thus 5.6 or 9.6 persons per sq. km. These agree very surprisingly well with the medieval index figure of 4.1 persons per sq. km. They also demonstrate fairly conclusively that the smaller estimates for the numbers of dwellings occupied at one time are the more probable, and that the subjective estimate of the Garn Boduan territory was rather too small. Further, the figures make it very likely indeed that almost all the people who drew their subsistence from the areas attributed to Garn Boduan and Carn Fadrun did live in those forts – though not necessarily throughout the whole year.

Places such as this, where the hill-forts dominate well-defined areas, are unusual. Generally their territorial boundaries can only be guessed at subjectively, so the results are useless for comparative purposes. The real boundaries can hardly ever be established beyond dispute, so what is needed is some completely objective method to estimate the way in which land was shared between adjacent hill-forts. D. L. Clarke (1968,

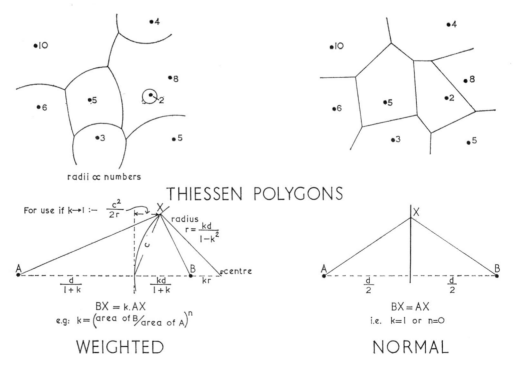

Fig. 28.

508–9, figs. 113–5) has apparently attempted something of this kind by fitting a honeycomb grid to the distribution pattern of sites, so that on average one falls in each cell. He does not explain the method in detail, but essentially it would seem to be a diagrammatic way of illustrating the average intensity of hill-forts per unit area. This approach seems open to the serious objection that each fort is treated as of equal importance, whatever its area, whereas it would seem self-evident that in general the boundary separating the territories of two communities should lie nearer to the smaller one.

One possible method which suggests itself as overcoming that difficulty is based on the use of what are essentially Thiessen Polygons, but with the distances from each fort to the boundary between them weighted to allow for their different areas (fig. 28); the necessary formulae are given in the diagram.

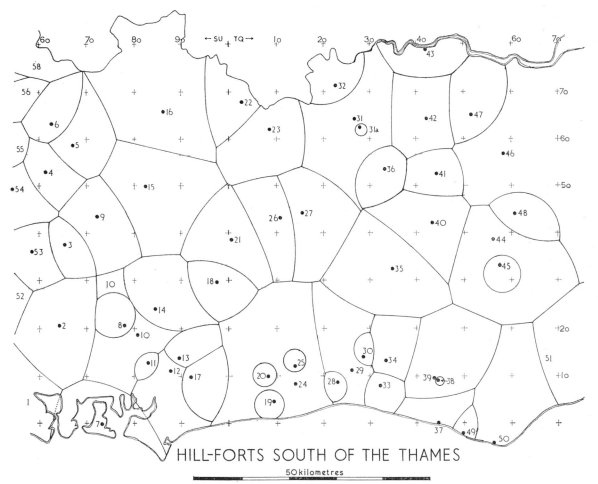

HILL-FORTS SOUTH OF THE THAMES

50 kilometres

WEIGHTED THIESSEN POLYGONS: RADII $\propto$ AREAS$^{0.25}$

Fig. 29.

This method has been applied, experimentally, to the hill-forts south of the Thames (List, see appendix). In order to make the trial as objective as possible, everything has been left out of account except the areas of the forts; for some of these, where the site is eroded, an estimate has been made of the probable original area. The results have not been as useful as was hoped; for example, they give no guidance to help sort out forts of different periods. They do give some information, though, which could not be obtained otherwise and should assist the classification of the forts. Again, if preferred, the figures obtained can be regarded as index numbers rather than as real quantities.

The chief difficulty in application is to decide the value which should be assigned to n. For a regular pattern of forts with two different areas only, $n = \frac{1}{2}$ gives a fairly constant ratio of polygon area to fort area, but for the actual distribution tested it seemed to place too much emphasis on the larger forts. The method has therefore been tried out for $n = \frac{1}{2}$ and $n = \frac{1}{4}$ (fig. 29); probably the best value lies between the two, for the smaller value seems to over-emphasise the territory of the smaller forts.

Considering the group of forts as a whole, the method gives a fairly objective estimate for the total area associated with them all; but a subjective approximation to the boundaries could not go far wrong. The result is of some interest, for it works out at 26 to 28 sq. km. per hectare enclosed (for $n = \frac{1}{2}$ and $n = \frac{1}{4}$ respectively). Considering this against the medieval population density, which is about 10 in this region, several alternative possibilities arise, which can only be answered by excavation combined with fieldwork. If the forts accommodated all the population then either the average regional population density was very low, only 2 or 3 per sq. km., less than in Lleyn, or the forts were very much more intensively occupied than – say – Hod Hill; alternatively there were a great many undefended farms and settlements in the region. The last seems the most probable, but even if the average of 10 per sq. km. is double what it should be, the number of undiscovered settlements must be very large indeed. A rough calculation, incorporating too many uncertainties to be worth quoting in full, suggests that every one of the 70 villages and 220 'finds' marked on the O.S. Iron Age Map would need to correspond to a settlement of about a hundred people.

Turning to individual forts and their associated polygons, it becomes difficult to generalise, for change in n from $\frac{1}{2}$ to $\frac{1}{4}$ may produce a very large movement of the polygon boundaries (fig. 30). Some forts, though, have 'territories' relative to their enclosed area consistently above the average for both values of n, and others consistently below; and these fall into groups. It is interesting to note that the group of forts with 'large' territories lie fairly consistently on the sands and gravels; they are the two Caesar's Camps (15, 16), Piper's Copse (18), Hascombe (21), St. George's Hill (23), Holmbury (26), Anstiebury (27) and Philpots Camp (35). Those with relatively small 'territories' are Squerryes Park (41) and Holwood Hill (42); the group round the Devil's Dyke (29) including Thundersbarrow (28), Wolstonbury (30), Hollingbury (33) and Ditchling Beacon (34). The three coastal forts, Castle Hill, Newhaven (37), Seaford Head (49) and Beltout (50) all seem to have exceptionally small polygons associated with them; but this may be the result of making a wrong allowance for erosion. Incidentally, the forts at Oldbury (46) and East Hill, Hastings (51) fall within the same sort of range (as indicated by sq. km. per hectare enclosed) as the rest, but

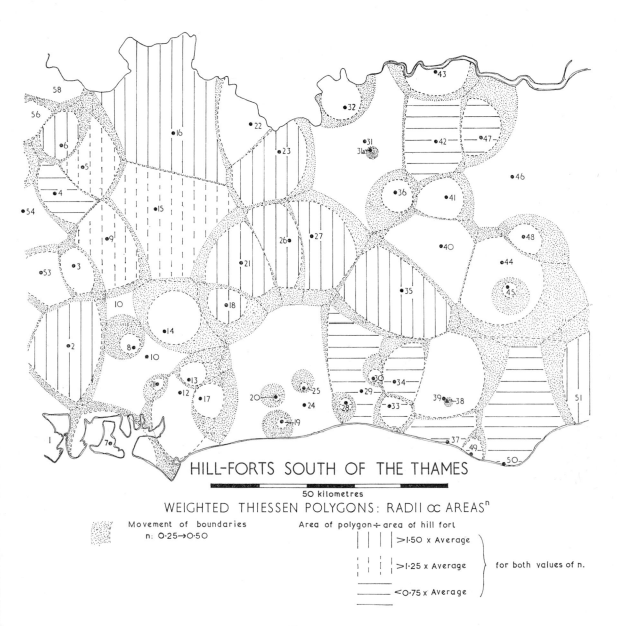

HILL-FORTS SOUTH OF THE THAMES

50 kilometres

WEIGHTED THIESSEN POLYGONS: RADII $\propto$ AREAS^n

Movement of boundaries
n: 0·25→0·50

Area of polygon ÷ area of hill fort

| | | | >1·50 x Average
| | | | >1·25 x Average   } for both values of n.
———— <0·75 x Average

Fig. 30.

Bigbury near Canterbury has the very much larger figure of 123 to 146 sq. km. per hectare, depending on n.

The way in which these forts fall into groups does suggest that this purely objective method of analysis gives results which have some real significance, but at present, it would be unwise to claim that it provides a clue to the real territorial boundaries. It is tempting to point out the close agreement between the River Adur and the theoretical boundary between the Devil's Dyke group (29) and Cissbury (24), or the way in which the north boundaries of Holmbury (26), Anstiebury (27), and Squerryes Park (41) correspond to the scarp of the North Downs, but there are so many hills and streams in this region, that a determined attempt to relate the boundaries of the polygons to natural features can hardly fail. The problem needs to be approached with great caution.

Throughout this paper, emphasis has been placed on the need for objective methods, preferably numerical. As indicated earlier, many archaeologists find this sort of approach distasteful. I believe that such a reaction arises from a misconception, so in conclusion I will give my personal view as to how field archaeology, as defined here, fits in to the study of archaeology as a whole.

The basic function of archaeology is to reconstruct the way in which people lived, including the changes in their modes of life during the passage of time. This reconstruction may lead to the discovery of 'laws' relating to such changes, and conversely the discovery of such 'laws' may help the reconstruction. At present, though, the most generally acceptable way of presenting the reconstruction is in the form of a narrative synthesis of the material.

Confusion arises from the assumption that such a form must therefore be the best way of presenting the basic data. I believe this to be completely wrong. Intuition and even imagination can properly be used in preparing the narrative reconstruction, and may be of value not only in producing a readable account but in suggesting hypotheses which deserve investigation. This applies not merely to wide-ranging syntheses but even to detailed descriptions of single earthworks. What is essential, though, is that the actual facts shall be presented as objectively as possible. If, without warning, subjective interpretations are passed off as facts, or inaccurate surveys as correct, the fundamental material on which all progress must depend becomes unreliable.

APPENDIX

HILL-FORTS SOUTH OF THE THAMES (figs. 29–30)

| | | | | | Polygons | | | |
| | | | | | n=$\frac{1}{2}$ | | n=$\frac{1}{4}$ | |
No.	10km	G.R.	Name	Fort Area ha	Area sq. km	Sq. km per ha	Area sq. km	Sq. km per ha
1	SU40	482 061	Hamble Common	12.0	—	—	—	—
2	SU62	641 206	Old Winchester Hill	5.6	254	45.4	297	53.1
3	SU63	656 374	Medstead	1.6	55	34.2	86	54.7
4	SU65	613 529	Winklebury	6.8	98	14.4	105	15.4
5		671 584	Bullsdown	4.0	134	33.4	158	39.5
6	SU66	626 630	The Frith	1.6	68	42.6	117	73.3
7	SZ79	732 999	Tourner Bury	2.6	66	25.4	176	67.8
8	SU72	780 204	Torberry	2.8	15	5.5	66	23.4
9	SU74	723 434	Dicket's Plantation	5.2	176	33.8	205	39.4
10	SU81	807 183	Harting Beacon	12.0	615	51.2	183	15.2
11		830 127	Goose Hill	0.6	6	9.7	21	35.0
12		877 110	The Trundle	5.0	160	32.1	112	22.3
13		897 137	Court Hill	1.6	22	13.9	71	44.4
14	SU82	846 240	Hammer Wood	4.0	102	25.5	206	51.5
15	SU85	825 500	Caesar's Camp, Farnham	10.2	483	47.5	394	38.6
16	SU86	863 657	Caesar's Camp, Easthampstead	9.8	614	62.8	556	57.0
17	SU90	920 097	Halnaker Hill	1.6	35	22.0	107	67.0
18	SU92	978 295	Piper's Copse	0.6	46	77.0	127	214.0
19	TQ00	092 043	Highdown	0.7	4	6.0	32	45.8
20	TQ01	081 100	Harrow Hill	0.3	1.5	5.0	21	70.0
21	TQ03	004 386	Hascombe	2.2	140	63.5	218	99.1
22	TQ06	026 676	St. Ann's Hill	4.7	108	23.1	128	27.2
23		085 618	St. George's Hill	5.3	196	37.1	236	44.7
24	TQ10	139 080	Cissbury	19.5	718	36.5	358	18.4
25	TQ11	139 120	Chanctonbury	1.0	2	2.5	17	16.5
26	TQ14	104 430	Holmbury	3.2	133	41.5	169	52.7
27		153 440	Anstiebury	4.4	200	45.4	259	59.0
28	TQ20	229 084	Thundersbarrow Hill	1.2	6	5.1	23	19.2
29	TQ21	260 111	Devil's Dyke	15.2	283	18.7	200	13.2
30		284 138	Wolstonbury	2.0	7	3.5	23	11.5
31	TQ26	269 640	Carshalton N.	24.0	641	27.0	348	14.5
31a		279 623	Carshalton Hospital	1.3	1	0.9	5	4.0
32	TQ27	224 711	Caesar's Camp, Wimbledon	4.3	66	15.2	97	22.5
33	TQ30	322 078	Hollingbury	3.0	33	10.9	58	19.2
34	TQ31	333 130	Ditchling Beacon	5.5	90	16.3	115	20.9
35	TQ33	349 332	Philpots Camp	6.2	304	48.1	372	60.0
36	TQ35	331 532	Cardinal's Cap (Area est.)	1.5	36	23.8	108	71.5

| | | | | Fort Area ha | Polygons | | | |
| | | | | | n=$\frac{1}{2}$ | | n=$\frac{1}{4}$ | |
No.	10km	G.R.	Name		Area sq. km	Sq. km per ha	Area sq. km	Sq. km per ha
37	TQ40	446 000	Castle Hill, Newhaven (Area est.)	15.0	90	6.0	75	5.0
38		444 089	The Caburn	1.4	1	0.4	3	2.0
39		438 092	Ranscombe (Unfin.) (Area est.)	8.0	213	26.6	283	35.4
40	TQ44	432 417	Dry Hill	9.2	243	26.4	220	23.9
41	TQ45	443 522	Squerryes Park	4.8	76	15.9	106	22.0
42	TQ46	421 640	Holwood Hill (Caesar's Camp)	17.2	238	13.8	199	11.5
43	TQ47	420 787	Charlton (Area est.)	4.3	68	15.9	122	26.0
44	TQ53	561 382	High Rocks	8.8	196	22.2	405	46.0
45		577 329	Saxonbury	0.6	8	13.3	48	80.0
46	TQ55	582 566	Oldbury	49.0	2100	43.0	1380	28.2
47	TQ56	518 646	Hulberry	10.0	81	8.1	167	16.7
48	TQ64	607 438	Castle Hill	3.3	34	10.2	104	31.5
49	TV49	495 978	Seaford Head (Area est.)	7.0	13	1.9	22	3.1
50	TV59	560 956	Beltout (Area est.)	30.0	433	14.4	289	9.6
51	TQ80	833 099	East Hill, Hastings	9.1	415	45.5	777	85.5
52	SU42	484 276	St. Catharine's Hill	9.2	—	—	—	—
53	SU53	584 362	Oliver's Battery	3.6	94	26.2	130	36.0
54	SU54	544 494	Cadbury	16.0	—	—	—	—
55	SU55	526 567	Bowry Walls	3.6	—	—	—	—
56	SU56	525 696	Ramsbury	2.8	—	—	—	—
57	SU57	511 723	Grimsbury	3.6	—	—	—	—
58		520 780	Perborough Castle	5.4	—	—	—	—
59	SU41	413 170	Chilworth Ring	2.0	—	—	—	—
60	SU42	445 233	Cranbury	2.0	—	—	—	—
61	TR15	117 575	Bigbury	10.7	1315	123.0	1565	146.0

Note. Areas of polygons are rounded off, but ratios to fort areas are calculated from original figures. Nomenclature of camps as on O.S. Iron Age Map.

BIBLIOGRAPHY

Alcock, L. 1965. 'Hill-forts in Wales and the Marches', *Antiquity*, XXXIX, 184 ff.

Allen, D. F. 1958. *The Origins of Coinage in Britain* in Frere 1958, 97 ff.

Caerns, III. *Inventory of Ancient Monuments in Caernarvonshire*, vol. III, RCAM (Wales) (HMSO 1964).

Clarke, D. L. 1968. *Analytical Archaeology*, London.

Cole, J. P., and King, C. A. M. 1968. *Quantitative Geography*, London.

Fox, A. 1958. *South-Western Hill-forts* in Frere 1958, 35.

Frere, S. S. 1958. *Problems of the I.A. in Southern Britain*, CBA, London.

Glam. I. *Inventory of Ancient Monuments in Glamorgan*, RCAM (Wales) Forthcoming.

Haggett, P. 1965. *Locational Analysis in Human Geography*, London.

Hogg, A. H. A. 1956. 'Hill-fort on Conway Mountain', *Arch. Camb.*, CV, 49–80.

Hogg, A. H. A. 1960. 'Garn Boduan and Tre'r Ceiri', *Arch. Journ.*, CXVII, 1–39.

I.A. Map. *Map of Southern Britain in the Iron Age*, OSO, 1962.

Pearson, K., and Blakeman J. 1906. 'A Mathematical Theory of Random Migration', *Drapers' Co. Research Memoirs*, XV, Biometric Series III.

Piggott, S. 1931. 'Ladle Hill', *Antiquity*, V, 474.

Wheeler, R. E. M. 1953. 'An Early Iron Age "Beach-head" at Lulworth', *Ant. Journ.* XXXIII, 1–13.

V.C.H. Sussex. *Victoria History of the County of Sussex*, vol. I, 1905, 453–470.

BRITISH POTIN COINS: A REVIEW

By D. F. ALLEN

INTRODUCTION

'THE Ancient British coinage made of an alloy of tin and copper has never been accurately dated.' These are the opening words of a paper I wrote in 1936, and they remain substantially true today, 35 years later.[1] That article was in other respects inadequate, even misleading. Though I have mentioned them incidentally[2], I have never since devoted an article to these strange objects. Unlovely though they are, they deserve a more thorough treatment.

TECHNIQUE

The coins are all chill-cast in a bronze with a high tin content.[3] The percentage of metals, in different examples analysed, varies. Tin runs from 7% to 27%; copper from 70% to 90%; lead from 1% to 3%; iron from 0·1% to 2%; nickel and bismuth are never more than 1%. The common description, 'tin coins', is a misnomer and should be abandoned; the substitute, 'speculum', describes a particular metal composition and is also a misnomer. If 'chill-cast high-tin bronze' is too much of a mouthful, we can, like the Germans, adopt the well established French name for their comparable coins, to which there is no equivalent term in English, 'potin'.

Potin coins differ from all other British coins, except the late series from Hengistbury and Holdenhurst, in that they are cast in moulds.[4] Though none have yet been found, the moulds were certainly of clay. They appear to have been individually made by hand; no two coins have ever been found from the same mould in Britain, nor, I believe on the Continent. It looks as if the moulds were used only once and discarded. Somewhere, probably in Kent, a vast heap of broken moulds must await discovery.

The coins bear evident traces of how they were made. They were, like their continental counterparts, cast in strips and chopped into individual coins afterwards. The metal remaining from the runnels joining one coin to another was not cut away; all the coins retain projecting 'tangs' at either end, except the last in the line, which has only one. From the proportion of these single tang coins it can be deduced that the average strip probably contained five or six coins. The tangs are always on the centre line. It

[1] D. F. Allen, 'British Tin Coinage of the Iron Age', *Transactions of the International Numismatic Congress*, London, 1936, 351–7 (Allen, 1936).

[2] D. F. Allen, 'The Belgic Dynasties of Britain and their Coins', *Archaeologia XC* (1944), 12; 'The Origins of Coinage in Britain: A Reappraisal', in S. S. Frere, *Problems of the Iron Age in Southern Britain*, 1961, 122–3; (*Origins*). Ordnance Survey, *Map of the Iron Age in Southern Britain*, 1962, 22 (O.S. Map).

[3] G. F. Hill, 'A Note on the Composition of British Coins', *Numismatic Chronicle*, 1917, 316–8; F. C. Thompson, 'A Note on the Composition of British Pre-Roman "Tin-Money",' *Numismatic Chronicle*, 1962, 111–2; R. W. Tylecote, 'The Method of Use of Early Iron-Age Coin Moulds', *Numismatic Chronicle*, 1962, 108. See also R. A. G. Carson, *Numismatic Chronicle*, 1950, 149. *Cf.* the analysis of potin coins found in Gaul; A. Blanchet, *Traité des Monnaies Gauloises*, 1905, 43 (Blanchet), quoting J. Déchelette, *Revue Numismatique*, 1899, 169–72.

[4] J. P. Bushe-Fox, 'Excavations at Hengistbury Head, Hampshire', *Soc. of Ant. Research Rep. III*, 1915, 69–70; G. F. Hill, *Numismatic Chronicle*, 1911, 46–56.

is probable that a number of strips formed, as it were, branches of a tree on the moulds, but the tangs remaining are not long enough to demonstrate how they were arranged.

Two matching moulds were used; the coins were not made by a *cire-perdue* process. This is plain from inspection of the coins. The moulds never fitted one another precisely and it is easy to see where marginally they failed to coincide. There are some continental potin coins where the correspondence has gone badly astray.

In Gaul the moulds were often made, so it has been thought, by impressing into them strips of coins already cast.[5] These coins are usually thick and lumpy. British coins, although derived from the same tradition, are thin and flat and the process of making the moulds was clearly different. For such low value coins, of which the surviving numbers (at least 2,000, probably more) imply an enormous issue, the process must have been quick and simple. Professor E. G. Turner of University College and I have done some experiments to ascertain how they were made.[6]

The thickness of the coins, where there is no design, is normally about half a millimetre. The design is raised on either side by another half a millimetre or so, making a total thickness of something like a millimetre and a half. It is clear from this that the depression in the moulds on each side was extremely shallow, as one might say paper-thin. The first step in manufacture was to make this round and flat depression for each coin, together with the runnels joining one to another.

Once the depressions were made, the next stage was to add the designs. In Britain these were drawn on by hand, in a number of strokes with a tool of the character of a stylus. Experiments on modelling clay show that anyone accustomed to the use of a stylus on a wax tablet would have been able to draw the patterns at great speed. One can, in fact, detect a kind of handwriting in the nuances. I found that I could draw them at the rate of about five seconds a side, and with practice could certainly have improved on this. While parts of the designs were drawn freehand, it is also clear that a compass was sometimes used to describe the circles and to ensure accurate correspondence. British coins provide no evidence for the use of matrices to produce identical moulds, nor of the comparable technique of impressing moulds with strips of actual coins.

The coins offer no direct evidence as to how the depressions were at first made. (I shall describe the order of the coins later, but must at this stage assume a relative chronology.) The depressions on the earlier coins are not surrounded by a raised circle, and there is no trace of a central compass mark on either side. The depressions must, therefore, have been made in the clay by impressing some flat circular object, a smooth stone, perhaps, worked into the appropriate shape. Even after surrounding circles have become general, there are on the early coins no or only minimal traces of a central compass point.

At a certain stage a new and intriguing process was introduced which leaves

[5] Blanchet, 57, for clay moulds of potin coins found at the Chaté de Boviolles, Meuse; they appear to be lost. I am told that, provided the moulds were used only once, sun-dried clay moulds would have served as well, or better, for casting the coins than moulds which were oven-baked.

[6] I take this opportunity of expressing my thanks to Professor E. G. Turner for his experiments and valuable suggestions.

clear traces on the coins. It has long been observed that the background of some of the British coins is marked with a curious criss-cross graining. Sir John Evans deduced from this, wrongly, that the moulds were sunk in wood and that the linear designs were burned into these moulds.[7] Even if wooden moulds could have stood up to the necessary temperatures (which is impossible) a close inspection of the graining makes it obvious that it does not represent the texture of wood. This objection also applies to the theory put forward by Commander R. P. Mack that the depressions were sunk in the mould from wooden blocks.[8] The surface of those coins on which the graining is most clearly seen indicates a texture which I at one time took to be a woven fabric. It was first suggested by Dr. J. P. Wild that the material in question was papyrus[9] and Professor Turner's experiments confirm this conclusion.

From a blank sheet of ancient papyrus Professor Turner cut a strip identical in shape with the indentations for a strip of coins. He then impressed this into a slab of modelling clay by pressing it in with a flat surface. He found that the papyrus came away readily and intact, leaving in the clay a clear impression of cross-graining identical in character with that on the coins. If the same piece of papyrus is used to make an indentation on another slab of clay, the two resulting moulds fit exactly (pl. III, a, b, c). Moreover the thickness of the sheet of papyrus, and hence of each indentation, was 0.7 millimetres, making a thickness of the coin of about 1.4 millimetres, which agrees very closely with the actual thickness. The moulds, prepared in this way, were then ready for the freehand addition by stylus of the designs.[10]

Improbable as this process may sound, it is borne out by enlarged photographs of the coins (pls. I, a, b, II, a, b). These demonstrate that the graining ran right to the edge of the indentations, where it ceased; it also ran through the runnels, and, one must presume, from coin to coin. Although the graining gives a criss-cross effect, it can plainly be seen that all the threads on one side are parallel and that the threads in the other direction are showing through. Since papyrus was made by welding together under pressure two films from the reed laid in contrary directions this is exactly the effect to be expected; it is also exactly the effect produced by Professor Turner's experiments. The designs are always cut through the graining and they can only have been added subsequently. Traces of graining are detectable on many coins which are not nearly as clear as the enlargements illustrated; if the papyrus strip were used more than once to make impressions it would gather moisture and surface adhesions, but it is possible that the material was originally waxed or otherwise coated, and that where the graining shows most clearly the coating has come away.

The alternative possibility, that the papyrus was left in the clay when the moulds

[7] J. Evans, *Coins of the Ancient Britons*, 1860, 124; *Numismatic Chronicle*, 1855, 18; *Supplement*, 1891 (Evans).

[8] R. P. Mack, *The Coinage of Ancient Britain*, 1953, 5. The second edition (1964) omits this suggestion (Mack).

[9] J. P. Wild, 'Papyrus in Pre-Roman Britain?', *Antiquity XL*, 1966, 139–42, pl. XXIII; see also response of H. W. M. Hodges, 308, pl. XLVII; L. R. Laing, *Coins and Archaeology*, 190–1.

[10] The experiment in a sense was unnecessary. In excavations at Paphos 11,000 clay seal impressions were found, which had been attached to papyrus documents, and which bear papyrus impressions on the back. These look identical with the markings on British coins. (See pl. III, d–e, for sample photographs kindly supplied by Dr. K. Nicolaou.)

were baked, and burned away in the baking will not work, because it is inconsistent with the subsequent addition of the drawing. I do not think the designs could have been scratched on to baked clay.

Graining ends as suddenly as it began and is accompanied by changes in the design which confirm that it is linked with the layout of the moulds. The essential change is that on both sides there is now a firm centre point on a smooth background and the outer circle is drawn by a compass around this point; the rest is still added by hand. Whatever purpose the graining served is now replaced by the presence of measurable points from one coin centre to another. The vast majority of surviving coins are of this kind. The central point, initially discreet, gradually grows in size and, before the end, becomes the dominating feature of the designs on both sides, a development accompanied by a progressive simplification and straightening of the lines. After the circle had been drawn, only the minimum had to be added by hand; I could draw the final designs in three seconds a side or less.

The processes behind these strange coins are, thus, more sophisticated than appearances suggest. Each coin bears, as it were, the individual hand-writing of the maker, his personal signature. For instance, I can detect two hand-writings on the grained coins, one of whom was right-handed, the other probably left-handed. Perhaps we should deduce that the makers, at least at one stage, were literate, being familiar with papyrus and the stylus.

ORIGINS IN GAUL

It is necessary to start with prototypes because, like all Celtic coins, British potin coins have an origin in something that had gone before. But most of what has previously been written on the prototype, by myself as much as by others, is misleading.

Potin coins in Britain follow after a long line of cast potin coinage in France, the history of which has not been well worked out. It starts from the bronze coinage of Massalia, some time in the second century B.C. There are three denominations of struck bronze coins of Massalia, each with a head of Apollo, long-haired, to left on the obverse and a bull butting to right on the reverse. The potin coinage of Gaul developed from the middle size, which is scarce, somewhere at the head of the Rhone Valley or between it and the Loire.[11] The first imitations are detectable by the visible presence of the letters MA above the bull, and one such has actually been found at Marseilles (pl. IV, 1–2).[12] Imitations soon omit the legend but are readily distinguishable by the modelling of the head and the bull, which face in the original directions.

From this beginning, which in all probability lay in the late second century B.C., the coinage developed in several directions, typologically and geographically. What may be called the main stream retained the bull in a form close enough to the original Massalia animal, but generally turned to the left (pl. IV, 3–7).[13] The head acquires

[11] Blanchet, 249, no. 18. Find-spots: Néris, Allier; Alise St. Reine, Côte d'Or; Soings, Loiret; St. Amand-Montrond, Cher; Gergy, Sâone et Loire; forêt de Compiègne.

[12] J. B. Colbert de Beaulieu, Ogam, *Tradition Celtique VI*, 1954, 200.

[13] R. Forrer, *Keltische Numismatik der Rhein und Donaulande*, 1908, reissued 1968, 92, fig. 170–4, esp. 172 (Forrer).

a sunken eye and a pointed nose and chin, which have earned for it the name of 'tête diabolique'. At some stage the size of coin was reduced from the norm of 16–17 milli-metres (pl. IV, 8–10), and at another the head improved (pl. IV, 11). The distribution of these coins is very wide, examples being found in most parts of Gaul, but the centre of distribution seems to be on the Loire at such sites as Amboise.[14] The group as a whole has been well mapped, but the chronological movements in it are not yet fully elucidated.[15]

Peripheral to this series are a number of others, none yet properly studied, on which the bull takes different and usually more degenerate forms; their diameter is 16–18 millimetres. Some of these begin to approach the characteristics of the earliest British potin coins (e.g. pl. IV, 12–15, cf. 16–18).[16] It is these unlocated and undated coins which are the true forerunners of the British potin series. But because so little is known about them, they have been almost entirely overlooked. Some, at least, probably belong to the north-western part of Gaul, though not to Belgic Gaul. I should not be surprised if their home proved to be in Normandy.

It has been customary for many years to seek the derivation of British potin coins in the enormous series of coins which in the standard literature are classed to the Sequani and described as either 'grosse tête' or 'quadruped deformé' (pl. IV 19–24, cf. variants, 25–27).[17] These are large coins often with a diameter of c. 20 millimetres, markedly heavier than the early imitations of the bronze coins of Massalia. They are characterised by the reduction of the wreath of Apollo to two parallel lines. They belong to Burgundy, Franche Comté, North Switzerland, Baden and Württemberg[18]. There is no reason to think that these are ancestral to British potin coins. All they have in common is the butting bull, derived from a common source, and even this animal soon turns into a kind of horned horse (pl. IV, 23, 24), totally unconnected with British coins.[19] Maps relating to this type of potin coin have been published to indicate the point of origin of British potin coins and they are thus positively misleading.[20] The importance of 'Sequani' coins in the story is confined to the fact that they are more readily datable than most other potin coins, and by analogy may have some bearing on the starting date of British potin coins.

GAULISH ORIGINALS IN BRITAIN

Few early Gaulish potin coins with the bull have been recorded from Britain, four findspots and six specimens in all. Four coins from two findspots are of tête diabolique

[14] Blanchet, 250, no. 22.

[15] R. Forrer, *Keltische Numismatik der Rhein und Donaulande*, supplementary vol. II, 1969, 34, map 2 (Forrer II), or J. B. Colbert de Beaulieu, 'Les Potins dit "à la tête diabolique", un monnayage indigène de la Gaule envoie du Romanisation', *Revue belge de Numismatique*, CXVI, 1970, 97–123; but I would re-verse the order of the two types illustrated.

[16] E.g. Forrer, 92, fig. 170, but few have been reproduced.

[17] Blanchet, 248, nos. 14–15, figs. 109–7; Forrer, 281, fig. 483.

[18] The principal findspot is Mont Beuvray, Nièvre, where two-thirds of the coins found (over 700) were of this type. Findspots are more numerous than those mentioned by Blanchet.

[19] Forrer, 281, fig. 482; Blanchet, 246, no. 1, fig. 102. The records unfortunately lump Forrer 482 and 3 together, although their distribution and history are distinct.

[20] Allen, 1936, 354; Dolley, see note 24, 78.

character, two of an earlier vintage (pl. IV, 30, 31, cf. 32).[21] There is no concentration of findspots, nor can these properly be treated as a body of prototypes. No-one can yet say precisely where in northern or central France they originated. The implication is that they were all casual imports, not a causative force in the introduction of British potin coinage.

BRITISH TYPOLOGICAL SEQUENCE

It is at present customary to arrange British potin coins in two classes, I and II. So far as it goes, there is nothing wrong with this classification, which corresponds with a detectable stage in the development of the coinage. But within each of these classes, even a superficial inspection of the coinage shows a wide range of variation. There have been two attempts at a more sophisticated arrangement. The first by Mr. R. A. G. Carson, when he published the Sunbury Hoard, is simple and usable, but fails to distinguish some of the earlier types.[22] The second, by Mr. R. H. M. Dolley, devised for the Snettisham Hoard, is ingenious but over-elaborate and very difficult to use.[23] I have, therefore, worked out a new series of 15 types, which are lettered from A to P (omitting I so as to avoid confusion with the old Class I). The first 10 of these correspond to the old Class I, the last 5 to Class II (figs. 31–32).

One of the more obvious differences between the coins is whether the types face left or right. Most varieties contain examples with either side facing either way, though one arrangement is usually the more common. So the basic classification of letters disregards which way the types face. If one wishes to refine, one may add arrows after the letter, thus: L⇄, to indicate that the obverse faces left and reverse right.

While I am confident that in the broad the classification represents the progression of British potin coins from their continental-style origin to their final decadence, it would be ridiculous to expect individually hand-made coins to conform precisely to the standard forms of the classification. Assignment of individual coins to a lettered type must, at the margins, be subjective. It is, however, plain that the coinage as a whole conforms so closely at any one stage to a norm that most of it must have originated in a single, so far unlocated, factory.

The first type (Type A, pl. V, 44, 45; Type B reverse) is readily identifiable because of its general resemblance to continental coins of the tête diabolique family: it would pass muster in France as a peripheral variant, were it not found only in Kent.[24] The face, to the left as always on continental coins of this class, is in relief, while the bull to

---

[21] I have records of coins from St. Neots, Cambs., (Fitzwilliam Mus., unpublished) and South Ferriby, Lincs. (Hull Mus., see Hull Museum Publication no. 214, pl. II, 25). Both are of early varieties recalling the type described in notes 11–12, but without the legend MA. In addition three coins from the Penzance hoard, now in the British Museum, are of *tête diabolique* type (*Num. Chron.*, 1961, 98, fig. 1, 2–4). A coin found at Weston-under-Penyard is recorded by Evans, 482, as being similar. A coin in Deal Castle Museum, a local find, may also be related, weight 2.50g; the exact type appears to be unpublished.

[22] R. A. G. Carson, 'A Hoard of British "Tin" Coins from Sunbury on Thames', *Numismatic Chronicle*, 1950, 148–9.

[23] R. H. M. Dolley, Appendix: 'The speculum ("Tin") Coins in Hoard C' in R. Rainbird Clark, 'The Early Iron Age Treasure from Snettisham, Norfolk', in *Proceedings of the Prehistoric Society XX*, 1954, 72–86 (Dolley).

[24] Mack, 1964, 22a (where its size is reduced).

left on the reverse remains a recognisable four-legged animal, with a degree of modelling.

It is only after this very rare type that the characteristic flat linear style of British potin coins begins. To say that it had no parallel on the continent would be to overlook a type which has a linear outline on the obverse round a modelled centre though on the reverse the bull has become a horse (pl. IV, 29, cf. 28); but it seems to be an analogous development without direct connection.[25] On British potin coins the design is from the first reduced on both sides to simple lines, stylus drawn.

The early obverses (Types B and C, pl. V, 46, 47) are done in two lines and a circle, representing the profile and the back of the head with, not always centrally placed, the eye. I have little doubt that in origin these lines are meant to reproduce, in linear form, a tête diabolique originally drawn in relief. Later, the outline of the head is drawn in a single line (Type D, pl. V, 48–50).

The reverses are equally linear; the bull, right-facing as on the Massalia originals, is reduced to a formula, the hindleg being united in a single stroke with the ground line. The S of the tail is often accompanied by an extra crescent, a recollection perhaps of legend or symbol above the bull's back on the coins of Massalia.[26] On what look like the earlier coins the bull has a single fore and hindleg (Type C, pl. V, 46, 47), the formula adopted on both tête diabolique and quadruped deformé coins, but, by the stage of the regular outline head, the bull in Britain had settled down, as it began, to a four-legged beast (Type D, pl. V, 48–50, cf. 51), and so it remained throughout.

Coins of Types A to D are all scarce; they occur in the hoards, but worn and often broken and have not been recognised as the early phase which they certainly represent. They are thicker, heavier and broader than the coins that follow; indeed the sequence of British potin coins is as well indicated by the progressive reduction of their diameter from c. 18 (Type A) to c. 11 (Type P) millimetres as by any other criterion; it is more constant than the concurrent reduction in weight.

After Types A to D the coinage became more standardised; it survives in larger numbers. In Type F (pl. V, 51, cf. 50, of which Type E is a scarce variant with added crescents below) the circular central eye, still drawn freehand, contains no trace of a compass point, though it is during this class that a drawn outer circle surrounding the type on obverse and reverse first appears. The outline of the face begins to show the marks of a familiarity with penmanship, looking readily either way. The body of the bull, also looking either way, is marked by a single curved line drawn in one stroke from tail to head, to which the four legs are appended, one bent. The ground is a separate line.

It is during the currency of Type F that the curious phenomenon of papyrus graining first appears. The designs, facing left, have the round eye without compass point and the bull's body in a single curving line (Type GB, pl. I, a, b; II, a, b; V, 53, 54). With these go Type GA (pl. V, 52), an infrequent variety always with papyrus graining, on which the round eye is replaced by three dots, but which otherwise is indistinguishable from Type GB. A second hand is represented by Type

[25] H. de la Tour, *Atlas de Monnaies Gauloises*, XXX, 7388, Forrer, 10, fig. 9 (de la Tour).

[26] For symbols see the larger Massalia denomination, de la Tour IV, 1476, 1495, 1515, etc.

K

Fig. 31. Types of British Potin Coins, A–G.

Fig. 32. Types of British Potin Coins, H–P.

GC, which faces right (pl. V, 55), and on these coins the graining, though retained on the reverse, apparently disappears from the obverse.

There are, however, open-eyed coins, on which the bull's curvilinear back is to a greater or lesser degree squared up. The tail is drawn in a single stroke with the hind-leg, the head and body being marked by another stroke which meets it at a sharp angle (pl. V, 56, 57). Since these characteristics are never found on coins with papyrus graining, I assume the coins with squared up bull to be subsequent (Type H). On the reverse of some of them a trace of the compass point, used to draw the surrounding circle, is clearly seen.

Overlapping with the coins from Type E or F to H are a series of coins on which the eye contains a marked central point, as it were a pupil to the eye, which certainly grew out of a compass point, now seen regularly on the reverse. A number of these coins have bulls with curvilinear backs, though not always drawn in a single stroke from tail to head (Type J, pl. V, 58). Much commoner, however, are those on which the design is squared up into an almost geometrical pattern composed of individual strokes, rather like a Chinese character (Type L, pl. V, 59–62). (There is a minor variant with two crescents below, Type K, to be compared with the open-eyed Type E.)

There is little doubt that in general Type L, far the commonest of the whole series, is later than the in many ways similar Type H. I imagine Types J and K to be roughly contemporary with Types F and G, but at present I do not see how this can be proved. What is demonstrable is that Type L was the principal, if not the only, type currently in issue when a wave of hoards were buried. Although the records are not perfect, all the hoards of British potin coins so far found appear to have been buried at exactly the same stage; they contained only coins of Class I under the old classification and all ended with at least some of Type L, of c. 15–16 millimetres diameter.

The main characteristic of the remaining coins, Class II under the old classification, is a great increase in the size of the compass point, which now becomes a central boss, a main feature of design. The bull is progressively reduced to a square or parallelogram with first two, later one, crescent above. One or two crescents still usually represent the features of the face and the neck becomes the fulcrum of the design; but it is still always possible to see which way the coin faces. Type M is of nearly the same diameter as Type L, c. 14–15 millimetres, Type N (pl. V, 63, 64) is narrower, c. 12 millimetres. On Type O (pl. V, 65, 66) for the first time the crescents are reduced from two to one. Type P (pl. V, 67), the end of Class II, with a diameter of c. 11 millimetres, is the *reductio ad absurdum*, by which stage we are almost on the threshold of the Roman occupation.

DISTRIBUTION

A steady accumulation of finds in recent years has established firmly that British potin coins, both of Class I and Class II, are coins of north Kent [27] (figs. 33, 34).

Excluding hoards, Class I is found along the whole of the coastal belt of Kent, north of the Weald, across the Medway and into the eastern borders of Surrey. There is a

---

[27] For old distribution maps see Allen, 1936, 354, Dolley, 79, fig. 15, O.S. Map, 32, no. 8, Mack, 1964, 8 Map 4 and, for Class II only, Woods (see note 43), fig. 19.

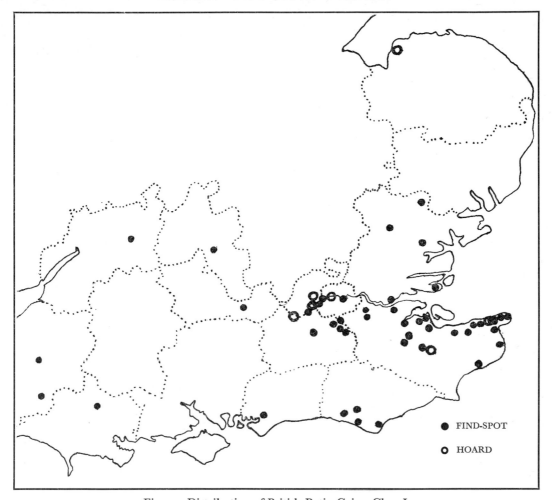

Fig. 33. Distribution of British Potin Coins, Class I.

minor diaspora in several directions. A small spread runs across Essex northwards; there is a pocket in Sussex, south of the Weald. A few found their way along the Thames in the direction of the Bristol Channel, others to hill-forts of Hampshire, Dorset and Somerset.[28] None have been reported abroad.

The distribution of the hoards is particularly interesting. Four hoards have been found along the Thames at the extreme west of the main distribution, two near the Nore at the extreme east and one towards the Weald at the extreme south. One has been found, totally displaced, near the Wash. Something must have happened in Kent, during the currency of Type L, to cause burial of the hoards exclusively on the margins or outside the proper area of distribution of the coins.[29]

[28] Appendix I, Class I, Isolated Finds.   [29] Appendix I, Hoards.

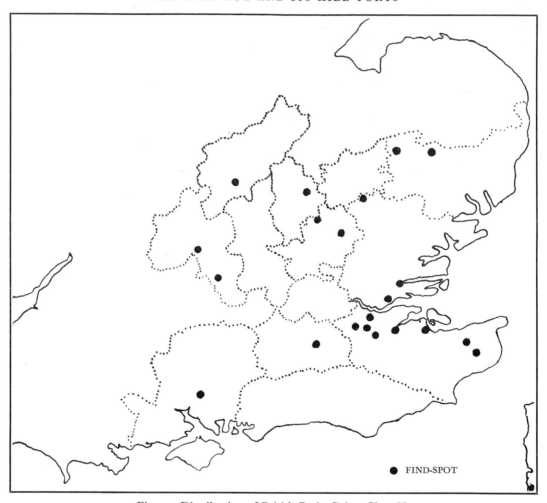

Fig. 34. Distribution of British Potin Coins, Class II.

Class II, of which there are no hoards[30], has been thought to belong to East Anglia, but this is certainly not so. The distribution in north Kent and east Surrey is less dense, but otherwise indistinguishable from Class I. The diaspora, however, takes an entirely different form. Apart from a minor pocket on the south Essex coast (one may compare the finding of coins of Dubnovellanus on both banks of the estuary[31]) the coins are spread north and west of Kent into the home counties and East Anglia.[32] Two are reported from Mont César, Oise.[33] The different distribution in the period following the hoards is so marked that it must have a meaning.

[30] If we disregard a small concentration in a house excavated at Rochester, which may count as a scattered hoard.

[31] Mack, 275–7 (Essex) compare with Mack, 279–86 (Kent). For distribution see O.S. Map 28 (Map 4) or

Mack, 1964, 96 (Map 4) compare 164 (Map 15).

[32] Appendix I, Class II.

[33] *Revue Archéologique* NS 41, 1881, 136, no. 53, pl. VIII (2 examples). (Nos. 48–50 are relevant *tête diabolique* prototypes.)

THE HOARDS

Only two hoards are preserved intact, those from Sunbury (*c.* 359 coins)[34] and Snettisham (145 coins)[35]. Some illustrations and a representative selection survive from the two Quex Park or Birchington hoards (600 coins at least in the second)[36]. The coins from the Eel Pie Island or Brentford hoard have mostly been dispersed (266 coins at least), but enough are on record to establish its character.[37] A few contemporary illustrations survive of the St. James's Park hoard, and few coins are now labelled as coming from it, which do not entirely agree.[38] Four coins survive from the Lenham Heath hoard.[39] I have a note of the small Gunnersbury hoard (12 coins), now stolen.[40]

Putting this material together, it is certain that the Sunbury, Snettisham, Quex Park, Eel Pie Island and Gunnersbury hoards ended with Type L, which was in each instance the predominant type. In the case of Sunbury and Snettisham, Type L constituted more than a third of the total. At St. James's Park the coins now surviving seem to agree with this, though not the early drawings, while of the four Lenham Heath coins, one is of Type L. It is reasonable to suppose that all eight hoards had an approximately similar composition, and that they all ceased whilst the prolific Type L was in circulation. In other words, Type L, as typology suggests, came at the end of Class I.

If the hoards do not provide much information from internal evidence with regard to the history of the coinage, they are, nonetheless, critical for an understanding of its dating.

DATING

A sequence such as the British potin coins cannot be dated accurately, but it should be possible to aim at dating certain fixed points. These are the beginning, the introduction of papyrus graining, the hoards and the termination. If the argument here and there is involved or far reaching, this is because one must clutch at straws.

CLASS II

It will be easiest to work from the known to the unknown and therefore to take points in reverse order. There is no doubt whatever that Class II coins belong to the final phases preceding the Roman conquest of Britain. They were found at the Lullingstone, Farmingham and Faversham, Kent, Roman Villas[41] in the earliest levels, and the finds from other sites such as Owslebury, Hampshire[42], and Hardingstone, Northamptonshire[43], again imply a mid 1st century A.D. date. On the other hand the general

---

[34] In the London Museum; see n. 22.
[35] In the Norwich Castle Museum, see n. 23.
[36] In the British Museum (18), Birchington Museum (*c.* 30), Ashmolean Museum (1), Nat. Museum Antiquities, Edinburgh (2), etc.; Evans 125, 484, pl. H, 1, 2, 4, 6, 7.
[37] In the London Museum (5), *Archaeologia*, LXIX, 1917–18, 18; Sotheby's Sale, 8th December, 1915, lot 280.
[38] In B. N. Paris (4); V. Newbery Collection (2), etc. Contemporary drawings of 6 in possession of N. Rhodes ('Found in excavating a sewer for the New

Palace in St. James's Park, 15th September, 1827'). Evans, 125: *Num. Journ.*, I (1837), pl. I 2.
[39] In British Museum; *Num. Journ.*, I, 1837, pl. I 1.
[40] See Appendix III. Dolley, 85 (the promise was not fulfilled till now).
[41] Neither yet published.
[42] J. R. Collis, Preliminary Report, *Antiquaries Journal*, XLVIII, 1968, 31; Allen, *British Numismatic Journal*, XXXVI, 1967, 10, fig. 5.
[43] P. J. Woods, *Excavations at Hardingstone, Northants, 1967–8* (Northants C.C. 1969), 38 (Woods).

distribution in north Kent is not specifically a Roman one. It may be concluded, therefore, that Class II coins belong to the early part of the 1st century A.D., up to the time of the Roman conquest, and that some of them remained above ground and in circulation in Kent after the conquest.

The diaspora of coins of Class II may very well be a post-conquest phenomenon, indicating the direction in which the men of Kent were swept, as soldiers, camp followers or slaves. Most come from the territory of the Catuvellauni, a few from the Dobunni and the Iceni, all areas to which, in the early days of the occupation, Roman troops were undoubtedly despatched.

THE HOARDS

Moving backwards in time we come to the phenomenon of the eight hoards, concentrated on the outskirts of the homeland of the coinage. There is no direct evidence for the date of any of these hoards except that from Snettisham.[44] If one assumes, as one must, that all the finds made there were buried at the same time, one must consider the date of the hoard of 12 gold coins, the torques and, in particular, the torque with the gold coin inside. The key type for dating the Snettisham hoards is the quarter-stater I have called Gallo-Belgic DC, because not only was this the latest of the coins in the actual coin hoard, but it was also the type of the coin found inside the torque. There is additional evidence about it, unpublished, in the Weybourne hoard[45] (pl. VI).

This hoard of gold coins has been washed by the sea out of the cliff at Weybourne on the Norfolk coast, about 25 miles east of Snettisham, over the last thirty years. Coins have been picked up on the beach. The hoard will have contained at least 60 coins but I have full records of 33. Of these 30 are uniface gold staters of the type of Gallo-Belgic E (pl. VI, 1–30), while the remaining three are examples of Gallo-Belgic DC (pl. VI, 31–33). This is the same type of coin as was found in the Snettisham hoard and inside the Snettisham torque. Indeed it could well be that, despite the absence of Gallo-Belgic E at Snettisham, the Snettisham and Weybourne hoards were buried at about the same time. A single specimen of the same type of quarter-stater, moreover, was found in the Le Catillon hoard, which was presumably buried in 56 or 51 B.C.[46]

The dating of Gallo-Belgic DC quarter-staters has been a matter of inference, but their presence with Gallo-Belgic E in the Weybourne hoard confirms a suspected association. They were, in effect, the quarter-staters for Gallo-Belgic E, a type of coin which can be dated with fair accuracy as the form of coin current in north-east Gaul, and in Britain, at the time of Caesar's campaigns.[47] A particularly important indication of date is that three were found at Amiens in a hoard of Roman denarii datable to

[44] R. Rainbird Clarke, 'The Early Iron Age Treasure from Snettisham, Norfolk', *Proceedings of the Prehistoric Society*, XX, 1954, 68–71, but see *Origins*, 122–3.

[45] *Origins*, 164, records some 15 coins from Sheringham and Weybourne. These were undoubtedly the beginnings of a hoard which is being progressively washed from the cliff. Something like 60 coins appear to have been found, mostly Gallo-Belgic E, but several Gallo-Belgic DC. Examples are illustrated in pl. VI; for available particulars see Appendix V.

[46] *Origins*, 111, 297, Gallo-Belgic D. For the Le Catillon hoard see J. B. Colbert de Beaulieu, 'Le Trésor de Jersey 11', *Revue belge de Numismatique*, CIII, 1957, 47–88.

[47] *Origins*, 114, Gallo-Belgic E.

c. 30 B.C.[48] They must by then have been surviving stragglers in Gaul. Working back from the Amiens hoard through the Weybourne hoard to the Snettisham hoard, one can be fairly sure that these were not buried much later than 30 B.C. and there is no numismatic reason why they should not have been buried a number of years earlier.

I am inclined to think, therefore, that the Snettisham gold coin hoard, one of several found round the Norfolk coast, which from its composition could well have been put together in Kent, was displaced either at the time of Caesar's invasion of Kent, or, less likely, as a result of the fear of further Roman invasion in or about 34 B.C.[49] One may also compare the Carn Brea hoard, of very similar composition to the Snettisham hoard, which also probably originated in Kent, and was also buried at just about the same time. If this deduced dating for the gold is near the truth, it carries with it the implication of a similar dating for the hoard of British potin coins found at Snettisham; and since we have seen that the composition of all the potin hoards from Britain is the same, it implies a burial date for all of them, not later than the 30's, and perhaps as early as the 50's B.C. (There may also be implications for the Snettisham gold torques, but this is not the place to pursue them.)

If Caesar's famous mention to *aes* in Britain refers to these coins, as seems more likely than not, then we have an historical confirmation for what is at least indicated by the other evidence.[50]

The conclusion is plain: the group of hoards of potin coins found on the outskirts of the Kentish homeland of the coinage were probably buried on the occasion of Caesar's invasion by people fleeing in different directions. The ordinary people mainly escaped up the Thames towards the interior of the country. Richer people, carrying gold hoards, managed to get further afield. But if this dating seems improbably early, then we must seek the occasion in some other Kentish disturbance in the first century B.C., of which there are other possible reflections in the coinage, such as the arrival there of Eppillus, son of Commius.[51] In any event, the hoards appear to be of the middle to late first century B.C., leaving only the degenerate Class II coins to cover the succeeding years up to the Roman conquest.

CLASS I

It may be suggested that the dating proposed for the hoards and Class II presents an insoluble problem for the dating of Class I, which must be later than the ill-defined date of its Gaulish prototypes. What has been written in recent years about continental potin coins has tended to depress their date.[52] I do not think that this reasoning has been correct. As is well known, both butting bull and horned horse types, the

[48] *Revue Numismatique,* 1910, 101. M. Crawford, *Roman Republican Coin Hoards,* 128, n. 458; (the statement that the Gaulish coins are of silver is incorrect).

[49] *Origins,* 111, 122. Of the four recorded hoards whose contents include Gallo-Belgic E, two (Ryarsh and Folkestone) are from Kent and two are from the east coast (Weybourne and Grimsby). The Grimsby hoard, too, was much larger than has hitherto been recorded.

[50] Caesar, *de Bello Gallico,* V, 12. *Utuntur aut aere, aut nummo aureo, aut taleis ferreis ad certum pondus examinatis pro nummo.*

[51] D. F. Allen, 'The Belgic Dynasties of Britain and their Coinage', *Archaeologia,* XC, 1944, 33–4.

[52] J. B. Colbert de Beaulieu, *Annales de Bretagne,* LXVIII, 1961, 42–53; LXX, 1963, 49–51; Forrer II, 35; *Les Monnaies Gauloises des Parisii,* 1970, 126–7; 'Les Potins dits à la Tête Diabolique', *Revue belge de Numismatique,* CXVI, 1970, 114–7.

latter at least in one of its later versions (cf. pl. IV, 21 and V, 40, approximately), occurred in the dated deposits at Alesia and must therefore have been in existence before 52 B.C.; but it seems certain that their origin is a good deal earlier. It is impracticable, in a study of British potin coins, to repeat all the arguments which I shall use elsewhere in relation to the 'quadruped deformé' potin coins found at La Tène.[53] In that context it will be necessary to take the finds as a whole, and to correlate the silver and potin coins found there with one another as well as with the many other antiquities from the site. These show, with little doubt, a cut-off date in the range of 60–75 B.C. for regular potin coins with the butting bull converted into the horned horse (the type of pl. IV, 23, 24, which are found in quantity at La Tène, whereas pl. V, 33–39 are in steep decline and 40–43 virtually absent). The date partly depends on the association, which can be demonstrated from hoard evidence, of regular horned horse potin coins with approximately datable silver coins of Kaletedou.[54] Working backwards, some at least of the potin coins which have an actual butting bull must be earlier than this; and, as we have seen previously, it is from these, the progenitors of the 'tête diabolique' coins, that the British potin series ultimately derives.

The typological sequence, therefore, suggests an origin very early in the first century B.C., or conceivably earlier still for the progenitors of the 'tête diabolique' series, and this date has recently obtained a remarkable confirmation, which, at first, like others, I was inclined to disbelieve. A hoard of silver monnaies-à-la-croix from Lattes, Gard, has been found which contained a single tête diabolique coin of potin.[55] The types and weights of monnaies-à-la-croix in the hoard suggested to me (though others have since disputed this) a date of c. 125–120 B.C., or not very long after.[56] Continental potin coins undoubtedly remained long in circulation (many of the early ones are worn almost smooth), but I am convinced that they had an appreciably earlier origin than most informed writers on the subject currently accept.

The presence of a potin coin of horned horse type with one of another type in grave 49 of the San Bernardino cemetery at Ornavasso may also be regarded as qualified evidence of a relatively early date for this type. Although views differ both as to the date when the cemetery came into use and when it ceased, the most convincing

[53] Not yet fully studied, but examples are to be found in V. Gross, *La Tène*, 1887, pl. XI, and E. Vouga, *Les Helvetes à La Tène*, 1885, pl. VIII. Examples now in Neuchâtel, Biel, Berne, Zürich, Geneva.

[54] Blanchet, 246, fig. 102 (horned horse or antelope), the type characteristic of La Tène; *cf.* 248, fig. 106–7 (bull), the type characteristic of Mont Beuvray. The Kaletedou coins found at La Tène, almost the only silver coins found there, cease with the type having a Δ below the horse and contain only one of the common type with the wheel in this place, clearly the latest. The Houssen, Colmar, hoard of 1849 (R. Forrer, *Monnaies Gauloises ou Celtiques trouvées en Alsace*, 1925, 40–1) shows this type to be contemporary with horned horse potin coins, easily the commonest potin type found at La Tène. There is ample evidence that Kaletedou coins are pre-60 B.C. and that the Δ type typologically precedes the wheel type. In the Chantenay hoard of 1861 (Blanchet, 583), buried *c.* 36 B.C., Kaletedou coins alone

are described as worn. It follows that the origin of the horned-horse potins, like the Δ type Kaletedou silver coins, is appreciably earlier than current literature suggests, and probably lies in the 60s or 70s B.C., even though many of the coins were not lost or buried until much later.

[55] R. Majurel, J. Arnal and H. Prades, 'Deux Nouveaux Trésors de Lattes (Hérault)', *Ogam*, XIX, 1967, 397–433; J. C. M. Richard, in 'Les monnaies gauloises "à la croix" et le trésor de Lattes', *Jahrb. für Numismatik und Geldgeschicte*, 20, 1970, 49–62.

[56] D. F. Allen, 'Monnaies-à-la-croix', *Numismatic Chronicle*, 1969, 47–9. But see: J. C. M. Richard, 'Les Trésors de Lattes', *Bulletin de la Société française de Numismatique*, 1968, 321–2; K. Castelin, 'Die Kreuzmünzen in Süddeutschland', *Sweizerischen Numismatischen Rundschau*, IL, 1970, 77–108, esp. 91f.

date for its end and replacement seems to be in the decade up to 70 B.C.; but even if a suggested later date is preferred, it is clear that all the coins found in the graves were old when buried.[57]

Moreover, British potin coins, with their four-legged right-facing bulls, undoubtedly start at a relatively early date in the total potin sequence. Most early 'tête diabolique' coins, such as those from the Ouldes, Indre et Loire, hoard[58], have the single-legged bulls facing left. The history of the British potin coin is, therefore, to be seen as unrolling in parallel with the long series of 'tête diabolique' coins; if the concept of potin coins reached Kent, the most advanced part of Britain, sharing kings and tribes with Gaul, at a fairly early date in the first century B.C. (simultaneously, in fact, with some of the gold coinages of Belgic Gaul[59]) there is ample time for all the developments represented by Types A to L, including the papyrus-grained Type G. The early types, as often happens are rare; perhaps it was some time before so novel a concept and the petty trade it implies took root.

Thus, by a very different route, I come back to a conclusion I reached in my initial paper on this subject, namely that the beginnings of potin coinage in Britain have been put much too late, relying on the valid deduction that the end was late.[60] The truth seems to be that in British potin coinage we have an example of the longevity of the barbarous in British tradition, long after the sophistication of the times would have warranted something better.

Nothing could demonstrate this sophistication better than the papyrus, the stylus, and even the handwriting of its makers; one might almost detect their humour in some of the draughtsmanship. If this dating of the hoards is even approximately right, the papyrus, as a step in coin manufacture, came and went before Caesar.

CONCLUSION

In this account I have attempted to analyse the techniques, trace the origins, follow the development and date the most self-consciously barbarous of all British coin products. We have seen that it is essentially from start to finish a coinage of north Kent, the part of Britain with probably the closest links with France. We can be sure that it lasted right up to the Claudian conquest; we can deduce, albeit in a roundabout way, that it went underground in hoards during Caesar's campaign, which will have affected Kent more than anywhere else. We can surmise, without direct evidence, but on continental analogies, that it started in a small way near the beginning of the first century B.C.

It was, without question, the first small change coinage in Britain, and hence the first evidence for the retail market of the kind of which there were so many in Gaul, a step, incidentally, in the direction of urbanisation. Outside Kent it has, in the main, been found in the *oppida* or settlements. Who issued it, and by what authority it obtained and retained its value we cannot know. Those who wrote these minimal value cheques or banknotes on the clay did not add the cashier's signature. As in Gaul, where

[57] J. Déchelette, *Revue Archéologique 3*, XL, 1902, 277; C. A. Moberg, 'Between La Tène III', *Acta Archaeologica*, **23**, 1953, 13f.; M. Crivelli, *Zeit für Schweiz. Arch. und Kunstges.*, 21, 1961, 109, pl. 45, 57 D; J. B. Colbert de Beaulieu, *Annales de Bretagne*, LXX, 1963, 49–51.

[58] Blanchet, 250, 568.

[59] *Origins*, 105–7; Gallo-Belgic C, Mack, 26, 30.

[60] Allen, 1936, 356.

the volume of potin coins was vast, there is rarely any direct connection between them and other contemporary coinages which proudly bore the names of the kings or magistrates which made them.

Acknowledgments

It is impossible to express acknowledgment to all those who, over the years, have contributed in one way or another to this paper and the illustrations which accompany it. I should like to say, however, that the conclusions on technique would have been impossible without the assistance at an earlier stage of Dr. J. P. Wild and more recently of Professor E. G. Turner. The new classification would have been impossible without the index of Celtic coins kept by Professor S. S. Frere at the Institute of Archaeology, Oxford. A debt is owed to Mr. R. H. Wilkins for much of the photography. Help over the chronology of La Tène will be acknowledged in another place.

APPENDIX I

FIND-SPOTS OF BRITISH POTIN COINS

A. Isolated Finds

CLASS I, Types A–L

Find-spot	Type	Ref.	Museum
KENT			
Barming	Cl. I	Allen, 1936, 357	—
Broadstairs	L	Noted 1965	—
Burntwick Island	L ?	*B.N.J.*, XXVII, 1953, 211	—
Canterbury	L	Excavations	Canterbury
Deal	Cl. I	*V.C.H.*, Kent I, 330, 335	—
Faversham	Cl. I	Noted 1965	—
Folkestone (3)	L	Winbolt, *Roman Folkestone*, 80	—
Gravesend	A	*Origins*, 205	Gravesend
Greenhythe (3)	H + Cl. I (2)	*Arch. Cant.*, LXXXI, 1966, 188	—
Hoath*	Cl. I (G.Bt.)	Cove Jones Sale, 1911, lot 281; Roth Sale, 1918, lot 23	—
Maidstone	K	Allen, 1936, 357	B.M.
Margate	Cl. I	Allen, 1936, 357	—
Radfield	L	Noted 1969	—
Reculver	GB	Allen, 1936, 357	B.M.
Richborough	L	*Rich. Excav. Rep. II*, 1928, 120, n. 2499	B.M.
Rochester (6)	Cl. I (incl. A and L)	Found 1962	Stratford, Essex
Swanley	Cl. I	Noted 1969	—
Ulcombe	C	*Origins*, 205	Maidstone
Upchurch	L ?	*B.N.J.*, XXVII, 1953, 211	—

* Recorded as Hoare, Hants, which does not exist; clearly a misprint for either Oare or Hoath, Kent.

Find-spot	Type	Ref.	Museum
SURREY			
Addington	L	Noted 1969	Croydon
Ashtead	Cl. I	Allen, 1936, 357	—
Coulsdon	Cl. I?	*Origins*, 206	—
Croydon	Cl. I	*Origins*, 206	—
Woldingham (1970)	C	Inf. from Surrey Arch. Soc.	—
BERKS			
Weycock/Waltham-St. Lawrence	F (or H?)	Evans, 125; *Arch. Journ.* VI, 1849, 120	—
HAMPSHIRE			
Hengistbury Head (7)	(incl. 2 L)	Inf. from Dr. D. P. S. Peacock	Southampton
DORSET			
Hod Hill (2)	GA, L	Evans, 125, 484	Farnham
ESSEX			
Dunmow (2)	L	Evans, 485, *Trans. Essex Arch. Soc.*, XIX, 250	Ashm., B.M.
East Tilbury	L	Inf. from Mrs. M. U. Jones, Mucking Excavation Committee, Thurrock	—
Gestingthorpe	C	Noted 1968	—
Great Wakering	L (or H)	*Origins*, 204	Southend
Wickford	L	Excavations at Beauchamps, 1970	W. Rodiwell
Witham (sev.)	Cl. I	Allen, 1936, 355, 7	—
LONDON†			
Acton	H	*Origins*, 205	Gunnersbury
Barn Elms	F(?)	*Arch. J.*, LXXXVI, 1929, 89	London
Hammersmith (7)	C(2) L(4)	*Arch. J.*, LXXXVI, 1929, 88	London
London Bridge	H	R. Goodburn, 1970	—
Richmond	L	—	London
HERTFORDSHIRE			
Braughing (3)	H or L	Excavations, 1971	C. R. Partridge
OXFORDSHIRE			
Islip	L	*Berks., Bucks., and Oxon Arch. J.*, IV, 1898, 43, pl. v	—

† These are presumably not strays from the Eel Pie Island hoard. The Barn Elms coin, found before 1929, is associated with a pile dwellings site; six of the seven Hammersmith coins (conceivably a hoard, but if so, curiously composed) were found in 1916, presumably close to one another, while the isolated Richmond coin was found in 1929. The Acton coin is possibly a stray from the Gunnersby hoard, but was recorded separately by Brooke.

Find-spot	Type	Ref.	Museum
SOMERSET			
Glastonbury	L (or Class II?) frag.	Bulleid and Gray, Glastonbury, 393–4	Glastonbury
Ham Hill	L	Bulleid and Gray, Glastonbury, 394; *Num. Chron.*, 1949, 167	Taunton
SUSSEX			
Chichester	Cl. I	Allen, 1936, 357	
Eastbourne	K	Evans, 485; *Sussex Arch. Coll.*, XXIX, 1879, 112, pl. iii, 17	Lewes, Farnham, Pitt-Rivers, Oxford
Lewes (Caburn) (*c.* 12)	Cl. I (incl. F, J, L)	Evans, 485. *Archaeologia*, XLVI, 1881, 471, 495, pl. xxv, 61–3; *Sussex Arch. Coll.*, LXVIII, 1927, 6–8	—
Newhaven (Caburn?)	L	—	Brighton
South Malling	H	*Origins*, 206	Lewes

CLASS II, Types M–P

Find-spot	Type	Ref.	Museum
KENT			
Bridge	Cl. II	Noted 1960	—
Canterbury (sev.)	N, O, P	*J.R.S.*, XXXIX, 1949, 111; *Arch. Cant.*, LXI, 1949, 35; *B.N.J.*, 1949, 94, etc.	Canterbury
Farmingham (3)	O, P	Noted 1963	—
Keston (2)	O, P	Noted 1966	—
Lullingstone (2)	O	*Origins*, 207	Lullingstone
Otford	P	Noted 1966	—
Radfield (2)	M, O	Noted 1969	—
Rochester (7)	O, P	Noted 1963	M.O.W.
SURREY			
Walton-on-the-Hill	O	*Surrey Arch. Coll.*, XLVIII, 1953, 151, pl. v	—
BEDFORDSHIRE			
Sandy	Cl. II	Evans, 485	—
ESSEX			
Billericay	P	Noted 1971	Billericay Arch. and Hist. Soc.
Great Chesterford (2)	M	*Origins*, 206	B.M.
Mucking (2)	O, P	Noted 1967	M.O.W.
Wickford (2)	O, P	Noted 1957	Colchester

Find-spot	Type	Ref.	Museum
HAMPSHIRE			
Owslebury	P	B.N.J., XXXVI, 1967, 10	—
HERTFORDSHIRE			
Baldock	Cl. II	J.R.S., XXIII, 1933, 202	Letchworth (now stolen)
Braughing (4)	P	Evans, 485	B.M.
NORTHAMPTONSHIRE			
Hardingstone	P	Woods (see note 42), 38	—
OXFORDSHIRE			
Dorchester	M	B.B.O. Arch. J., IV, 79	Ashmolean
Woodeaton	N	Noted 1968	Ashmolean
SUFFOLK			
Bardwell (sev.)	O, P	Evans, 485	B.M., Bury
Mildenhall	M	—	B.M.
FRANCE			
Mont César, Oise (2)	P	Blanchet, 251, 492	—

B. Hoards

CLASS I, Types A–L

KENT

1. Lenham Heath, 1781. Number not recorded.
   Evans, 125; *Numismatic Journal*, I, 1837, 222, pl. i. 1; *Revue Numismatique*, II, 1839, 311, pl. xiii. 14; R. Ruding, *Annals of the Coinage of England*, pl. A2.
   Four examples in the British Museum.

2. Quex Park, Birchington I, 1853. Number not recorded.
   Evans, 125, pls. H1, 2, 4, 6, 7; *Numismatic Chronicle*, XVI, 1953–4, 184.
   One example in British Museum, one in Ashmolean Museum, two in National Museum on Antiquities, Edinburgh (probably all from Birchington I). Others dispersed. (A note of Martin Tupper, reported by A. C. W. Lowther from an original manuscript, records a hoard as found at Farley Heath in Christmas 1852 which contained Class I, and possibly from his description Class II coins. In view of the coincidence of date I have rejected this find-spot.)

3. Quex Park, Birchington II, 1853. About 600 in rectangular box. Evans, 484.
   42 in Birchington Museum. Others presumably dispersed.

LONDON

4. St. James's Park, 1827. Number not recorded.
   Evans, 125; *Numismatic Journal*, I, 1837, 222, pl. i. 2; *Revue Numismatique*, II, 1839, 311, pl. xiii. 9; R. Ruding, *Annals of the Coinage of England*, pl. A1.
   One in Bibliothèque Nationale, Paris, no. 9538 (perhaps more); two in V. Newby Collection; three in R. P. Mack Collection; one in Hunterian Museum, Coates Coll., Glasgow. Others dispersed.

(Early drawings seem to show only types with open eye; e.g. drawing belonging to Mr. N. Rhodes. Coins in collections marked as from the hoard, however, have the pellet in the centre.)

5. Eel Pie Island, Twickenham, nine coins; perhaps the same find as that recorded as from Brentford, 1860, as at least 266 coins, probably many more.
   Archaeologia LXIX, 1917–8, 18 for Eel Pie Island; Sotheby's Sale 8.12.1915, lot 280 for Brentford. Seven from Eel Pie Island, one from Brentford in London Museum; eight from Brentford in British Museum; two from Brentford in R. P. Mack Collection. Others from Brentford dispersed. Treated as one hoard.
   (The seven coins from Eel Pie Island are 1 GB, 1 H, 5 L.)

6. Gunnersbury, *c.* 1950. 12 coins, wrapped in fabric (see Appendix II), J. E. Vulliamy, 'The Archaeology of Middlesex and London', 139; *Proceedings of the Prehistoric Society*, XX, 1954, 85.
   Was in Gunnersbury Museum.

MIDDLESEX
7. Sunbury, 1949. About 360 coins (some fragmentary) in three pots. *Numismatic Chronicle*, 1950, 148–9; *British Numismatic Journal*, XXVI, 1957, 339–40; *Proceedings of the Prehistoric Society*, XX, 1954, 72. *c.* 359 (*c.* 30 fragmentary rendering exact number uncertain) in London Museum.

NORFOLK
8. Snettisham, 1948–50. Total of at least 145 coins (116 described). *Proceedings of the Prehistoric Society*, XX, 1954, 85.
   In Norwich Castle Museum.

Plates I to VI

PLATE I

a

b

(a, b) Coin in Royal Scottish Museum, no provenance.

PLATE II

a

b

(a, b) Coin from Brentford Hoard, London Museum.

PLATE III

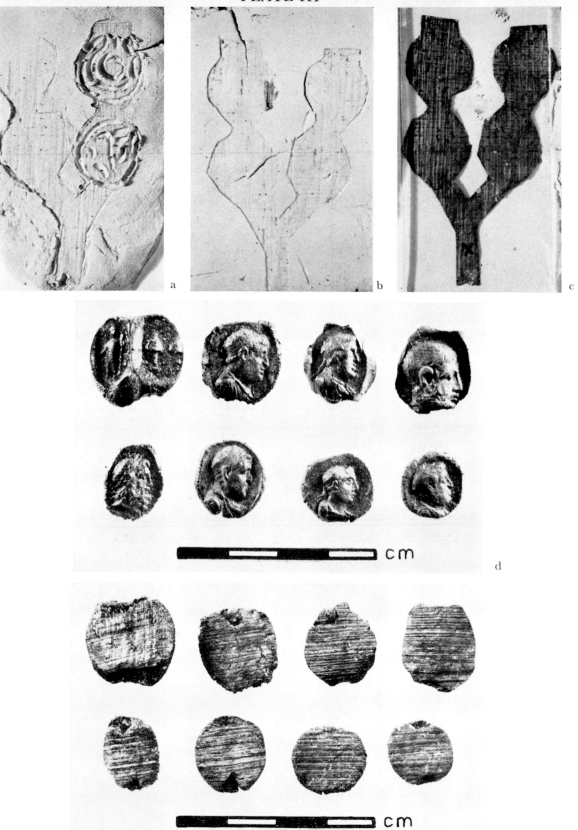

a

b

c

d

e

(a, b, c) Papyrus experiment.

(d, e) Clay seals from Paphos with papyrus impression on reverse.

PLATE IV

Gaulish Potin Coins, 1–32.

PLATE V

Gaulish Potin Coins, 33–43; British Potin Coins, 44–67.

PLATE VI

The Weybourne, Norfolk, hoard.

COMPARATIVE ANALYSIS OF HOARDS

Types	Lenham Heath, Kent	St. James's Park, London	Birchington, Kent, I	Birchington, Kent, II	Eel Pie Island or Brentford	Gunnersbury	Sunbury	Snettisham
A	—	—	—	—	1†	—	—	—
B	—	—	—	—		—	—	—
C	—	—	1	—		—	1	2
D	1	2	1	11	1	—	7	1
E	1	—	—	—	—		—	1
F	—	5	5	4	1	1	51	4
G { A			—	2	—		2	—
G { B	—	—	2	6	3	—	16	6
G { C			—	2	1		5	—
H	—	2	3	2	4	4	66	21
J	1	1	1	12	2	—	42	6
K	—	—	—	1	—	—	4	1
L	1	3	4	1	13	6	125	54
M	—	—	—	—	—		—	
N	—	—	—	—	—		—	
O	—	—	—	—	—		—	
P	—	—	—	—	—		—	
?	?	?	*	?‡	?	1	c. 40	20
Total	Many	Many	Many	c. 600	266‡	12	c. 359	c. 145

† This coin is on a Brentford ticket, but the weight disagrees, and it is possible that it was actually from one of the Birchington hoards.

* An odd, double sized piece, so far unique, with obscure designs which bear no resemblance to the standard type.

‡ It is possible that, alone of the recorded hoards, Birchington II was buried at an earlier stage in the coinage than the others. This assumes that the sample of coins preserved at Birchington Museum is typical of the whole. But although all the other hoards have or appear to have had in them more coins of Type L than of any other, there is still one undoubted coin of this type in the Birchington Museum, which we must assume to have come, like the rest, from Birchington II.

L

APPENDIX II

THE TYPE ILLUSTRATIONS IN FIGS. 31 AND 32 ARE TAKEN FROM COINS AS FOLLOWS:

A	From Gravesend, Gravesend Museum
B	Snettisham Hoard, Norwich Museum
C1	Fitzwilliam Museum
C2	From Ulcombe, Maidstone Museum
C3	Snettisham Hoard, Norwich Museum
C4	Snettisham Hoard, Norwich Museum
C5	From Gestingthorpe, Essex
D1	Hunterian Museum
D2	Quex Park Hoard, Birchington
D3	Snettisham Hoard, Norwich Museum
E	Snettisham Hoard, Norwich Museum
F1	Snettisham Hoard, Norwich Museum
F2	Brentford Hoard, R. P. Mack
F3	St. James's Park Hoard, old drawing
F4	Ashmolean Museum
F5	St. James's Park Hoard, Hunterian Museum
F6	Snettisham Hoard, Norwich Museum
F7	Quex Park Hoard, Birchington
GA	R. P. Mack; Leeds University
GB1	R. P. Mack
GB2	Aberdeen University
GB3	Snettisham Hoard, Norwich Museum
GC1	R. P. Mack
GC2	Quex Park Hoard, Birchington
H1	Snettisham Hoard, Norwich Museum
H2	Snettisham Hoard, Norwich Museum
H3	Snettisham Hoard, Norwich Museum
H4	R. P. Mack
J1	Brentford Hoard, R. P. Mack
J2	Ashmolean Museum
J3	Snettisham Hoard, Norwich Museum
J4	Snettisham Hoard, Norwich Museum
J5	Hunterian Museum
J6	Snettisham Hoard, Norwich Museum
J7	Snettisham Hoard, Norwich Museum
K1	Snettisham Hoard, Norwich Museum
L1	Brentford Hoard, Ashmolean Museum
L2	Snettisham Hoard, Norwich Museum
L3	Snettisham Hoard, Norwich Museum
L4	Snettisham Hoard, Norwich Museum
L5	St. James's Park, R. P. Mack
L6	Snettisham Hoard, Norwich Museum
L7	From Broadstairs, Kent
M1	R. P. Mack
M2	From Radfield, Kent

M3   R. P. Mack
N1   C. R. Lister
O1   From Keston, Kent
O2   From Lullingstone, Kent
P1   From Keston, Kent
P2   From Rochester, Kent

APPENDIX III

THE GUNNERSBURY HOARD

This hoard was in Gunnersbury Museum, Acton. It is recorded that it had been found in Gunnersbury Lane, Acton Hill, near Millhill Road, wrapped in sacking, which was not preserved. It was said that 'bronze age urns' had been found nearby. It was presented to Gunnersbury Museum by Major Salter, some years before 1955, when it was shown to me. The coins have since been stolen and the only record, therefore, is my note.

My notes were made according to R. H. M. Dolloy's classification in his publication of the Snettisham coins; translated to my current classification, I would interpret these as:

F	(27·4g)	L	(22·4g)‡
H	(20·7g)	L	(24·3g)‡
H	(19·6g)	L	(24·6g)
H?	(23·0g)‡	L	(29·4g)
H	(26·1g)	L	(24·1g)‡
H	(20·3g)	L	(38·3g)*

It is possible, but improbable, that this was a stolen parcel from the Eel Pie Island hoard.

APPENDIX IV

CONCORDANCE OF EVANS AND MACK REFERENCES WITH THE NEW CLASSIFICATION

Class I	A	Mack² 22a	—
	B	—	—
	C	Mack 21	Evans H3
	D	Mack 22	—
	E	—	—
	F	—	Evans H2
	GA	Mack² 13	Evans, p. 125
	GB-C	Mack 9, 10	Evans H6
	H	—	Evans H4, 7
	J	—	Evans H1
	K	—	—
	L	Mack 12, 17, 17a	Evans H5
Class II	M	Mack 23	—
	N	—	—
	O	Mack 24	Evans H8
	P	Mack 25	—

‡ Coins with single tang below neck.

* Uncompleted reverse mould, only the body, the ground and the crescents being drawn, while the tail and legs were omitted. (This is interesting as it shows the order in which the strokes were made.)

APPENDIX V

PARTICULARS OF COINS ILLUSTRATED, THEIR WHEREABOUTS AND PROVENANCES

(DFA = the author; Mack = Commander R. P. Mack Collection; the remainder, except those marked Private, are in museums as indicated.)

Plate I	a, b	Royal Scottish Museum, no provenance, 1·77g. (enlarged).
Plate II	a, b	London Museum, from Eel Pie Island (Brentford) hoard (N1063), 2·21g. (enlarged).

Plate IV   1–2   Gaulish potin coins with legend MA.

       1. The Hague   2. DFA   3·26g.

       3–11   Tête diabolique series, reducing in size.

3. BM	3·33g.		8. BM	2·51g.
4. BM	3·54g.		9. DFA	1·67g.
5. DFA	2·76g.		10. DFA	2·93g.
6. DFA	2·90g.		11. DFA	1·56g.
7. DFA	2·96g.			

       12–15   Variants of tête diabolique series.

12. DFA	2·55g.		14. DFA	2·21g.
13. DFA	3·12g.		15. DFA	3·57g.

       16–18   Comparable variants.

16. BM	2·93g.		18. Fitzwilliam 3.85g.
17. Hunter 'Tin' 2			
3·60g.			

       19–27   Grosse tête, quadruped déformé series.

19–22 Butting bull.

19. DFA	3·44g.		21. DFA	5·05g.
20. DFA	4·37g.		22. BM	4·45g.

23–24 Horned horse.

23. BM	4·36g.		24. Cardiff 5368
			4·85g.

25–27 Development of grosse tête, quadruped déformé series.

25. DFA	4·52g.		27. BM	5·37g.
26. DFA	3·13g.			

       28–29   Parallels for outline head.

28. DFA	3·50g.		29. DFA	2·75g.

       30–32   Found in Britain.

30. Fitzwilliam, found at St. Neots,	2·94g. (frag.)
31. Hull, found at South Ferriby,	2·12g.
32. Worthing Museum (loan), found at Clapham, Sussex (cf. 44–5)	

Plate V   33–43   Gaulish potin coins continued.

33–35   Wreathed or netted head, quadruped déformé.
33. BM   4·69g.   35. DFA   2·80g.
34. Cardiff 5390   8·57g.

36–39,   Inscribed.
43   36. Hunter (Coates) 95, Q. Doci   4·60g.
37. BM Q. Doci   4·66g.   39. BM TO (girix)
                                    3·18g.
38. BM Q. Doci   4·25g.   43. BM TOG (irix)
                                    2·23g.

40–42   Uninscribed, netted hair, reduced size.
40. BM   2·35g.   42. DFA   2·49g.
41. BM   2·81g.

44–67   British potin coins.

44–45   Type A.
44. Gravesend, found at Gravesend   2·73g.
45. BM from the Brentford hoard   2·11g.

46–47   Type C.
46. Private   2·08g.   47. Private   1·93g.

48–50   Type D.
48. Private   1·66g.   50. Private   1·68g.
49. Hunter   2·01g.

51   Type D or F.
51. Norwich, from the Snettisham hoard   2·09g.

52–55   Type G.
52. Mack, GA   1·61g.   54. Mack, GB   2·16g.
53. Private, GB   1·36g.   55. Private, GC   1·02g.

56–57   Type H.
56. Private   2·15g.   57. Mack   2·30g.

58   Type J.
58. Private   1·14g.

59–62   Type L.
59. Mack   2·06g.   61. Ashmolean 1·58g.
60. Ashmolean   1·53g.   62. Private, Dumpton Gap,
                                  Broadstairs, 1953   1·88g.

63–64   Type N.
63. Mack   1·47g.   64. Mack   1·19g.

65–66   Type O.
65. Lullingstone, from Roman villa
66. Bury St. Edmunds, found at Bardwell, Suffolk

67   Type P.
67. Private   1·09g.

Plate VI   Coins from the Weybourne, Norfolk, hoard.

1–30   Gold staters, Gallo-Belgic E, all of the variety with straight line exergue and cup and ball ornament below. Weights to nearest half grain, as recorded:
1. 94·0; 2. 95·5; 3. 94·5; 4. 92·5; 5. 93·0; 6. 92·5; 7. 93·5; 8. 93·0; 9. 94·5; 10. 93·5; 11. 95·5; 12. 93·5; 13. 93·0; 14. 92·0; 15. 93·7; 16. 94·0; 17. 95·0; 18. 92·0; 19. 92·5; 20. 93·0; 21. 96·0; 22. 94·0; 23. 94·0; 24. 93·5; 25. 93·0; 26. 91·5; 27. 91·0; 28. 94·0; 29. 90·0; 30. 93·0 grains.

31–33   Gold quarter-staters, Gallo-Belgic D, weights as recorded:
31. 22·0; 32. 20·2; 33. 22·0 grains.

34   Fragment from gold ornament, possibly part of a hollow torque.

HILL SETTLEMENTS, SOUTERRAINS AND THE CHRONOLOGY OF THE IRON AGE IN BRITTANY

By PIERRE-ROLAND GIOT

THE multiplication of hill-forts during the Iron Age is, in Armorica as elsewhere, one aspect of the tendency at that period for establishments of all kinds, earthworks, settlements, ritual sites or industrial areas to retire to hill-tops or to naturally strong positions.

It should nevertheless be pointed out that many of these sites exhibit a long continuity of occupation, just as many hill-forts were often reoccupied during the Middle Ages. A good example of such hill-top sites is given by the *oppidum* of Toul-Goulic at Trémargat (Côtes-du-Nord), in the interior of Brittany. Here, an intensive occupation during the Middle and Late Neolithic is shown by the discovery on the plateau inside the defences of flints, also of numerous flakes of A-dolerite, and of polished stone axes (imported from the axe factories of Plussulien, 16 km. away as the crow flies). There are in addition, some traces of Bronze Age occupation, in the form of a palstave, discovered amidst a chaos of granite boulders, and some pottery sherds possibly of this period which were found in conjunction with Iron Age sherds in the earthen defences. The southern gateway has shown more traces of medieval habitation than the northern.

Such a continuity is also quite usual in the coastal promontory forts and fortified headlands of Brittany. In Finistère there are the examples of Kermorvan, near Le Conquet; Lostmarc'h at Crozon; Kastel-Koz at Beuzec-Cap-Sizun; Kastel-Meur at Cléden-Cap-Sizun; Pointe du Raz at Plogoff. An ecological problem is posed by the distribution of neolithic industries on the tops of nearly all cliffs; the example of the Cap d'Erquy (Côtes-du-Nord) is the most curious: in the soil under the Late Hallstatt fortification of 'Fossé Catuélan', burnt twigs gave a radio-carbon date of Middle Neolithic age, the deforestation having thus long preceded the building of the wall. At Pointe du Blair, Baden (Morbihan), the big fortification called 'Mur des Vénètes' blocks a long necked promontory which included a small megalithic tomb; around this a lot of Late Neolithic material has been found, and also traces of Late Bronze Age or Hallstatt occupation, rather like those at the Camp du Lizo at Carnac; and few traces of Late Iron Age occupation in fact. Similarly at Kermorvan, Lostmarc'h, probably at Kastel-Koz, at Le Raz, Le Blair and Le Lizo, there are passage graves located on hill-tops.

One should also stress the existence of a whole series of other establishments, too modest to be considered as characteristic hill-forts. They are often on small islands, or headlands, with partly natural defences, sometimes only summarily completed by a localised earthwork. They may include traces of habitation or occupation dating at least in part from the Iron Age. The high cliffs of île Agot, Saint-Briac (Ille-et-Vilaine) made any further fortification unnecessary; but it and other islets could have been accessible at low tide during the Iron Age (even if they are not so nowadays), and so some defences may have been necessary, such as in the case of Raguenès, at Nevez

155

(Finistère) and Ile-Gaignog – or Guennoc – at Landéda (Finistère). The latter island has its crest occupied by a line of megalithic cairns with multiple passage graves. It was inhabited during the Hallstatt period (re-use of the chambers of the passage graves, and the building of a circular enclosure between two cairns), and again during La Tène times (general re-use of the passage graves with destruction of their covering; the construction of numerous quadrangular houses in the enclosure of which the bank is raised; other houses between the cairns, and also, in a very simplified form in more exposed areas).

Among diverse modest promontory fortifications, one can draw attention to those of Kastel-Ac'h at Plouguerneau (Finistère), and of the off-shore islands of the Mor Braz (Belle-Ile, Houat, and Hoëdic, all in the Morbihan department). However, one hesitates about the double rampart of the île du Château, in front of Port-Blanc at Penvénan (Côtes-du-Nord), which is associated with a natural defence on a granitic rock – locally one distinguishes between Kastel-Koz and Kastel-Nevez, this last being a medieval or even sub-modern redoubt (Richard II, act ii, scene 1: Port-le-Blanc). One also hesitates about the île du Bindy at Logonna-Daoulas (Finistère).

In the coastal parts of the Trégorrois (Côtes-du-Nord), where the granitic rocks form a very rugged landscape with some tors, traces of occupation perched up in improbable places are numerous. The parish of Plougrescant is rich in such places: An Tour, the Rocher de Saint-Gonéry near Porz-Bugalez, the Pointe du Château, and especially the rocks near the Gouffre de Kastel-Meur, fronted by a levelled earthwork. At Perros-Guirec, the Château du Diable, near Pors-Rolland, shows a filling up of the system of rocks with earth and pebbles so as to form small platforms. The occupation of the eastern summit of the cairn of Barnenez, at Plouézoc'h (Finistère), above the chambers of passage graves I and J, and of the top of the cairn of île Carn, at Ploudalmézeau (Finistère), indicate a similar theme.

The île Gaignog shows an early type of enclosure, with a very low wall or bank. This type of structure seems to appear in Armorica during the Late Bronze Age or the Hallstatt period, but its use can go back much further. A good example, currently being investigated, at Le Cordier, Brandivy (Morbihan), includes two tangential enclosures, one subcircular, the other subrectangular, with a lot of Hallstatt finds about. Here also the banks were very low, less than a metre, with an internal packing of dry stones. At Goarem-Cosquer, near Berrien (Finistère), the interior of the enclosure only showed traces of a medieval settlement; the bank was preceded by a ditch, and charcoal at mid-depth in the fill of this ditch has given a radiocarbon date of the third century B.C., which shows that the enclosure had been built beforehand. As a general rule, one should be careful not to mistake the protohistoric enclosures, with small banks, often without ditches, for defaced medieval courts.

The siting of establishments on hill-tops, or rather on the slope's border, is demonstrated by numerous recent discoveries of sites invisible in the field, but being shown up in section or plan by rural works, road trenches or quarry tip removal. Thus complete systems of deep ditches are revealed, which enclosed areas of various forms (no doubt combined with destroyed banks) where one discovers shallow pits, hearths and traces which could correspond, at least in part, to huts. The sites of Toulhouarn, at Guisseny, and of Menez-Loqueltas near Elliant (Finistère) have multiple parallel ditches of this sort. The sites of Miniou, at Bonen, and of Bellevue, near Saint-Connan (Côtes-du-Nord) only have hearths, but in the last case one should mention a pit containing some fifty bipyramidial iron ingots. The pottery associated with these sites belongs to different phases of the beginning of the La Tène period.

Near the coast, apart from the strictly defined promontory sites, there are remains of small banks very often of indeterminate date, which seem to enclose small plateaux or platforms. These occur at various altitudes, and quite a few are probably relics of protohistoric structures. We can mention the systems of banks described at Kélouer, near Plouhinec (Finistère), or at Pors-Carn, Penmarc'h (Finistère), and which are older than the sand-dunes. It is true that banks must have also enclosed cultivated fields, exactly like the modern banks of the Breton landscape, and indeed some have been discovered associated with Iron Age objects, fossilised under dunes, at the Theven of Plougoulm (Finistère), and also at Port-Blanc near Penvénan (Côtes-du-Nord). This shows how deeply rooted this kind of rural landscape is in the Armorican Massif.

*   *   *

The Iron Age Armorican souterrains constitute a very characteristic element of the regional culture, and a very well known one, thanks to modern excavations, especially so since until discovery, the contents of the souterrain is naturally protected from most kinds of damage. They should not be confused with the 'souterrains-refuges', all post-Roman, of other parts of France. Their geographical distribution coincides with the limits of the three tribes of the extreme west, the Osismii, the Veneti and the Coriosolitae, who can be considered as the original Armoricans (and among whom other specific traits are to be found, such as the funeral stelae of the early La Tène period). It is to be noticed that eastwards from this distribution, practically nothing is known of the Iron Age local cultures before late La Tène times, itself only poorly represented. In the distribution zone of the Armorican souterrains, their density together with the frequency of discoveries at present (a mean of five per year) gives a good idea of the distribution of settlements.

Usually there is nothing on the ground today to give a clue to the location of the souterrains. The common method of discovery is for a plough-horse (or nowadays a tractor), a cart or a machine to break through the weakened roof – a few results are also obtained by road- or quarry-working. The souterrains are artificially cut out of the subsoil of weathered rocks, and their layout is largely dependent upon the character and structure of the underground masses of rock. Some cases in the Morbihan, around La Trinité-sur-Mer, where the rock is too solid to be hollowed out, look like trenches with sides lined with dry-stone walling, covered by cap-stones, very similar to Cornish fogous.

More often these souterrains are near the top of well-drained hill-crests, and are thus sufficiently dry. There are nevertheless some lower down on slopes in less favourable positions, or on low plateaux. Associations of souterrains and enclosures have been found: at Kermeno near Grandchamp (Morbihan) the underground cavity was outside the enclosure; at Kermoysan near Plabennec (Finistère) it was inside. Some souterrains appear in section in retreating cliffs associated with promontories or fortified islets: at the île Gaignog near Landéda, at Lanvoy near Hanvec (Finistère), in the oppidum of Le Vieux-Passage near Plouhinec (Morbihan).

There may be only one chamber or up to half a dozen, linked by small tunnels. The first room is reached by a vertical shaft, or an oblique corridor; there may be two orifices, of one or other kind, at each end. The chambers or crypts are sub-rectangular, oval or elliptical in form, according to the material of the walls; they may be in a suite, a series, or as diverging crypts. There is one case where a unique shaft serves two U-shaped branches, each finishing with a chimney. The sizes vary: at the minimum a metre in the three dimensions, but the length of the rooms may be up to 5 or 6 m., the breadth 3 m., and the height 2 m., or more. The greatest known depth below the ground surface is 4 m.; there exist vertical shafts over 3 m. The natural ceiling is usually at least 1 m. thick at the time of construction, but owing to the disintegration of the rock, it tends to get dangerously near the surface, coming down grain by grain or block by block, and it fills up in the rooms with unpacked débris.

For a long time it was believed that these souterrains had funeral functions, which would be in fact exceptional, or secondary; there is a unique case where it is known to be possible. They were quite often occupied, for hearths are found especially at the bottom of the vertical shafts. It is difficult to say if these hearths result from industrial activities – there are indications of this – or if sometimes the souterrains have been really inhabited. It has been thought that they may have been used as places of refuge during troubled periods (they are in fact much too old to have been in such use during the Gallic wars, as was at one time believed). They may possibly be cellars or store-pits, especially in the drier sites; in some chambers one finds quantities of fragments of big utilitarian pots, often enough sherds to almost completely reconstruct these vessels (which were probably broken *in situ*), and so may possibly have been storage-pits. But in the majority of souterrains the thin occupation layer at the bottom of the crypts, contains no object or fragment, or very little at all which came there strictly during the phase of occupation.

Commonly these cavities are sealed by a deliberate filling-in of their openings. This operation is so systematic, organised and methodical that it would seem right to question the mysterious reason which is the cause of this. It is not very usual at the desertion of a habitation site, to remove all superficial traces, filling both the ditches around the souterrains with the refuse and waste, and the ashes after the intentional burning down of the wooden buildings. The filling of the apertures may begin with an organised piling up of blocks of stone (often re-used kitchen hearths), and completed with thrown in material just near the surface. In most other cases, there is a stratified core, the material of the fill having all been thrown in, more or less mixed up, earth, stones or cinders and ashes. Amidst this packing, there can be all sorts of remains from the surface occupation: wattle-and-daub, stones from hearths, querns, loom weights, sherds of pottery and other artefacts.

Most often the chambers and tunnels contain absolutely nothing left from their period of occupation, and all that one finds come from this fill. And, in the more rare occasions where there are some objects in the occupation layer, it is possible to ascertain that there are sherds of more recent pottery types amongst the material of this fill.

*   *   *

Though on occasion quite unproductive, it can be seen that the Armorican souterrains are on the whole the best of our sources of information on the pottery of the Iron

Age in Brittany. Yet the pots that can be totally reconstructed are rare, and are generally large storage jars of the commonest types. The systematic rescue excavation of souterrains, as their discovery proceeds, has in the last few years multiplied tenfold our knowledge of Armorican ceramics; together with the rescue of some coastal habitation sites rich in refuse-heaps.

Iron Age metal artefacts are scarce in Armorica, a most curious shortage, which cannot be merely the effect of bad conservation conditions in the coastal regions; consequently, the only truly general foundation for the regional chronology of the sites is provided by the ceramics, themselves very often influenced by metal prototypes.

In fact, the pottery styles of the Late Hallstatt and of the first phase of Early La Tène cemeteries with cinerary urns, are not to be found in the souterrains. Likewise, the pottery of Late La Tène (strictly speaking, the last century B.C.), is also unknown from these sources. The phenomenon of the souterrain seems to have lasted for three or four centuries at the most. The mean of 16 radiocarbon dates obtained from the rich discoveries of charcoal from 14 souterrains is 2350 years B.P., which shows clearly the tendency to date these places towards Early La Tène times.

These indications among others, confirm the present-day interpretations of the Amorican Iron Age chronology, causing the abandonment of the idea, so classic for a long time, of a regional time-lag because of the peninsular position of that country, and its apparent isolation from current continental influences. If the coarser pottery shows the slow evolution of local traditions, the fine ceramics show the high quality of Armorican workmanship. It is influenced by impressed decorative motifs from metal-working techniques as almost as early as that of the great centres of La Tène culture. One further problem is that of the local persistance of some of these patterns; but it seems now that these survivals may have been of less duration than was previously thought. This explains why in Late La Tène times the pottery is everywhere so uninteresting. At that period, the finest craftsmen were the die-sinkers.

BIBLIOGRAPHY

References to recent work will practically all be found in:

Annales de Bretagne (Notices d'Archéologie Armoricaine), LXV, 1958 and onwards, chiefly for excavation reports on souterrains. Brief notes on new sites of most kinds will be found under: P.-R. Giot, 'Chronique de Préhistoire et de Protohistoire finistériennes', *Bulletin de la Société Archéologique du Finistère*, LXXXVII, 1961 and onwards; P.-R. Giot, 'Chronique de Préhistoire at de Protohistoire des Côtes-du-Nord', *Société d'Emulation des Côtes-du-Nord*, XCV, 1967 and onwards. For the Morbihan, one should go through the *Bulletin de la Société Polymathique du Morbihan*.

ROMAN AMPHORAE IN PRE-ROMAN BRITAIN

By D. P. S. PEACOCK

SUMMARY

This paper is an attempt to assess certain economic and chronological aspects of the later British Iron Age from amphora evidence. During the first half of the first century and perhaps as early as the latter part of the second century B.C., amphorae of best southern Italian wine were received at Hengistbury Head, Hampshire. During and after the pacification of Gaul in the mid-first century B.C., it is probable that southern Britain became regarded as hostile territory and trade was diverted to the east, where the initial recipients may have been the Trinovantes, with whom Rome made an alliance.

In the last decade B.C. the scope of importation to eastern Britain was increased to include quantities of fish sauce and later olive oil from the Spanish province of Baetica as well as wines from Italy and other areas in the Mediterranean. This commerce, the Baetican in particular, increased in importance and eventually figured significantly in the economic life of Roman Britain.

INTRODUCTION

Amphorae, used for transporting perishable commodities such as wine, olive oil, fish sauce (e.g. *garum*) and salted products, were an important form of trade-packaging in the Mediterranean Roman world. The distribution of these containers stretches along the eastern fringes of the Atlantic Ocean from Scotland to the Canary Islands and thence across parts of three continents to the Coromandel coast of India, as Sir Mortimer Wheeler (1946) has shown. This impressive span, approaching 6,000 miles, is a vivid testimony not only to the acumen of Roman merchants but also to the demand for Mediterranean luxury foodstuffs well beyond the Imperial frontiers.

Study of amphorae thus provides an opportunity to assess certain external contributions to the economies of barbarian peoples and to establish chronological horizons, for amphora forms varied with the passage of time as a result of both typological evolution and the ascendancy and decline of different production regions. With regard to amphorae as chronological indices, I share neither the pessimism of Callender (1965) nor the excessive optimism of Uenze (1958), for whom they were an ideal dating medium. It is true that these vessels appear to have evolved slowly and undoubtedly the individual amphora might have had a long life serving other functions when its primary purpose had been fulfilled. However, under favourable conditions of preservation amphorae have been found with painted inscriptions (*tituli picti*) indicating the date and often the provenance of the contents. They are thus a unique class of ceramics, certain types having precise written evidence of chronology and origin. Used with care and preferably in quantity, the amphora can I believe, be an invaluable source of information.

At present the main drawback in interpreting amphora evidence is our very rudimentary knowledge of these vessels. André Tchernia (1967:234) remarked that of the numerous types known, only two could be ascribed with certainty to their source region.

Although this situation has improved, due largely to the researches of Fausto Zevi and Tchernia himself, the statement remains true in essence. This paper is thus a preliminary and very tentative attempt to assess certain chronological and economic aspects of the later British Iron Age from amphora evidence. I have drawn heavily upon the works of others, but have included notes on my recent petrological work which serve to amplify the data. This study continues and full publication of the new evidence will be delayed until a larger sample of amphorae has been examined.

PART I

AMPHORA TYPOLOGY, CHRONOLOGY AND PROVENANCE: A REVIEW OF THE EVIDENCE

In this section I propose to review what is known of the typology, chronology and origin of the principal amphora types exported to Britain before the Roman conquest, *viz.* mainly Camulodunum forms 181–7 (Hawkes and Hull, 1947). However, form 187, the globular amphora, will not be discussed in detail since in Britain it is *par excellence* the amphora of the second century A.D., and best left until pertinent to review all the evidence.

The classification of amphorae

Amphora classification is fraught with difficulties. The most widely accepted system is that of Dressel (1899), but as Zevi (1966:214) has pointed out, this was intended not so much as an absolute classification of universal application, as a sketch to accompany a corpus of amphora inscriptions from Rome. It has nevertheless formed the basis of most subsequent classifications (e.g. Pélichet, 1946; Lamboglia, 1955). Callender's (1965) scheme has little to commend it since it is excessively conflated and the divisions are not always logical, while the recent work of Joncheray (1970) is intended as a guide to assist under-water archaeologists in preliminary identification.[1] In Britain we are fortunate in having the excellent Camulodunum type series, but this does not cover all the variations known from other British Iron Age sites and it is confusing to use an insular nomenclature when relating to continental material. I have attempted to overcome these difficulties by listing some of the alternative terminology at the beginning of each section.

1. ITALIAN TYPE AMPHORAE
(Dressel 1, Callender 1, Camulodunum 181, Républicaine III (Benoit, 1957))

(a) *Typology*

This type (fig. 35, 1–2) is characterised by a heavy spindle-shaped body and paste which is thick and reddish often with whiter surfaces. The collar rim and long flattened rod-like handles are characteristic.

Loeschcke (1942:84) indicated two distinct varieties, while Lamboglia (1955) isolated three, two of which (Dressel 1A and B) are of interest to us in Britain. Dressel

[1] See now, however, the useful work by M. Beltrán Lloris (1970), *Las ánforas romanas en España*, Zaragoza.

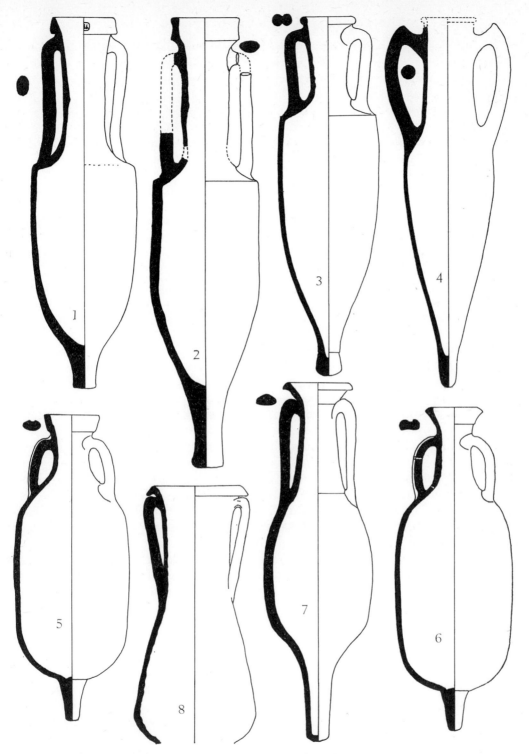

Fig. 35. Amphora types (scale 1/10). No. 1, Grand Congloué, Marseilles (after Benoit, 1961);
No. 2, Hertford Heath (after Holmes and Frend, 1957); Nos. 3-7, Camulodunum (after
Hawkes and Hull, 1947); No. 8, Caerleon (after Wheeler and Wheeler, 1928).

type 1A (fig. 35, 1) is smaller, characterised by a short jutting rim triangular in cross-section, a rounded shoulder angle and a stumpy base. The B variety (fig. 35, 2) is larger with a near vertical collar rim, a sharper shoulder angle and a longer basal spike often slightly expanded at the extremity.

(b) *Provenance and petrology*

The provenance of most of these vessels is securely tied by *tituli picti* to the Caecuban and Falernian wine-producing regions of Italy (Zevi, 1966:214), situated west of Terracina and east of Capua respectively.

Petrologically three principal fabric varieties can be distinguished, of which fabric 1 is predominant and fabric 3 rare.

Fabric 1. Frequent inclusions of quartz (discrete and polycrystalline grains), potash felspar (including sanidine), volcanic rock and glass fragments, some green or occasionally colourless augite, a little plagioclase felspar and accessory garnet.

Fabric 2. Abundant large crystals of green or colourless augite, yellow-brown garnet, quartz, sanidine, volcanic rock fragments and a little basaltic hornblende. Easily recognisable in the hand-specimen as the fabric appears to contain black sand.

Fabric 3. Quartz, potash and some plagioclase felspar, biotite, granite fragments. Distinguished in the hand-specimen by glistening flecks of mica.

The existence of so few variations is surprising, suggesting amphora factories. It appears that the precept of Varro (*De Re Rustica*, I, 22.1) recommending that everything possible should be made on the estate may not have been adhered to in this respect.

Fabrics 1 and 2 are found in both the A and B forms, although no examples of Dressel 1A in fabric 2 have yet been found in Britain. Elizabeth Ettlinger's (1960) suggestion that the two forms originated in different production regions is thus invalid. Nor is it possible to correlate the two fabrics with the Caecuban and Falernian districts respectively. A group of sherds collected from Uenze's (1958:7) site at Mondragone in the heart of the Falernian region contained both fabrics, suggesting indiscriminate use of the two products.

Various attempts have been made to limit the provenance of these vessels petrologically. Collot (1918) and later Lais (1943) drew attention to the presence of volcanic materials in the fabric indicating an Italian source. Bouscaras (1954) erroneously reasoned that a vessel from the sea off Agde (Hérault) originated at either Capo di Bovo (Latium) or Monte Somma (Campania) on an association of leucite and augite in the fabric. Maréchal (1966:124) has rightly drawn attention to the wide Italian distribution of green augite, a persistent feature of fabrics 1 and 2, but his suggestion of an origin on the Island of Ischia in the bay of Naples, although very feasible for fabric 2, remains unverified as no petrological description of the supposed raw materials or of kiln waste has been published.

Fabric 3 which occurs rarely in form B, is characterised by inclusions of granitic origin. Since it can be difficult to distinguish one granite from another, the group may include vessels from a number of sources. However, such material is unlikely to have come from the Caecuban and Falernian regions, and if production of this form is restricted to Italy, a source in the southern toe of the country is more probable. The wine-producing localities of Thurii and Consentia (Frank, 1940:136, 147) lie on the fringes of a granite massif. Zevi (1966:214) reminds us of an uncertain *titulus pictus* from Rome implying contents of wine from Rheginum, the ancient Reggio-Calabria, which lends support to a southern Italian source.

(c) Contents

The principal contents of these vessels were undoubtedly Caecuban and Falernian wine, ranked by Pliny (*Nat. Hist.*, XIV, 8) among the finest. However, a vessel recovered from the sea off the Archipel de Riou, Provence, contained *Spondylus* shells suggesting occasional use for other commodities (Benoit, 1962:164).

(d) Chronology

Zevi (1966:212) lists nine dates between 102 and 13 B.C. and another possibly of 129 B.C. Production as early as the last quarter of the second century B.C. is however, confirmed by finds from Entremont, destroyed in 123 B.C. (Benoit, 1968). The termination of production, of particular relevance to Britain, is unfortunately difficult to assess with accuracy. Despite the fact that four of the nine dates listed by Zevi are Augustan, there can be little doubt that production was falling during this period. Where these vessels have been found in Mediterranean wrecks carrying fine ceramics the association is invariably with Campanian ware *not* Arretine, suggesting attenuation of trade during the ascendency of the latter. Associations of Dressel 1B with Campanian ware are known from the following wrecks: Albenga (Lamboglia, 1952), Ile Maire 4 (Benoit, 1962), Drammont A (Benoit, 1960), Point de l'Ermitage (Tchernia, 1969). A decline in popularity during the Augustan period is also confirmed by excavations of Rhenish forts. Oberaden (12–8 B.C.) produced fragments of nine vessels (Loeschcke, 1942), Haltern (11 B.C.–A.D. 9) yielded only one (Stieren, 1932), while none are recorded from Augsburg-Oberhausen approximately contemporary with Haltern (Ulbert, 1960). The evidence thus points to a termination of production early in the last decade B.C. and there is certainly no indisputable case for the continuation of this form after the end of the first century B.C. It should be noted that the Stanfordbury amphorae (p. 182), dating to the second quarter of the first century A.D., were erroneously attributed to this form by Callender (1965:8).

Relative dates for types A and B were suggested by Lamboglia's (1955) excavations at Ventimiglia on the Italian-French border. Dressel 1A was predominant in the earliest levels while increasing quantities of Dressel 1B appeared after about 70 B.C. On the basis of this work Uenze (1958) constructed a scheme for the typological evolution and chronology of Dressel 1 amphorae with which he attempted to date certain late La Tène sites north of the Alps. However, as Elizabeth Ettlinger (1960) has pointed out, he has in some instances impressed upon the material far greater chronological precision than the evidence warrants.

At present it seems safe to regard Dressel 1A as characteristic of the first half of the first century B.C., Dressel 1B appearing about 70–50 B.C. As Zevi (1966:214) has noted

Dressel was obviously aware of the differences, referring to amphorae of the first half of the first century as *formae 1 similis*.

2. GRECO-ROMAN AMPHORAE (KOAN TYPE)
(Dressel 2–4, Callender 2, Camulodunum 182–3, Républicaine II (Benoit, 1957))

(a) Typology

This amphora group, produced or distributed in Italy and the west, was based upon prototypes from the Greek Island of Kos (*cf.* Grace, 1961: figs. 57–60).

Vessels of this type (fig. 35, 3) can be distinguished by their simple beaded rim and bifid handles which are often angular or rise to a peak before joining the neck just below the rim. Hawkes and Hull (1947) recognised two forms each with sub-categories, but this group is so variable that detailed taxonomy is somewhat arbitrary, dependent upon the criteria selected. The typological diversity often makes it difficult to assign individual pieces to a precise place in Dressel's classification.

The paste is usually reddish with paler surfaces, but many varieties occur.

(b) Provenance and Petrology

Zevi (1966:216) regards the evidence of provenance derived from *tituli picti* as confused and inadequate. Diverse sources are indicated, principally in Campania and Southern Italy, but wines from Spain (the Lauronense) and the Provincia (the Baeterense from ancient Béziers) also appear to have been carried. The forms Dressel 2 and 3 both contained the Baeterense, Lauronense and Amineum (Campanian) wines which is surprising as one might have expected the two forms to be characteristic of different regions.

However petrology clarifies the matter to a certain extent. The 21 examples sectioned can be divided into eight fabric types. Although in some cases raw materials for the fabrics might have been found within a short distance of one another, the geological differences are often so great that a wide geographical origin is implied, although it is not yet possible to pin-point any one source with certainty.

Fabrics 1–3 continued in use suggesting that the factories which had produced Dressel 1 amphorae continued, although the style of their products had radically changed. The general picture appears to be one of an expanding wine industry: Dressel 1A exists in two fabrics, Dressel 1B in three and with the advent of Greco-Roman types at least eight fabrics are indicated.

The geographical diversity of production sites probably accounts for the many typological variations, although it is not yet possible to correlate differences in fabric and form.

(c) Contents

There is no evidence to suggest that the contents of these vessels was other than wine.

(d) Chronology

Zevi (1966) records 14 *tituli picti* ranging between 16 B.C. and A.D. 146, but the

majority fall in the first half of the first century A.D. This accords well with the archaeological evidence as the form is ubiquitous on sites dating from the last decade of the
first century B.C. to the early second century, e.g. Oberaden (Loeschcke, 1942),
Haltern (Loeschcke, 1909), Hofheim (Ritterling, 1913), Caerleon (Wheeler and
Wheeler, 1928).

In view of the diversity of production sites it is futile to erect an evolutionary scheme
for the development of this type: each centre must be isolated and studied independently. Similar forms may have been produced at different times in different centres,
while no doubt in some cases a variety of typological traits were in vogue contempor-
aneously.

Zevi ascribes consular dates to the typological variations distinguished by Dressel,
but each has too few dates for even tentative conclusions to be drawn.

3. GRECO-ROMAN AMPHORAE (RHODIAN TYPE)
(Camulodunum 184, Callender 7)

(a) *Typology*

This type of amphora, which is much less common than the preceding, is based
upon prototypes from the Island of Rhodes (Grace, 1961: fig. 62).

The characteristics (fig. 35, 4) are the simple beaded rim and the long single rod
handles which rise to a sharp peak. It is a highly distinctive type which is close to
Dressel forms 5 and 43, although not accurately represented in his scheme.

The fabric is variable in colour, ranging from buff or reddish with paler surfaces, to,
in rare instances, off-white.

(b) *Provenance and Petrology*

Unfortunately little is known of the *tituli picti* on this type. The evidence listed by
Callender (1965:16) refers to Pompeii form VIII, which though related, is not the
same.

Tchernia (1969:470) has suggested that these amphorae may have been made on
Rhodes itself. While the petrology does not preclude this possibility, a wide variety of
sources is again indicated. The 13 sherds sectioned can be conveniently divided into
six groups of differing origin. The Rhodian type thus exhibits similar diversity of origin
to the Koan, but since most of the fabrics are different there appears to have been
little overlap of the two styles.

(c) *Contents*

The contents of this type are unknown, but presumably wine was carried.

(d) *Chronology*

Although this form is frequently found on sites of the mid-first century A.D. (e.g.
Claudian Hofheim (Ritterling, 1913) and Hod Hill (Richmond, 1968)) occurrences
at Oberaden (Loeschcke, 1942: type 79) and Haltern (Loeschcke, 1909: type 67)
suggests that it was established by the last decade of the first century B.C., while that
from Caerleon may indicate production after *c.* A.D. 75 (Wheeler and Wheeler, 1928:
186).

4. SOUTHERN SPANISH AMPHORA TYPES
(Dressel 7–11, 38, Camulodunum 185–6, Callender 6, 8, 9, Pélichet 46)

(a) Typology

This group comprises types of diverse character which nevertheless form part of a variable related series.

The commoner forms found in Britain are illustrated in fig. 35, 5–8. Fig. 35, 5 and 6 show Camulodunum forms 185A and B, a characteristic feature of which is the vertical groove down the handle, while fig. 35, 7 and 8 are Camulodunum form 186 distinguished by the hollow spike and long flattened recurved handles. This type exists in a number of varieties of which the rim is generally characteristic. Fig. 35, 7 is Camulodunum 186A with slender body and bell mouth, while fig. 35, 8 shows the typical broad neck and hooked rim of form 186C. Form 186B is intermediate, having a broad neck and short everted rim (Hawkes and Hull, 1947).

Camulodunum 185A (fig. 35, 5) occurs in a hard buff fabric with numerous inclusions, while the remainder are generally finer, off-white in colour, sometimes pink or with a reddish core, the surface usually bearing a pale, fine, off-white slip.

(b) Provenance and Petrology

Although *tituli picti* occur frequently on amphorae of this class, the information they bear is of a different nature, providing little direct evidence of source. In an excellent analysis Zevi (1966:229–46) has demonstrated the inscriptions to be similar in style to those on globular amphorae (Dressel 20). The work of Bonsor (1931) and Clark-Maxwell (1899) has shown the latter to be a characteristic product of the valley of the Guadalquivir between Seville and Cordoba in Spain, and thus a source in Baetica is also implied for the group under consideration. Since these amphorae usually contained marine products rather than wine or oil, an origin along the Baetican coast is implied and sea-food factories are frequent here (Ponsich and Tarradell, 1965: fig. 1). A source in this region is confirmed by the discovery of kilns near Cadiz (Jiménez-Cisneros, 1958) and at Algeciras (Sotomayor, 1969).

Callender (1965, 15) tentatively suggested an Italian source for his form 6 (*cf.* fig. 35, 8) on the basis of an inscription apparently referring to Vesuvian wine and the large number occurring at Pompeii. However, Schoene (1871) from whom Callender's information is derived, may have wrongly attributed some of the *tituli picti* ascribed to this form. I have petrologically examined two examples of this type from Verulamium, one of which is illustrated by Callender (1965: pl. Ic). The vessels contain no volcanic matter diagnostic of an Italian source, but have a composition indistinguishable from the fabrics of Camulodunum 185B/186.

The fabric of Camulodunum 185A (fig. 35, 5) resembles that of globular amphorae, tentatively implying that this type had an inland origin and thus may not have contained sea-food. The fabrics of the remainder are similar in that thin sections reveal little but quartz and baked clay, but there are textural differences implying diverse origins. Variations can sometimes be distinguished in the hand-specimen: for example, occasional coarser wares with large quartz grains (up to 2 mm. across) exist in Camulodunum 186.

The heavy mineral analyses (Peacock, 1967) tabulated below help to clarify the situation.

TABLE I

No.	Type	Zircon	Rutile	Tourmaline	Apatite	Epidote	Garnet	Andalusite	Kyanite	Staurolite	Anatase	Topaz	Sillimanite	Amphibole	Augite	No. grains counted
1.	Globular	13.7	4.3	0.9	0.9	3.3	66.1	6.4	0.5	—	0.2	0.3	0.3	2.8	0.3	578
2.	Camulodunum 185A	22.5	2.6	4.4	3.4	1.8	44.4	13.1	—	1.3	—	—	2.6	3.1	0.8	383
3.	Camulodunum 185B	39.0	3.9	0.5	3.1	23.5	13.3	13.3	0.5	—	—	0.3	0.3	2.4	—	413
4.	Camulodunum 186 sp.	70.6	13.3	—	0.9	0.1	6.2	5.3	0.3	—	0.6	1.3	0.4	0.7	0.1	677
5.	Camulodunum 186 sp.	47.9	4.2	—	21.6	1.6	19.5	—	—	—	—	—	—	4.7	0.5	190

The globular amphora (stamped ARAXI EM) from Roman Dorchester contains a very high percentage of garnet like other vessels of this type I have analysed. This may thus be a characteristic of the deposits in the Guadalquivir drainage basin. Since the second analysis of Camulodunum 185A also contains much garnet, a Guadalquivir origin appears to be confirmed, although a source around the mouth of the river cannot be eliminated on this evidence.

The third analysis (Camulodunum 185B, type specimen) has a high tenor of epidote, a mineral which Mabasoone (1963) has shown to be abundant in the Guadalete drainage area. An origin around Cadiz is likely though again it is impossible to decide mineralogically between a littoral and inland origin.

Analyses 4 and 5 are of finer and coarser fabrics of Camulodunum 186 sp. The former shows a high zircon content, the latter a high apatite. Although the sources cannot yet be determined, they are different from one another and from the other three analyses.

Further work is obviously necessary and this will undoubtedly amplify the number of fabric types. However, the general implications are clear: the amphorae were made along a considerable stretch of the southern Spanish coast and the diversity of production centres is probably one of the more important factors influencing typological variation.

(c) *Contents*

Tituli picti indicate that the principal contents of these vessels were fish-based products such as *garum*, *muria* and *liquamen* (Zevi, 1966: 231).

(d) Chronology

This group was at the height of popularity during the first century A.D., but as Zevi (1966: 239) has stated, its precise range and particularly that of the typological variants is difficult to establish with certainty. However, the industry was exporting before Oberaden (12–8 B.C.) and persisted until at least the first quarter of the second century A.D., as shown by examples from Caerleon (Wheeler and Wheeler, 1928: fig. 23, 78), Leicester (Kenyon, 1948: fig. 33, 1) and Tarsus (Goldman, 1950: fig. 790).

That Camulodunum forms 185 and 186B are at least partly contemporaneous is demonstrated by the frequent association of these types at, for example, Snailwell (Lethbridge, 1953), Camulodunum, and in the wreck off La Tour Sainte-Marie, Corsica (Tchernia, 1969: 489).

Little can be added to Hawkes' and Hull's (1947: 252) chronology of the individual types. However, it should be noted that a form close to 185, usually though not invariably, pre-Claudian, was found at Augustan Oberaden which extends the range (Loeschcke, 1942: type 82). Numerous variations of form 186 exist and although the distinctions A, B and C are often useful it can be difficult to place individual pieces. The possibility of geographically diverse origins influencing the typology releases us from the need to arrange these vessels in a strict evolutionary sequence and thus permits slight revision of the dating. The example from Haltern (Loeschcke, 1909: type 69) attributed to form 186A was held as evidence for the priority of this class. However, it is in reality intermediate between A and B, and forms related to 186B occur at Oberaden (Loeschcke, 1942: type 80–1). Thus amphorae on the 186A/B theme appear to have been current from before *c.* 10 B.C. to the late first century A.D. Form 186C is common in deposits of the early second century A.D., but its presence at Pompeii (Schoene, 1871: form VII) attests an origin before A.D. 79.

5. THE GLOBULAR AMPHORA
(Dressel 20)

This form, which occurs in pre-Roman contexts at Camulodunum, has been discussed extensively by Callender (1965).

The work of Bonsor (1931) and Clark-Maxwell (1899) indicates a source along the Guadalquivir between Seville and Cordoba. Olive oil may have been the principal commodity transported (Tchernia, 1964).

Callender (1965) claims that the form altered little typologically throughout its long life, but Tchernia (1967) has put forward an acceptable scheme for the evolution of the rim.

6. SUMMARY

The evidence outlined above forms the basis for assessing the significance of amphorae in pre-Roman Britain. Table II summarises the salient points.

TABLE II

Type	Provenance	Contents	Chronology
Italian (Dressel 1)	Campania and southern Italy	Fine quality wine	c. 129 B.C. – c. 1 B.C.
Greco-Roman			
Koan	Many areas, probably mainly Italy	Wine	c. 16 B.C. – c. A.D. 149
Rhodian	Many areas, probably mainly Italy	Probably wine	c. 10 B.C. – late 1st century A.D.
South Spanish	Coast between Cadiz and Malaga	Garum and marine products	c. 10 B.C. – early 2nd century A.D.
Globular	Guadalquivir between Seville and Cordoba	Olive oil	Predominantly 2nd century in Britain, but common in 1st century A.D. and present in early levels at Camulodunum.

PART II

AMPHORAE AND THE LATER IRON AGE IN BRITAIN

A catalogue of pre-Roman sites producing amphorae constitutes the appendix, in which details of individual pieces and find-spots are given. In this section I propose to attempt a tentative synthesis of the evidence. The emphasis will rest upon Dressel 1 types since these are the most informative at present.

That Dressel 1 is common in Gaul is demonstrated by figure 36, constructed largely from information recorded in the literature. The distribution naturally shows a predilection for the Mediterranean coast and the Provincia, but a scatter of finds occurs up to about 150 miles (250 kms.) north of the frontier. The spread seems to be fairly even, but when the productivity of individual sites is taken into account, the most prolific lie in a well-defined area stretching from the present day Burgundy to the frontier of the Provincia. This is hardly surprising for the Aedui and their dependents, whose territory this was, were more or less constant friends and allies of Rome after a treaty of 121 B.C.

In Britain, Dressel 1 amphorae are tightly concentrated in an area north of the Thames constituting present day Hertfordshire and Essex, but there is a thin scatter in southern counties (fig. 36), particularly in Hampshire and the Isle of Wight.

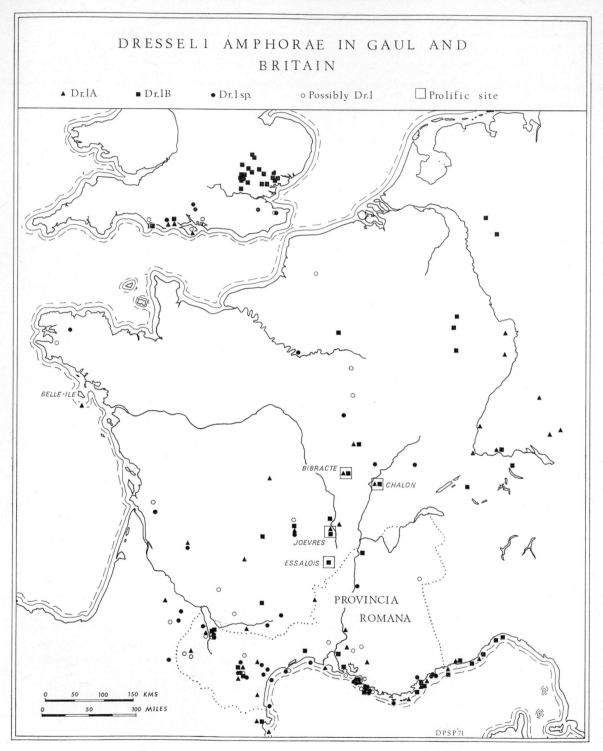

Fig. 36. Distribution of Dressel 1 amphorae in Gaul and Britain.

1. Southern Sites Producing Dressel 1 Amphorae

None of these is prolific with the notable exception of Hengistbury Head, which also has the distinction of being the only British site to produce quantities of Dressel 1A, although a single sherd, possibly of this type was found on neighbouring Green Island in Poole Harbour and a few more were recovered from Knighton, near Brading, Isle of Wight. The evidence thus suggests that Hengistbury was receiving amphorae of best southern Italian wine during the first half of the first century and perhaps even the latter part of the second century B.C. The typological variation shown by the rim sherds (fig. 37) is more than can be expected from a single or even a few cargoes and thus trade over a considerable period is implied. The change from Dressel 1A to the B form cannot be precisely dated and thus the few Dressel 1B sherds could have arrived just before the middle of the first century, though equally they could imply continuation of trading into the latter part of the century on a greatly reduced scale.

Caesar (*B.G.* III, 8) records Venetic ships sailing to Britain and thus there is a possibility that the goods were delivered by Armorican intermediaries. Certainly Hengistbury shows good evidence of contact with Armorica. It has produced more graphite coated ware than any other British site and Bushe-Fox's (1915) Class B cordoned ware which is present in quantity, would also be at home across the Channel (Wheeler and Richardson, 1957: 47). The fabric of this pottery contains much mica, a mineral which is scarce in the raw materials available around Hengistbury, although a common feature of Breton Iron Age pottery (Giot, 1960: 190).

However, if wine was received through the Veneti very little appears to have been retained in Armorica as Dressel 1 amphorae are scarce (see fig. 36). It thus seems reasonable to postulate a direct trade link between Italy and Hengistbury, albeit with due tributes paid to the Veneti, since Caesar (*B.G.* III, 8) indicates that they were masters of the English Channel. The wreck or wrecks off Belle Ile, Morbihan, bearing Dressel 1A amphorae (André, 1959, 1961) could have been bound for Britain as feasibly as Armorica.

Since the amphora evidence from Hengistbury suggests disruption or at least severe attenuation of trade about the middle of the first century, it is tempting to see a connection with the disastrous Venetic uprising of 56 B.C. Had the commerce been in the hands of the Veneti it would certainly have suffered, though equally Rome is unlikely to have encouraged direct trade with southern Britain after this date in view of the support given to the Veneti. In any case, during and after the conquest of Gaul, Britain, the next in line, would have been regarded as hostile territory.

The remaining material from southern Britain is sparse and fragmentary and thus little can be added to the information given in the appendix.

2. Dressel 1 Amphorae in East Anglia

The distribution of Dressel 1 amphorae in eastern Britain is given in fig. 36 and in more detail in fig. 38. Where species is determinate all vessels are of the B form and hence most probably belong to the second half of the first century B.C. Again, derivation from Continental tribes is unlikely because of the scarcity of amphorae in neighbouring territories across the Channel (fig. 36).

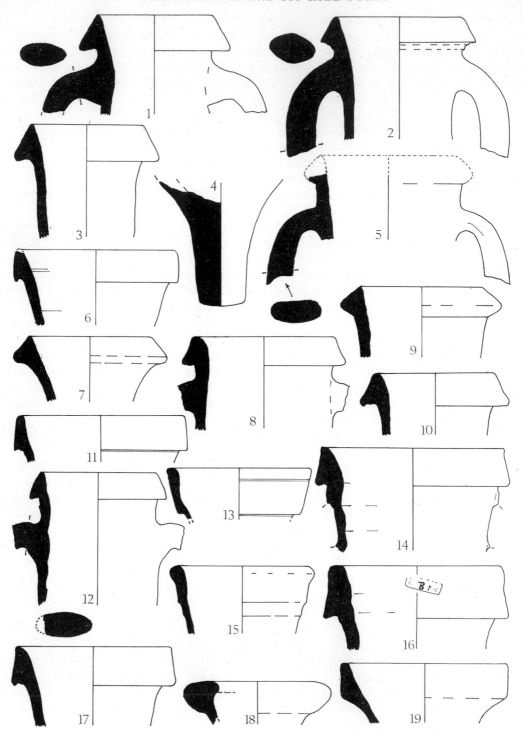

Fig. 37. Amphorae from Hengistbury Head, Hampshire. Scale 1/4.

It is remarkable that most of the amphorae from eastern Britain are complete or practically so. The reason is that they almost certainly come from graves, as it is difficult to account for their preservation otherwise. Stead (1967) has shown that amphorae are a feature of the rich flat graves he has designated the 'Welwyn type'. The sites of the complete vessels shown on the map (fig. 38) may thus mark Welwyn type graves of which they are the only surviving evidence. The distributional correspondence supports this.

Dressel 1 amphorae and Welwyn type graves containing them are concentrated in a belt stretching from the Essex coast to central Hertfordshire, but they do not reach the Verulamium and Wheathampstead region (fig. 38). The area defined may thus have acted as both a cultural and an economic unit and hence could be a tribal territory.

It has been customary to equate the rich Hertfordshire graves with the Catuvellauni, but this must now be questioned on chronological grounds. Stead (1967) has suggested that Welwyn type burials containing Dressel 1 amphorae and no other types, date (on the basis of associated metal-work) between about 50 and 10 B.C. and with this the amphora evidence is in complete accord. Graves such as Welwyn A and Hertford Heath could date from the decade or so after Caesar's invasion while the others may be a little later. The burial from Mount Bures, north of Colchester, is certainly later than those from Hertfordshire since the Dressel 1 amphora was associated with a number of Dressel 10 vessels and Gallo-Belgic pottery. It is probable that the burial took place towards the end of the last decade B.C. (p. 184). A similar, although perhaps slightly earlier date applies to the Lexden tumulus (p. 183) which can perhaps be regarded as a Welwyn type grave over which special circumstances warranted the erection of a barrow. However, the Dressel 1 amphora from Park Field, Lexden, and particularly the pair from Danbury, west of Maldon, could represent graves on the eastern fringe of the distribution contemporary with those in Hertfordshire. Thus during the period 50–10 B.C. Welwyn type graves containing Dressel 1 amphorae may have been constructed over the whole of the area in question. The distribution clearly antedates the eastwards expansion of the Catuvellauni under Cunobelin and probably even the temporary incursion of Tasciovanus suggested by rare coins with a Camulodunum mint mark (Allen, 1944: 15), although in any case this would have been too brief to be of significance here. Since eastern Essex at least was probably in Trinovantian hands during this period it is reasonable to suggest that the Dressel 1/Welwyn type grave distribution maps out the territory of the Trinovantes.

Further evidence can be advanced to support this hypothesis. No Dressel 1 amphorae are recorded from the Wheelers' (1936) extensive excavation at the Catuvellaunian stronghold of Verulamium, or its probable precursor at Wheathampstead, although in contrast small scale rescue work on a settlement at Crookhams, Welwyn Garden City, five miles or so to the east, produced sherds of at least two vessels (Rook, 1968). The evidence is slight but would well accord with a tribal frontier economically separating the two regions. Alternatively we must ascribe the Crookhams find to chance and assume that the Catuvellaunian aristocracy were provided in death with luxuries not enjoyed to any extent by the living. However, it is noteworthy that no Welwyn type graves were discovered in the Verulamium cemetery (Stead, 1969). There is of course, nothing new in suggesting a political boundary in this region for the Wheelers (1936:

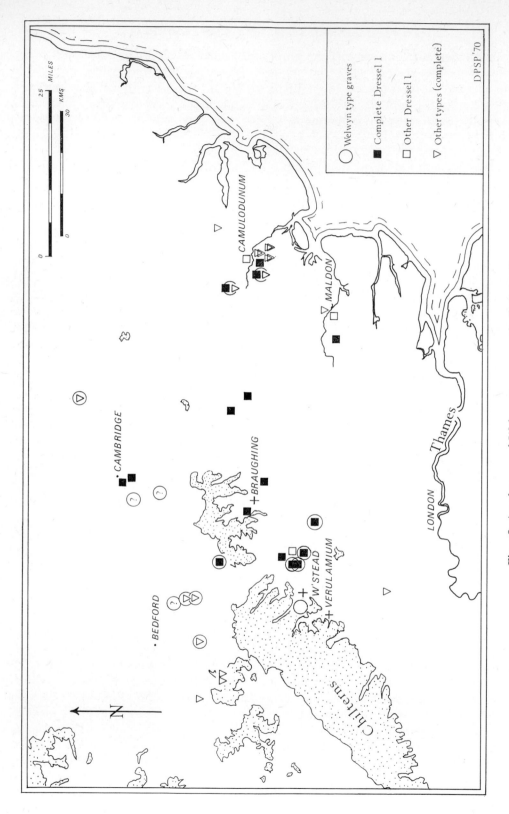

Fig. 38. Amphorae and Welwyn type graves in East Anglia.

20–3) interpreted the Beech Bottom Dyke, between Verulamium and Wheathampstead as a frontier work.

The hypothesis also satisfies the literary evidence. Rice-Holmes (1907: 702) long ago deduced that the stronghold of Cassivellaunus was near to the frontier with the Trinovantes which implies that their territory stretched as far west as Hertfordshire, since his oppidum must lie somewhere in this region even if a better contender than Wheathampstead eventually comes to light. Extensive territories stretching across Essex and Hertfordshire would befit a tribe described by Caesar (*B.G.* V, 21) as perhaps the strongest in these parts. The contents of the graves are also significant for they blatantly accord with a tribe befriended by Rome: I have already alluded to an analogous concentration of amphorae in the territory of the Aedui (p. 171).

Coin evidence offers another approach, though unfortunately the only coins that can be ascribed with certainty to the Trinovantes are those of Addedomarus, approximately contemporary with Tasciovanus and hence comparatively late. However, these roughly cover the area in question (Allen, 1944: map IV), but extend further to the west and north, as a result of trade or perhaps temporary fluctuation of the kingdom. The scarcity of finds in the central Essex-Hertfordshire region may be fortuitous. However, it is interesting that none of the graves from the Welwyn region date from after *c.* 10 B.C. and this might indicate that the centre of Trinovantian power was moved to the east, at or before this time, perhaps as a result of Catuvellaunian encroachment of the western marches.

Not all Welwyn type graves contain Dressel 1 amphorae: southern Spanish types were found in the Snailwell burial, while those from Stanfordbury contained an anomalous type of uncertain origin. A burial at Maulden Moor contained an amphora of unknown class. Complete examples of the Koan type were recovered from Woburn, Stanmore, Stratford St. Mary, Heybridge and Colchester, while a number of complete southern Spanish amphorae have been found around Colchester and another at Wavendon near Bletchley. All probably came from graves.

The distribution of these amphorae or of Welwyn type graves containing them covers much the same ground as Dressel 1 amphorae, but they are found beyond the limits of the latter (fig. 38). Their date is difficult to fix with precision but they are undoubtedly later than Dressel 1 and this is often confirmed by their grave goods: Gallo-Belgic pottery is not infrequently associated, whereas it is never found in graves containing just Dressel 1 amphorae. A date after Cunobelin's expansion eastwards is certain for the Stanfordbury and Maulden Moor burials which contained Samian. The graves may thus represent a dissemination of the Trinovantes or of Trinovantian ideas in the new enlarged Catuvellaunian kingdom. This suggestion is however, very tentative: the graves with Samian could post-date the Roman Conquest, while there is no associated dating evidence for many of the other amphorae. Some might be as early as Addedomarus or Dubnovellaunus or could again be post-conquest.

More work is needed to confirm this identification of the Trinovantes. The scientific excavation of Welwyn type graves in Essex would clarify the eastern end of the distribution, while in Hertfordshire, petrological comparison of coarse pottery on either side of the frontier might indicate whether different production centres were involved.

However, if my reasoning is correct, this historical tribe begins at last to emerge more fully into the archaeological record.

3. CAMULODUNUM: CHRONOLOGICAL AND ECONOMIC CONSIDERATIONS

Although the majority of Dressel 1 amphorae from Welwyn type graves fall within the date range 50–10 B.C., they are also present at Camulodunum, apparently in some-what later contexts. The form Camulodunum 181 (Dressel 1) comprises a full 10 per cent of all the early amphorae from the Sheepen site, which coin evidence suggests to be contemporary with Cunobelin (Hawkes and Hull, 1947).

If we take the conventional date of A.D. 10 for the foundation of Camulodunum, it is necessary to extend the date range of Dressel 1 *at least* a quarter of a century beyond the latest *titulus pictus* of 13 B.C. to account for the Sheepen material. This is possible but difficult to understand. From sometime around 16 B.C., Hellenising in-fluences began to transform the Italian amphora industry and since the Dressel 1 factories were involved in this, it is unlikely that the form would be available in quan-tity at such a late date (see p. 165). Furthermore if production persisted, it is surprising that more evidence was not found at, for example, Haltern. Arretine ware, was of course imported into Britain after it had ceased to be used by the army on the Rhine (Hawkes and Hull, 1947: 190) but it is difficult to imagine that amphorae containing best Falernian and Caecuban wine would be disposed of in a similar manner.

This apparent chronological conflict can be resolved in one of three ways.

1. Dressel 1 amphorae could have had a longer life than at present seems likely.
2. The eastwards expansion under Cunobelin and the foundation of Camulodunum could have taken place before A.D. 10. This however, would create other diffi-culties as Cunobelin's already lengthy reign would be extended to something over 40 years and there would be less time in which to fit the preceding reigns of Dubnovellaunus and Addedomarus.
3. The material could be rubbish survival from an earlier and hence Trinovantian occupation of the site.

Of these possibilities the third is to be preferred. Professor Hawkes has kindly drawn my attention to the thin occupation deposit found beneath the remains of a Period I rampart on the Sheepen site (Hawkes and Hull, 1947: 60). The sparse material from this layer was originally ascribed to Period I: 'no serious occupation of this area need be allowed for before the advent of the dyke-builders, to whom in fact these few leaving may well be assigned'. However, the amphora evidence implies that this deposit may have been a relic of much more extensive occupation of the site under the Trinovantes.

The Lexden tumulus (Laver, 1927), previously supposed to be that of Cunobelin himself, would also present a chronological difficulty if this attribution were correct. The amphorae comprise an association of Dressel 1B and Greco-Roman types, so the grave should date to the period of overlap of these forms in the last 15 years B.C. This agrees well with Ann Birchall's (1965: 254) independent suggestion of a date in the latter part of the first century B.C. on metal evidence, and with a *terminus post quem* of 17 B.C. provided by the medallion of Augustus (Laver, 1927: 251). The tumulus could antedate Cunobelin's arrival at Camulodunum, but its contents would be archaic indeed if the grave was constructed after about A.D. 40, the probable date of his death. If it is possible to name the occupant of the tomb, I would favour Addedomarus.

The economic standing of Cunobelin's kingdom is reflected in both the number and variety of amphorae from Camulodunum. Although some of the material is residual, much must be contemporary with Cunobelin and the quantity recovered contrasts markedly with the sparse fragments from the Dobunnic oppidum of Bagendon or from Atrebatic Silchester (see pp. 180, 181). The bulk of Roman trade with Britain appears to have been concentrated in the east, which lends support to Frere's (1967: 44) suggestion that Cunobelin was not anti-Roman in policy.

Finds from Mount Bures and the Lexden tumulus, suggest that Greco-Roman and South Spanish types were being imported before Cunobelin, but there can be little doubt that trade flourished after his accession. Of particular note was the commerce with the Spanish province of Baetica, from whence came fish sauces and olive oil. A vital trade link had been established and Baetican trade was to figure significantly in the economic life of Roman Britain.

*   *   *   *

As one whose work is frequently concentrated on museum collections I am acutely aware of the debt I owe to others. It is quite literally the spade-work of my predecessors which has made this study possible, and my great debt to Sir Mortimer can be gauged from the number of times I have had occasion to refer to his published works. It is thus a particular pleasure to offer this essay, imperfect though it is, as a contribution to mark his eightieth birthday.

Acknowledgements

This work would have been very difficult without the help of the many museum curators and individuals who gave me information or facilities to study material in their care. I should like to offer sincere thanks to Mr. K. J. Barton (Portsmouth), Mr. M. Biddle, Mr. J. W. Brailsford and Miss C. John (British Museum), Mr. D. T-D. Clark (Colchester), Mr. J. R. Collis, Miss M. Cr'aster (Cambridge University), Mr. A. G. Davies (Hertford), Mr. D. G. Davies (Verulamium), Dr. G. C. Dunning, Mr. L. R. Fennelly, Professor S. S. Frere (Cirencester), Mr. D. Gwatkin and Mrs. J. Greenaway (Reading), Mr. R. A. Hills, Mr. D. Kelly (Maidstone), Mr. J. Lavender (Christchurch), Sir George Meyrick, Miss L. Millard (Canterbury), Mr. R. N. Peers (Dorchester).

I am also greatly indebted to Professor B. W. Cunliffe and Mr. A. J. Parker for improving criticism of a draft of this paper.

APPENDIX

NOTES ON BRITISH IRON AGE SITES WITH AMPHORAE

I. *Counties south of the Thames*

CORNWALL

St. Mawgan in Pydar (Truro museum)

Fragments from huts dating from ? before the mid first century A.D. (Hut A) to the first half of the second century A.D. (Hut Z). Two of the sherds illustrated (Murray-Thriepland, 1956: fig. 31, 138) have been wrongly reconstructed. The handle (unstratified) is of Camulodunum 185 and hence southern Spanish, dating perhaps to roughly the first half of the first century A.D. The rim and also nos. 139 and 140 are of a type unknown in pre-Roman Britain and probably date from the latter part of the first century A.D.

DORSET

Maiden Castle (Dorchester museum)

A few small fragments of amphora body were associated with Iron C and occasionally B pottery (Wheeler, 1943: 103, 116). Four sherds from site D were sectioned. Three were similar to fabric 2 (p. 164) but contained rare shell fragments, while the fourth was of fabric 3. The vessels may have been of Dressel 1, since although the same fabrics occur in the Koan form, such vessels are rare.

Weymouth Bay

Body of a Dressel 1B amphora dredged from the sea-bed. Stamped P (Damon, 1890).

Green Island, Poole Harbour (Christchurch museum)

A rim sherd, possibly Dressel 1A and a body sherd both in fabric 1. They were associated with Iron Age pottery (mainly bead rim bowls) and shale working debris (Calkin, 1953: 53).

Hamworthy, Poole (Poole museum)

A large unstratified collection of Iron Age and Roman pottery includes six Dressel 1 handle fragments, two of which are in an atypical streaky, creamy-buff fabric. Less certainly pre-conquest are five fragments of Koan type amphorae (three bases, one shoulder, and one handle fragment) and globular amphorae, represented by four rim sherds and five handles, all unstamped.

GLOUCESTERSHIRE

Bagendon (Cirencester museum)

This site, dated between c. A.D. 20 and 50, yielded a rich collection of pottery amongst which were a few amphora sherds. The following have been examined.

1. Clifford, 1961: no. 76B. A fabric similar to that used for Camulodunum 185A, but softer and yellowish. Probably south Spanish. Two further body sherds are also present in this fabric and at least two vessels are represented in all.

2. Clifford, 1961: no. 76A. Thin sectioning reveals volcanic glass and sanidine felspar fragments suggestive of an Italian origin. This amphora was erroneously compared (Clifford, 1961: 230) with Camulodunum form 185B, which is of south Spanish origin (p. 169).

3. Five body sherds, possibly all from the same vessel, in a fine pink fabric with whiter surfaces. They are superficially similar to the finer south Spanish fabrics, but heavy mineral separation produced a flood of opaque grains making analysis difficult. It is not the same as the known south Spanish material.

4. Three body sherds possibly from the same vessel in a coarse red fabric with granitic inclusions.

HAMPSHIRE AND ISLE OF WIGHT

Hengistbury Head (Christchurch museum, British Museum, Private Possession)

All extant rim sherds are illustrated in fig. 37. Nos. 1–3, 5–12, 14 and 17 are of Dressel 1A in fabric 1 (p. 164). No. 19 is Dressel 1B in the same fabric, while nos. 13 and 15 are of the B form in fabric 3 (p. 164). No. 16, with an almost illegible stamp is intermediate between the A and B forms. Microscopically the fabric is anomalous with a 'pisolitic'-type structure. One Dressel 1A base in fabric 1 is illustrated (no. 4).

No. 18 is from a Spanish globular amphora perhaps of the first century A.D.

Further unillustrated material in the Red House Museum, Christchurch, comprises 11 Dressel 1 handle fragments or stubs, one grooved handle of south Spanish type (Camulodunum 185) and three handles from globular amphorae, one stamped ROMNI (Callender, 1965: no. 1541), another perhaps BELLCNA'PAGAEN (*cf.* Callender, 1965: no. 185D). The latter are probably of the second century A.D. A further six bases are present, three of Dressel 1, three conical. All the material is unstratified. It includes sherds from excavations by Bushe-Fox (1915), H. St. George Gray and stray finds.

Three more stamps are recorded by Bushe-Fox (1915: 53).

Owslebury

One Dressel 1 sp. handle fragment associated with saucepan pots. (Information J. R. Collis.)

Horndean (Portsmouth museum)

One Dressel 1 sp. shoulder fragment in fabric 1 associated with Iron Age pottery (Cunliffe, 1961: no. 8).

Winchester (Assize Courts)

One Dressel 1 sp. handle stub from the lower filling of a ditch. Associated with Iron Age pottery belonging perhaps to a late phase of the saucepan pot tradition. (Information M. Biddle.)

Silchester (Reading museum)

None of the amphorae from recent excavations at Silchester is certainly pre-conquest (Boon, 1969). A fragment like Camulodunum form 186 and a globular amphora rim from Claudio-Flavian levels (layer Aii) could be rubbish survivals from the earlier occupation. Another piece which may be early is a globular amphora body sherd dating from before A.D. 60. An unstratified handle of form Camulodunum 185 was also recovered.

The amphorae figured by May (1916, pl. LXVII) comprise globular vessels, Greco-Roman and one example of Camulodunum 186c, all of which may be post-conquest. One potential Dressel 1B rim is illustrated but this is unconfirmed as the specimen was not available for inspection.

Knighton, nr. Brading, Isle of Wight

Four Dressel 1A rims, two handle fragments and many body sherds associated with Iron Age pottery. (Information L. R. Fennelly.)

N

181

Gills Cliff, Ventnor, Isle of Wight (Carisbrooke Castle museum)

Amphora sherds, possibly Dressel 1, associated with Iron Age pottery including bead rim bowls (Benson, 1953).

KENT

Quarry Wood, Loose, near Maidstone (Maidstone museum)

A quantity of Iron Age pottery was recovered together with a single amphora body sherd, which bears a clear stamp EB. It is almost certainly of Dressel 1. (Information D. Kelly.)

Rose Lane, Canterbury (Canterbury museum)

The Belgic group from this site (Frere, 1954) includes three fragments in fabric 1, probably from different vessels. Although Greco-Roman vessels occur rarely in fabric 1, it would be unusual to find three of the same type associated and thus they are probably Dressel 1.

This group has been assigned to the years immediately preceding the Claudian conquest, but if Dressel 1 amphorae are present, it may date, at least in part, to before the latter years of the first century B.C.

Bridge Hill, Canterbury (Canterbury Museum)

A Dressel 1 handle and two body sherds in fabric 1, from a site producing Iron Age pottery, brooches, beads, speculum coin etc (Watson, 1963).

SOMERSET

Camerton (Taunton museum)

Amphorae occurred frequently in pre-Conquest levels. Wedlake (1958, nos. 273, 273A, 274, 275) illustrates examples, all of which appear to be of the globular type, although no. 273A is an unusual elongated variant.

II. *Counties north of the Thames*

BEDFORDSHIRE

Maulden Moor

Amphora found in 1798 together with 'several urns of different forms and sizes containing bones and ashes and fragments of the red pottery enriched with figures and other ornaments' (Lysons and Lysons, 1813: 24).

Woburn

Two Koan type Greco-Roman amphorae found at different times in the grounds of Woburn Abbey (Bedford, 1834). These are wrongly listed as Dressel 1 by Stead (1967: 60).

Stanfordbury (Cambridge University museum)

Two burials originally containing amphorae, but only one (from burial A, (Stead, 1967: 55)) now remains. This a small anomalous type which is difficult to place, but the petrology suggests a Spanish source. Dated to about the time of the Claudian conquest on associated Samian (Stead, 1967: 47; Dryden, 1845).

BUCKINGHAMSHIRE

Wavendon Heath, near Bletchley

South Spanish amphora with one handle missing (*cf.* Dressel, 9–11). Illustrated by Lysons and Lysons (1813: 24).

CAMBRIDGESHIRE

Jesus Lane, Cambridge (Cambridge University, Museum of Archaeology and Ethnology)
Body of Dressel 1 amphora. No details (Fox, 1923: 101).

Dam Hill, Trumpington (Cambridge University museum)
Dressel 1B amphora with rim and neck missing. No details (Fox, 1923: 101).

Snailwell (Cambridge University museum)
Welwyn type burial. Camulodunum 185A and two 186B amphorae associated with Gallo-Belgic imports (Lethbridge, 1953).

ESSEX

Camulodunum – Sheepen site (Colchester museum)
Dressel 1B amphorae (Camulodunum form 181) comprised 10 per cent of all amphorae from Periods I–III, but probably derive from earlier Trinovantian occupation of the site (see p. 178). Greco-Roman and south Spanish types were plentiful and may date largely from occupation during the reign of Cunobelin (Period I) though the possibility of some being residual cannot be disregarded.

Complete amphorae from the Sheepen region have not been plotted on fig. 38 as they may not have come from burials. They include the type specimens Camulodunum 186A, 182A (Colchester museum, 96.32, 97.32), another form 186A (Colchester museum, 212.30) and the type specimen Camulodunum 184 (Hawkes and Hull, 1947).

Lexden Tumulus (Colchester museum)
Amphorae from the burial are fragmentary, but as the sherds come from an area in the northern part of the grave, disturbed by an ancient opening (Laver, 1927) it is reasonable to suggest that the vessels were broken at a date subsequent to the interment. For this reason they are shown complete on fig. 38. The minimum number of vessels is as follows:

Dressel 1B   4 (fabrics 1 and 2)
Greco-Roman
   Koan   10
   Rhodian   1

The association of Dressel 1B and Greco-Roman amphorae suggests a date in about the last 15 years B.C. The absence of south Spanish vessels may be significant in a collection of this size. A possible explanation could be that the grave dates from before the establishment of contacts with Baetica. If correct it should be slightly earlier than the Mount Bures burial (p. 184).

The four Dressel 1B rims were sectioned: two were in fabric 1 and two in fabric 2.

Park Field, Lexden (Colchester museum PC. 700)
A Dressel 1B amphora with rim missing, illustrated by Hawkes and Hull (1947) as the type specimen of Camulodunum form 181. Found 1823. See Hull (1958: 252).

Lexden Park, Colchester (Colchester museum)
Two amphorae of form 186 (Hull, 1958: 252), one (Colchester museum, PC. 702) with rim and base missing.

Fitzwalter Road, Colchester (Colchester museum, 6.1964)
An almost complete amphora discovered in 1964 (Ann. Rep. Colchester and Essex museum, 1963–4). No details. The form is not accurately represented in the Camulodunum series, but it is a south Spanish vessel, close to Dressel types 9–11.

St. Clare Road, Colchester (Colchester museum 2058.31)

The type specimen Camulodunum 185A (this paper fig. 35, 5) found in a garden in St. Clare Road associated with a pedestal beaker and terra rubra. A Dressel IB rim sherd (Colchester museum 2059.31) stamped HI [E]? recorded by Hawkes and Hull (1947: 214) comes from the same locality.

Colchester region – no provenance (Colchester museum)

A complete amphora of form Camulodunum 185A; also the type specimen Camulodunum 183A (Hawkes and Hull, 1947).

Danbury, Maldon (Colchester museum)

A pair of Dressel IB amphorae in fabric 1 found together. No details.

Lindsell (Saffron Waldon museum)

A Dressel IB amphora in fabric 1 with rim missing. Associated with a cremation (Fox, 1923: 101).

Thaxted (Saffron Waldon museum)

A Dressel IB amphora in fabric 1 with rim missing. No details (Fox, 1923: 101).

Maldon (Colchester museum 2668.13)

A Dressel IB rim in fabric 1 with traces of pitch. Stamped PE.

Heybridge (Colchester museum, PC.699)

Koan type amphora in fabric 3 (*cf.* Dressel 1). Type specimen Camulodunum 183B (this paper, fig. 35, 3). No details.

Stratford St. Mary (Colchester museum, 437.32)

Koan type amphora in fabric 1 (*cf.* Dressel 1). Type specimen Camulodunum 183C. No details.

Mount Bures

Welwyn type grave containing a Dressel IB body and four south Spanish amphorae similar to Dressel 9–11, associated with a variety of grave goods including Gallo-Belgic pottery. The grave was probably only partially excavated (Smith, 1852). The association of Gallo-Belgic pottery and Dressel IB body suggests a date in the last 15 years B.C. A pre-Cunobelin date might also explain why the south Spanish amphorae cannot be precisely matched in the Camulodunum type series, if Smith's drawing is accurate. Like the Lexden tumulus, the burial dates somewhere between roughly 15 and 1 B.C. The differences between the two graves could be explained by assuming that the Lexden tumulus belongs to the earlier part of the period while Mount Bures is later.

HERTFORDSHIRE

Crookhams, Welwyn Garden City

Sherds of at least two Dressel 1 amphorae found associated with coarse and Gallo-Belgic pottery. In a gully discovered in a rescue excavation (Rook, 1968).

Verulamium (Verulamium museum)

Wheeler and Wheeler (1936, fig. 13, 29) illustrate the rim and neck of an amphora in a buff fabric close to that used for globular amphorae. This type, which occurs at Oberaden (Loeschcke, 1942: type 84) and Haltern (Loeschcke, 1909: type 71), may be the ancestor of the globular amphora.

Welwyn, Mardlebury (Hertford museum)
Body of a Dressel 1B amphora in fabric 1. No details.

Welwyn (British Museum)

Burial A:

Dressel 1B amphora in fabric 1, stamped SOS on collar (British Museum, 1911, 12–8.1). Associated with rich metal work and pottery. See Smith (1912) for details.

Burial B:

Five Dressel 1B amphorae, one stamped AA on collar (British Museum, 1911, 12–8, 15–19). Associated with rich metalwork and pottery. See Smith (1912) for details. Three of the unstamped amphorae were sectioned (nos. 17–19) and are of fabric 1.

Welwyn Garden City (British Museum)
Five Dressel 1B amphorae from a rich burial. See Stead (1967) for details. Four vessels examined. Stead, 1967: fig. 5, 1, 4 and 5 are in fabric 1, while fig. 5, 3 is in fabric 3.

Hertford Heath (British Museum)
One Dressel 1B amphora (this paper fig. 35, 2) from a rich burial. Also another rim and neck found nearby. See Holmes and Frend (1957) for details.

Little Hadham
Dressel 1 amphora now lost. See Stead (1967: 60).

Westmill
Three amphorae possibly Dressel 1. See Stead (1967: 60).

Baldock
Dressel 1 amphora in Welwyn type grave (Stead, 1968).

MIDDLESEX
Stanmore Park (British Museum)
Complete Koan type amphora with stamp MAR OF on spike. The fabric is identical with Dressel 1 fabric 2 (see p. 164) (Brailsford, 1964: fig. 17, 11).

BIBLIOGRAPHY

Allen, D. F. 1944. 'The Belgic Dynasties of Britain and their coins', *Archaeologia*, 90, 1–46.

André, J. 1959. 'Trois amphores romaines "pêchées" au large des côtes Morbihannaises', *Ann. Bretagne*, 66, 64–68.

André, J. 1961. 'Notes d'archaeologie sous-marine: amphore romaine au large de Belle-Ile', *Ann. Bretagne*, 68, 95–97.

Bedford, Duke of. 1834. 'Roman amphora found in the park at Woburn Abbey', *Archaeologia*, 25, 606–7.

Benoit, F. 1957. 'Typologie et épigraphie amphoriques, les marques de Sestius', *Riv. Studi Liguri*, 23, 247–85.

Benoit, F. 1960. 'Nouvelles épaves de Provence (II)', *Gallia*, 18, 41–56.

Benoit, F. 1961. 'L'épave du Grand Congloué a Marseille', *Gallia*, Suppl, 14.

Benoit, F. 1962. 'Nouvelles épaves de Provence (III)', *Gallia*, 20, 147–76.

Benoit, F. 1968. 'Résultats historiques des fouilles d'Entremont, 1946–47', *Gallia*, 26, 1–31.

Benson, G. C. 1953. 'A Belgic occupation site at Gills Cliff, Ventnor', *Proc. I.O.W. Nat. Hist. and Arch. Soc.*, 4, 303–11.

Birchall, A. 1965. 'The Aylesford-Swarling Culture: the problem of the Belgae reconsidered', *Proc. Prehist. Soc.*, 31, 241–367.

Bonsor, G. E. 1931. *The archaeological expedition along the Guadalquivir, 1889–1901*, New York.

Boon, G. C. 1969. 'Belgic and Roman Silchester: the excavations of 1954–58 with an excursus on the early history of Calleva', *Archaeologia*, 102, 1–82.

Bouscaras, A. 1954. 'Recherches sous-marines au large d'Agde', *Riv. Studi Liguri*, 20, 47–54.

Brailsford, J. W., 1964. *Guide to the antiquities of Roman Britain*, British Museum, London.

Bushe-Fox, J. P. 1915. 'Excavations at Hengistbury Head, Hampshire in 1911–12', *Rep. Res. Comm. Soc. Ant.*, London, 3.

Calkin, J. B. 1953. 'Kimmeridge coal-money', *Proc. Dorset Nat. Hist. & Arch. Soc.*, 75, 45–71.

Callender, M. H. 1965. *Roman Amphorae*, Oxford.

Clark-Maxwell, W. G. 1899. 'The Roman towns in the valley of the Baetis between Cordoba and Seville', *Arch. J.*, 56, 245–305.

Clifford, E. M. 1961. *Bagendon – a Belgic oppidum*, Cambridge.

Collot, M. 1918. *Pro Alesia*, 4, 190.

Cunliffe, B. W. 1961. 'Report on a Belgic and Roman site at the Causeway, Horndean, 1959', *Procs. Hants Field Club*, 22, 25–9.

Damon, R. 1890. 'Roman amphora or wine jar', *Procs. Dorset Nat. Hist. & Arch. Soc.*, 11, 88–90.

Dressel, H. 1899. *Corpus Inscriptionum Latinarum*, XV, Pars 1, Berlin.

Dryden, Sir H. 1845. 'Roman and Romano-British remains at and near Shefford, Co. Beds', *Pubs. Cambs. Ant. Soc.*, 1, no. 8.

Ettlinger, E. 1960. 'Review of Uenze, 1958, Frührömische Amphoren als Zeitmarken im Spätlatène', *Germania*, 38, 440.

Fox, C. 1923. *The archaeology of the Cambridge region*, Cambridge.

Frank, T. 1940. *An economic survey of Ancient Rome. V, Rome and Italy of the Empire*, Baltimore.

Frere, S. S. 1954. 'Canterbury excavations, summer 1946: The Rose Lane Sites', *Arch. Cant.*, 68, 101–43.

Frere, S. S. 1967. *Britannia: A history of Roman Britain*, London.

Giot, P. R. 1960. *Brittany*, London.

Goldman, H. 1950. *Excavations at Gözlü Kule, Tarsus*, 2 vols, Princeton.

Grace, V. 1961. *Amphoras and the ancient wine trade*, American School at Athens.

Hawkes, C. F. C., and Hull, M. R. 1947. 'Camulodunum', *Rep. Res. Comm. Soc. Ant.*, London, 14.

Holmes, J., and Frend, W. H. C. 1957. 'A Belgic Chieftains Grave on Hertford Heath', *Trans East Herts. Arch. Soc.*, 14, 1–19.

Hull, M. R. 1958. 'Roman Colchester', *Rep. Res. Comm. Soc. Ant.*, London, 20.

Jiménez Cisneros, M. 1958. 'Beobachtungen in einem römischen Töpferbezirk bei Puerto Real, Prov. Cadiz', *Germania*, 36, 469–75.

Joncheray, J. P. 1970. *Classification des amphores découvertes lors de fouilles sous-marines*, Gap.

Kenyon, K. M. 1948. 'Excavations at the Jewry Wall Site, Leicester', *Rep. Res. Comm. Soc. Ant.*, London, 15.

Lais, R. 1943. 'Über die Herkunft römischer Amphoren aus Latènesiedlungen am Hoch – und Ober-Rhein', *Germania*, 27, 50.

Lamboglia, N. 1952. 'La nave romana di Albenga', *Riv. Studi Liguri*, 18, 131–236.

Lamboglia, N. 1955. 'Sulla cronologia delle anfore romane de età republicana', *Riv. Studi Liguri*, 21, 252–60.

Laver, P. G. 1927. 'The excavation of a tumulus at Lexden, Colchester', *Archaeologia*, 76, 241–54.

Lethbridge, T. C. 1953. 'Burial of an Iron Age warrior at Snailwell', *Procs. Cambs. Ant. Soc.*, 47, 25–37.

Loeschcke, S. 1909. 'Keramische Funde in Haltern', *Mitt. Alt. – Kommission für Westfalen*, 5, 101.

Loeschcke, S. 1942. In Chr. Albrecht *Das römische Lager in Oberaden II: Die römische und belgische Keramik*, Dortmund.

Lysons, D. and S. 1813. *Magna Britannia*, vol. 1.

Mabesoone, J. M. 1963. 'Observations on the sedimentology and geomorphology of the Guadalete drainage area (Cadiz, Spain)', *Geol. Mijnbouw*, 42, 309–28.

Maréchal, J. R. 1966. 'L'application des méthods scientifiques de laboratoire a l'étude de la céramique, de la métallurgie et de la verrerie romaines', *Melanges d'Archéolgie et d'Histoire offerts à André Piganiol*, 1, 123–154.

May, T. 1916. *The pottery found at Silchester*, Reading.

Murray-Threipland, L. 1956. 'An excavation at St. Mawgan-in-Pyder, North Cornwall', *Arch. J.*, 113, 33–83.

Peacock, D. P. S. 1967. 'The heavy mineral analysis of pottery: a preliminary report', *Archaeometry*, 10, 97–100.

Pélichet, E. 1946. 'A propos des amphores romaines trouvées à Nyon', *Zeit. Schweiz Arch. und Kunstgeschichte*, 8, 189–209.

Ponsich, M., and Tarradell, M. 1965. *Garum et industries antiques de salaison dans la Mèditerranèe occidentale*, Paris.

Rice-Holmes, T. 1907. *Ancient Britain and the Invasion of Julius Caesar*, Oxford.

Richmond, I. A. 1968. *Hod Hill*, vol. II, London.

Ritterling, E. 1913. 'Das Frührömische Lager bei Hofheim im Taunus'. *Ann. Verein für Nassauische Altertumskunde und Geschichtsforschung*, 40.

Rook, A. G. 1968. 'Investigation of a Belgic occupation site at Crookhams, Welwyn Garden City', *Hertfordshire Arch.*, 1, 51–65.

Schoene, R. 1871. 'Tituli vasis fictilibus', In *Corpus Inscriptionum Latinarum*. Ed. C. Zangemeister, vol. 4, *Inscriptiones Parietariae Pompeianae*, Berlin.

Smith, C. R. 1852. *Collectanea Antiqua*, vol. II.

Smith, R. A. 1912. 'On Late Celtic Antiquities discovered at Welwyn, Herts', *Archaeologia*, 63, 1–30.

Sotomayor, M. 1969. 'Hornos romanos de ánforas en Algeciras', *X° Congreso nacional de arqueologia*, Mahon, 1967, 389–99.

Stead, I. M. 1967. 'A La Tène III burial at Welwyn Garden City', *Archaeologia*, 101, 1–62.

Stead, I. M. 1968. 'A La Tène III burial at The Tene, Baldock, Hertfordshire', *Ant. J.*, 48, 306.

Stead, I. M. 1969. 'Verulamium, 1966–8', *Antiquity*, 43, 45–52.

Stieren, A. 1932. 'Römische Töpferöfen im Lager Haltern', *Germania*, 16, 112–5.

Tchernia, A. 1964. 'Amphores et marques d'amphores de Bétique à Pompei et à Stabies', *Mél. d'Arch. et d'Hist. École Franç de Rome*, 76, 419–49.

Tchernia, A. 1967. 'Les amphores romaines et l'histoire économique', *Journ. des Savants* (Oct.-Dec.), 224.

Tchernia, A. 1969. 'Recherches archéologiques sous-marines', *Gallia*, 27, 465–500.

Uenze, O. 1958. *Frührömische Amphoren als Zeitmarken im Spätlatène*, Marburg.

Ulbert, G. 1960. 'Die römische Keramik aus den Legionslager Augsburg-Oberhausen', *Materialhefte zur Bayerischen Vorg*, 14.

Watson, M. B. 1963. 'Iron Age site on Bridge Hill', *Arch. Cant.*, 78, 185–8.

Wedlake, W. J. 1958. *Excavations at Camerton, Somerset*, Bath.

Wheeler, R. E. M. 1943. 'Maiden Castle, Dorset', *Rep. Res. Comm. Soc. Ant.*, London, 12.

Wheeler, R. E. M. 1946. 'Arikamedu: an Indo-Roman trading-station on the east coast of India', *Ancient India*, 2, 17–124.

Wheeler, R. E. M., and Richardson, K. M. 1957. 'Hill-forts of Northern France', *Rep. Res. Comm. Soc. Ant.*, London, 19.

Wheeler, R. E. M., and Wheeler, T. V. 1928. 'The Roman amphitheatre at Caerleon, Monmouthshire', *Archaeologia*, 78, 111–218.

Wheeler, R. E. M., and Wheeler, T. V. 1936. 'Verulamium: a Belgic and two Roman cities', *Rep. Res. Comm. Soc. Ant.*, London, 11.

Zevi, F. 1966. 'Appunti sulle anfore romane', *Archaeologia Classica*, 18, 207–47.

HILL-FORTS IN ACTION

By A. L. F. RIVET

SUMMARY

A summary is given of all Caesar's accounts of attacks on hill-forts and Roman works during the Gallic Wars and an attempt is made to distinguish between normal Celtic methods of attack and defence and those which the Gauls learned from the Romans. It is suggested that what they learned may have affected the alterations made to British hill-forts in the period between Caesar and Claudius. Attention is also drawn to the inadequacy of some modern translations of Caesar for this purpose.

In my concluding address to the Conference, I mentioned two ways in which a study of the classical Greek and Roman authors can assist us in our understanding of Iron Age hill-forts, the one general and the other particular. In general, I suggested that what we are told of the behaviour of the Celtic nobility[1] might indicate that display as well as utility entered into their design and that elaborate gates, for example, might be regarded partly as 'boasting platforms'. More particularly, I suggested that closer attention should be given to accounts of hill-forts in action. It is the purpose of this paper to amplify this second point.

Our chief corpus of such actions is, of course, supplied by Caesar's *De Bello Gallico*, but this, no less than evidence from excavation, needs to be handled with due regard to stratigraphy. Caesar himself remarks on the readiness with which the Gauls learned and adopted Roman ways of fighting,[2] and his accounts of the greatest sieges, of Gergovia, Alesia and Uxellodunum, though important in themselves, come too late in the story to tell us very much about 'normal' Celtic methods. Fortunately he describes plenty of others, which took place earlier, and at the beginning of Book II (II:6) he makes a general statement, as follows:

'The Gauls and the Belgae use the same method of attack. They surround the whole circuit of the walls with a large number of men and shower it with stones from all sides, so that the defences are denuded of men. Then they form *testudo*, set fire to the gates and undermine the walls. They began to do this (he goes on) without difficulty on this occasion (i.e. at Bibrax).'

This passage, which is obviously of great importance to us, has suffered badly at the hands of the editors. A few have suggested, on stylistic grounds, that the whole of it is an interpolation[3] – though it is difficult to see who could have inserted it, or why. More important, from a very early date they have jibbed at *portas succendunt* ('they set fire to the gates') and substituted *portas succedunt* ('they come up to the gates');[4] but

---

[1] The relevant texts, with translations and comments, are conveniently collected in Tierney (1960).

[2] Caesar VII:22: *ut est summae genus sollertiae atque ad omnia imitanda et efficienda quae ab quoque traduntur aptissimum.*

[3] E.g. Meusel, quoted by Rice Homes, followed by Kraner and Dittenberger (1960) and Seel (Teubner, 5th edn., 1961).

[4] E.g. Aldus (1518); Oudendorp (1737); Delphin (1819); Rice Holmes (1914); Edwards (Loeb, 1917); Merguet (1961), s.v. *succedo* (where the fact that it *is* a conjecture is not mentioned).

having done this, they are confronted with the grammatical difficulty that the simple accusative *portas* will not do in Caesar, so that this too has been emended – by some to *portis*,[5] by one to *propius*[6] and by one by simple deletion.[7] In actual fact the manuscripts are completely unanimous in giving the reading *portas succendunt*,[8] and it is unfortunate that none of the English translations in common use follows it.[9] The argument seems to depend mainly on the alleged impossibility of the action.[10] Yet Caesar himself burnt the gates of Cenabum (No. 18 in list) and the Gauls used fire against the *hiberna* of Q. Cicero (No. 14) and against the Roman siegeworks at Avaricum (No. 22) and Uxellodunum (No. 30). There is no doubt that fire, in one form or another, was a normal weapon.

A rather more difficult problem, not discussed by the editors, is posed by the words *testudine facta*. This manoeuvre, whereby a number of men advanced with their shields locked together, in 'tortoise' formation, was a commonplace of Roman warfare, but its full success required both a high degree of training and the use of standard rectangular shields.[11] The Gauls are said to have used it at Alesia (No. 28), but it may be that Caesar only means that they were advancing with their shields held over their heads. This sort of *testudo* needs to be distinguished from the shed-like structures, also called *testudines*, which they built and used against the *hiberna* of Q. Cicero (No. 14) – something which they clearly borrowed from the Romans.

Another device which the Gauls were using at an early stage was that of filling up ditches, presumably to create causeways over which the attackers could advance. They are first represented as doing this in the attack by the Alpine tribes on the *hiberna* of Ser. Galba at Martigny (No. 5), and it is mentioned in four other engagements (Nos. 7, 14, 15 and 28). Two variations appear: in one (No. 7) simple bundles of brushwood (*sarmenta virgultaque*) seem to have been used, but in the other (No. 28) wattles (*crates*) are referred to.[12] Whether this was a truly native form of attack we do not know, since it is only at Bibrax that we have details of a Gaulish assault on a Gaulish, as opposed to a Roman, work. But although P. Crassus used it in his attack on the pseudo-Roman camp of the Aquitani (No. 9), Caesar nowhere represents it as a borrowing. It could have been a contributory cause of the spread of multivallation.[13]

Of more limited application, but evidently a native as well as a Roman practice, is the use of tunnelling. In the Gallic Wars this was employed by the Sotiates (No. 8) and by the Bituriges (No. 22), and in each case Caesar attributes it to the fact that

---

[5] E.g. Oudendorp (1737).

[6] Klotz (1910), 243–4 and in Teubner (4th edn., 1952).

[7] Kraner (1961).

[8] So Dinter (Teubner, 1st edn., 1890); du Pontet (O.C.T., 1900); Constans (Budé, 1947); Rambaud (Presses Universitaires, 1965). The only slight indication to the contrary is that the late 13th century translator into Greek, cited by Oudendorp, evidently read *succedunt*: he renders it τῶν πυλῶν τῆς πόλεως ἐπιβάντες.

[9] So Bohn (1873) has 'advance to the gates'; Loeb (Edwards, 1917), 'move up to the gates'; Penguin (Handford, 1951), 'move close up'; Mentor (Warner, 1960), 'move up to the gates'.

[10] So Meusel, quoted by Rice Holmes in his note on the passage: '*Succendunt* is obviously impossible.'

[11] On the adoption of the rectangular shield by the Romans see Webster (1969), 22 n.

[12] This passage has attracted comment and (inevitably) emendation: see Rice Holmes (1914) on VII: 79:4.

[13] As I suggested in a paper given to the Prehistoric Society Conference on European Hill-forts, 17th-19th April, 1959.

the Gauls involved were skilled miners. He himself used it at Avaricum (No. 22) and Uxellodunum (No. 30).

These, then, are some of the tactics which the Celts were using at the beginning of the campaigns but, as already indicated, they were quick to adopt Roman methods. At Noviodunum Suessionum (No. 2), in 57 B.C., they were amazed by the Roman mantlets and siegeworks, which they had never seen nor heard of before, and later in the same year they were astonished when they saw a Roman siege tower actually begin to move against the *oppidum* of the Atuatuci (No. 4). But already in 54 B.C. the Nervii were using circumvallation against the *hiberna* of Q. Cicero (No. 14), although they lacked the right tools for the job, and they also employed towers and ladders; and by the time of Avaricum (No. 22), in 52 B.C., the Gauls seem to have mastered the whole Roman armoury. To assist them in this they had the help not only of Roman prisoners (No. 14), but also of Spaniards who had fought against Pompey under Sertorius: in one case (No. 9) these men designed and constructed a camp on the Roman model, complete with a *porta decumana*.

All of this has interesting implications for us in Britain, and it would not be unreasonable to attribute some of the alterations which were made to British hill-forts in the last century of independence to the experience of the Gallic Wars. Commius, for example, had seen those wars from both sides of the hill, and there must have been many like him. In the meantime, of course, the Romans too had improved their methods, and it is interesting that, so far as we know, they never had to resort to circumvallation in the course of the Claudian wars of conquest. This may reflect the lower degree of urbanisation achieved in Britain, with a smaller concentration of population. There is little doubt that Caesar's figures for Gaul, like those of any other writer of war communiqués, are considerably inflated but, as Rice Holmes pointed out,[14] the fact that Caesar could allocate one prisoner to each man in a force of some 50,000 does indicate that a very large number of people were involved at Alesia (No. 28) – many more than can have been the case anywhere in Britain. Caesar's contemptuous description of the so-called *oppidum* of Cassivellaunus (No. 12) is well known; but it is also worthy of note that the place which he attacked in Kent (? Bigbury, No. 11) is not given even this degree of recognition – it is simply a place (*locus*) in the woods which had fortifications (*munitiones*). By contrast, the towns of the Bituriges (No. 21) could be called not merely *oppida*, but actually *urbes*.

The attached list includes all the attacks on hill-forts and Roman camps which are described by Caesar, arranged in chronological order. Although some of the identifications are doubtful,[15] it nevertheless seems worth while to supply map references for them, to assist the interested reader to study them on the ground; for Britain National Grid References are given, for Gaul the reference is to the Michelin 1/200,000 map, in the form sheet/fold. In the summaries I have tried to bring out everything which bears on the actual methods of fighting used. It hardly needs to be stated that these summaries are no substitute for a reading of Caesar himself; but from what has been

---

[14] See his note (1914) on VII: 71: 2.

[15] I am grateful to Mr. A. H. A. Hogg for assistance with some of them. But neither he nor I have visited them all.

said above it should also be clear that it is Caesar who needs to be read, not his editors or translators.[16]

No. 1
Date: 57 B.C.
Reference in Caesar: II:6–7
Place: Bibrax, an *oppidum* of the Remi
Probable identification: ?Vieux-Laon, St. Thomas (Aisne)
        or ?Vieux-Reims, Guignicourt (Aisne)
Map reference: 56/5
    or 56/6
Summary. Belgae began attack by the 'normal' method (see text). Caesar relieved Iccius and the Remi by sending in Numidian and Cretan archers and by diversionary attacks.

No. 2
Date: 57 B.C.
Reference in Caesar: II:12
Place: Noviodunum, an *oppidum* of the Suessiones
Probable identification: Pommiers (Aisne)
Map reference: 56/4
Summary. Roman direct assault repelled because of the width of the ditch and the height of the wall. Caesar built a camp, brought up mantlets, piled earth (?into the ditch or as a mound?) and built towers; whereupon the Suessiones, alarmed (*permoti*) by the scale of his preparations (for they had never seen nor heard of such things) surrendered.

No. 3
Date: 57 B.C.
Reference in Caesar: II:13
Place: Bratuspantium, an *oppidum* of the Bellovaci
Probable identification: Nr. Beauvais (Oise)
Map reference: 52/17
Summary. Surrendered without a fight.

No. 4
Date: 57 B.C.
Reference in Caesar: II:29–33
Place: *Oppidum Atuatucorum*
Probable identification: Hastédon, St. Servais (Namur), Belgium
Map reference: B.2/19
Summary. Promontory fort, protected by steep cliffs on all sides but one, where not more than 200 feet was defended by a high 'double wall' (*duplici muro*), on which the Atuatuci had placed heavy rocks and sharpened stakes. They had abandoned all their other *oppida* and *castella* and concentrated here. At first they made sorties, but Caesar shut them in with a wall 12 feet high and 15 miles [*sic*] in circumference. He then brought up mantlets, constructed a

---

[16] It is too easy to be misled. As a further example, the Penguin edition interprets the *concilium* at Alesia (no. 28) as an 'assembly'. This suggests an unlikely degree of democracy and it seems fundamentally improbable that Critognatus would have dared to suggest cannibalism quite so publicly.

siege-mound and built a tower some distance away. This provoked jeers from the Atuatuci, but when they saw it actually move, they were alarmed (*commoti*) and surrendered, throwing their arms into the ditch and opening their gates. However, they had treacherously kept some arms and at night they attacked the siegeworks. The Romans, whom Caesar had kept outside 'lest they should do injury to the inhabitants', were on the alert, killed 4,000 and drove the rest back inside. On the next day the gates, now undefended, were broken down and 53,000 people [*sic*] were sold into slavery.

No. 5
Date: 57 B.C.
Reference in Caesar: III:1–6
Place: Octodurus, *hiberna legionis XII* (Ser. Galba)
Probable identification: Martigny (Valais), Switzerland
Map reference: 74/9
Summary. Site in a valley overlooked by high ground. Seduni and Veragri attacked by hurling spears and stones, then by breaking down the palisade and filling up the ditch (*vallum scindere et fossas complere*). After a defensive rest, the Romans broke them with a charge, killing 10,000 out of 30,000. But Galba evacuated the position.

No. 6
Date: 56 B.C.
Reference in Caesar: III:12–14
Place: *Oppida* of the Veneti
Probable identification: Various, but evidently *not* all cliff castles
Map reference: 58 and 63
Summary. 'The sites of the *oppida* of the Veneti were generally such that, being placed at the end of spits and promontories (*in extremis lingulis promunturiisque*), there was no approach to them on foot when the tide had rushed in from the open sea, which regularly happens twice every 12 hours, nor by ships, because when the tide ebbed they were caught on the shoals. Thus in either case the storming of the *oppida* was made difficult. And if ever the Veneti did happen to be overpowered by the scale of our works – when the sea had been shut out by huge dams (*aggere et molibus*) and these had been brought level with the walls of the *oppidum* – and began to despair of their chances, then they carried off all their property to the next *oppida* and there again defended themselves with the same advantages of position. For a large part of the summer they did this the more easily because our ships were held up by storms . . . (here follows the description of the Venetic ships) . . . When several (*compluribus*) of their *oppida* had been stormed, Caesar realised that his labour was in vain and that the enemy could not be prevented from escaping nor harmed by the capture of their *oppida*, so he decided to await the arrival of his fleet.'

No. 7
Date: 56 B.C.
Reference in Caesar: III:18–19
Place: *Castra* of Q. Titurius Sabinus
Probable identification: (In the territory of the Venelli – i.e. Cotentin peninsula)
Map reference: 54/?
Summary. Camp well sited at the top of a slope a mile long. Gauls under Viridovix collected fascines of brushwood and bushes (*sarmentis virgultisque collectis*) to fill up the Roman ditches, but their burdens put them at a disadvantage and a Roman sortie from two gates broke them.

No. 8
Date: 56 B.C.
Reference in Caesar: III:21
Place: *Oppidum Sotiatium*
Probable identification: ?Sos (Lot-et-Garonne)
Map reference: 79/13
Summary. P. Crassus attacked with mantlets and towers. The Sotiates replied with sorties and by driving galleries (*cunicula*) under the Roman siege-mound and mantlets 'in which the Aquitanians are by far the most skilled, because there are copper mines (*aerariae secturaeque*) in many places in their territory.'

No. 9
Date: 56 B.C.
Reference in Caesar: III:23–26
Place: *Castra* of the Vocates and Tarusates
Probable identification: Unlocated
Map reference: 78, 79, 82
Summary. The leaders of the Aquitanians were men from Spain who had fought under Sertorius and were considered masters of military science: they chose their sites, fortified their *castra* and tried to cut off Crassus's supplies in the Roman manner (*consuetudine populi Romani*), hoping thereby to force him to withdraw. He began the attack by filling up the ditch and clearing the ramparts with missiles; but his cavalry reported that the rear of the camp, near the *porta decumana* [*sic*], was not so well fortified and his reserve cohorts broke in there. The total enemy strength is given as 50,000.

No. 10
Date: 55 B.C.
Reference in Caesar: IV:14
Place: *Castra* of the Germans (Usipetes and Tencteri)
Probable identification: Unlocated, but west of the lower Rhine
Map reference: ?
Summary. This camp contained baggage wagons (*carros impedimentaque*) and women and children. Caesar took it with a rush.

No. 11
Date: 54 B.C.
Reference in Caesar: V:9
Place: Fortification of the Britons
Probable identification: Bigbury, Harbledown, Kent
Map reference: N.G.R. TR117575
Summary. A place in woods 'excellently fortified naturally and artificially, which they had previously prepared, it seemed, for an internal war (*domestici belli causa*); for all the entrances had been blocked by felled trees laid close together' (it is not called *oppidum*, nor *castra*, nor *castellum*). The VII legion took it by forming *testudo* and throwing a mound against the fortifications.

194

No. 12
Date: 54 B.C.
Reference in Caesar: V:21
Place: *Oppidum Cassivellauni*
Probable identification: Devil's Dyke, Wheathampstead, Herts.
Map reference: N.G.R. TL186133
Summary. 'The Britons call it an *oppidum* when they have fortified with a rampart and ditch dense woods where they are accustomed to gather to avoid an enemy attack'; again it was 'excellently fortified naturally and artificially'. Caesar took it with an assault from two sides and the Britons withdrew on another side. Many cattle were found in it.

No. 13
Date: 54 B.C.
Reference in Caesar: V:26–37
Place: *Hiberna* of Sabinus and Cotta at Atuatuca
Probable identification: Tongres (Limbourg), Belgium
Map reference: B.3/15
Summary. Attacked by Eburones under Ambiorix and Catuvolcus, but after a Roman cavalry sortie they withdrew to parley. Having persuaded the Romans to leave the camp (despite the misgivings of Cotta), they ambushed them. Such few Romans as could regain the camp committed suicide.

No. 14
Date: 54 B.C.
Reference in Caesar: V:38–49
Place: *Hiberna* of Q. Cicero in country of the Nervii
Probable identification: Nr. Bavai (Nord)
Map reference: 53/5
Summary. Having cut off a timber-collecting party, the Eburones, Atuatuci and Nervii, with their clients, tried an immediate assault, but were beaten off. During the night Cicero completed his defences and built 120 wooden towers. Next day the Gauls attacked again and filled in the Roman ditch. Similar attacks followed for some days, while the Romans used the nights to prepare stakes with fire-hardened points (*praeustae sudes*) and palisade stakes (*pila muralia*) and to improve the towers. Having failed to persuade Cicero to withdraw, the Gauls surrounded the *hiberna* with a rampart 10 feet high and a ditch 15 feet wide. 'They had learnt this method from our practice in previous years and were instructed by some prisoners from our army; but having no supply of iron tools (*ferramenta*) suited to the task, they had to cut the turfs with their swords and remove the earth with their hands and cloaks. Their large numbers (later given as 60,000) could be gauged by the fact that in less than three hours they completed a fortification 3(?) miles long; and in the next few days, instructed by the same prisoners, they began to build towers equal in height to the rampart and to make grappling-hooks (*falces*) and sappers' huts (*testudines*).' On the 7th day, in a high wind, they began throwing hot sling-bullets of softened clay and fire darts (*ferventis fusili ex argilla glandis fundis et fervefacta iacula*). These set fire to the thatched buildings inside the *hiberna* and the Gauls began to move up their towers and *testudines* and to climb the rampart with ladders. The Romans did not waver and killed many Gauls 'because they crowded close to the foot

of the rampart and those behind prevented those in front from retreating'; and when the Gauls brought a tower up close, they cleared it with stones and set it on fire. Eventually Cicero got a message through to Caesar, who assembled a relief force, and the Gauls raised the siege.

No. 15
Date: 54 B.C.
Reference in Caesar: V:49–51
Place: Caesar's small *castra*
Probable identification: Nr. Bavai (Nord)
Map reference: 53/5
Summary. Caesar deliberately made the camp small (though it held 7,000 men, without baggage) and blocked the gates to simulate panic, thereby luring the Gauls into an unfavourable position. They threw weapons (*tela*) into the camp and called on his men to surrender. Then, not realising how lightly the gates were blocked, some began to cut at the rampart by hand while others filled up the ditches. Caesar then routed them with sallies from all the gates.

No. 16
Date: 53 B.C.
Reference in Caesar: VI:36–41
Place: Reused *hiberna* of Sabinus and Cotta at Atuatuca
Probable identification: Tongres (Limbourg), Belgium
Map reference: B.3/15
Summary. Camp manned by untried troops under Q. Cicero. While 5 cohorts and 300 convalescents were out foraging, German cavalry made an attack on the *porta decumana* so suddenly that the merchants who had gathered under the rampart had no chance of escape. Seeing that the Roman force was small, they then attacked from all sides and routed some of the forage party, but when the Roman defences were properly manned they withdrew.

No. 17
Date: 52 B.C.
Reference in Caesar: VII:11
Place: Vellaunodunum, an *oppidum* of the Senones
Probable identification: ?Le Donjon, Triguères (Loiret)
Map reference: 65/3
Summary. Caesar built a circumvallation round it in two days, and on the third it surrendered.

No. 18
Date: 52 B.C.
Reference in Caesar: VII:11
Place: Cenabum, an *oppidum* of the Carnutes
Probable identification: Orléans (Loiret)
Map reference: 65/16
Summary. Caesar arrived too late in the day to attack it. During the night the inhabitants began to leave it by a bridge over the Loire, but Caesar burnt the gates and sent in the troops he had held ready. Very few of the Carnutes escaped because of the narrowness of the bridge and the streets.

No. 19
Date: 52 B.C.
Reference in Caesar: VII:9–12
Place: Gorgobina, an *oppidum* of the Boii
Probable identification: ?Dun-les-Places (Nièvre)
Map reference: 65/16
Summary. Attacked by Vercingetorix, who abandoned the siege to relieve Noviodunum. No details.

No. 20
Date: 52 B.C.
Reference in Caesar: VII:12–13
Place: Noviodunum, an *oppidum* of the Bituriges
Probable identification: Nr. Neuvy-sur-Barangeon (Cher)
Map reference: 64/20
Summary. When Caesar began the attack, the Bituriges offered surrender, but when they saw the advance guard of Vercingetorix's forces they began to take up arms again, shut the gates and man the walls. The centurions who were in the *oppidum* seized the gates and evacuated their men safely. After Caesar had defeated the relief column, the Bituriges again surrendered.

No. 21
Date: 52 B.C.
Reference in Caesar: VII:14–15
Place: More than 20 towns of the Bituriges
Probable identification: Various
Map reference: 64, 65, 68, 69
Summary. The advice of Vercingetorix was to deny supplies to the Romans by burning all villages and farms (*vicos atque aedificia*) within range of foragers and to burn 'all *oppida* which were not made completely impregnable by their fortifications and situation . . . More than 20 *urbes* of the Bituriges were burnt in one day. The same thing happened in the other *civitates* and fires could be seen in all directions.'

No. 22
Date: 52 B.C.
Reference in Caesar: VII:15–28
Place: Avaricum, an *oppidum* of the Bituriges
Probable identification: Bourges (Cher)
Map reference: 69/1
Summary. Avaricum was not burnt because, the Bituriges argued, it was strong and 'it was about the fairest city of all Gaul, the defence and pride of their nation.' Its wall was a *murus Gallicus* (fully described in VII:23). Because it was largely surrounded by river and marsh (and the Gauls had broken down the causeways over the marsh) Caesar could not circumvallate it, but he built a siege mound and two towers and brought up mantlets. His operations were hindered by the success of Vercingetorix in denying him supplies and by the tactics of the defenders, largely imitating those of the Romans: they lassoed the Roman hooks and pulled them in with windlasses; they undermined the Roman mound with galleries 'the more cleverly because they have great iron mines and are thoroughly familiar with all kinds of underground working'; they built towers all along the wall and raised them to keep pace with the Roman works; they set fire to the Roman works; they countermined the Roman saps

O

and prevented their extension with fire-hardened stakes, hot pitch and large stones; and when, after 25 days, the Roman mound had grown to 330 feet wide and 80 feet high, they fired it from a tunnel and at the same time threw torches, dry wood and pitch on the top of it. Nevertheless they were driven to consider evacuation and were only dissuaded by the women. Finally, in a rainstorm, the Romans succeeded in occupying the whole wall. The Gauls re-formed in the market place (*in foro*) but then scattered to all parts of the *oppidum;* some were killed crammed into the narrow gateways, others were cut down in flight by the cavalry. Only 800 out of 40,000 survived.

No. 23
Date: 52 B.C.
Reference in Caesar: VII: 36, 41
Place: Roman *castra*
Probable identification: Nr. Gergovie (Puy-de-Dome)
Map reference: 73/14
Summary. Caesar had left C. Fabius with only two legions in the large camp while he dealt with the Aedui. Constant attacks, in which the Gauls used arrows and all kinds of missiles, put great pressure on them, but artillery (*tormenta*) was of great use to the defenders. Fabius was blocking up all but two of the gates and adding breastworks (*pluteos*) to the rampart when Caesar relieved him.

No. 24
Date: 52 B.C.
Reference in Caesar: VII: 36–53
Place: Gergovia, an *oppidum* of the Arverni
Probable identification: Gergovie (Puy-de-Dome)
Map reference: 73/14
Summary. The home town of Vercingetorix (VII: 4). As it was situated on a high mountain and difficult of access, Caesar decided not to begin a siege until he had secured his supplies, but in a preliminary action, in which the Gauls used archers and cavalry, he occupied a neighbouring hill to restrict their water supply and their foraging. Here he built his 'small camp' and linked it to his 'large camp' with a double ditch 12 feet wide. The Gauls had taken in an additional area on the slope below the *oppidum* with a 6-foot wall of large stones and were fortifying a narrow wooded ridge which adjoined the *oppidum* itself. Caesar made a feint on the left towards this ridge, thus drawing off the defenders of the *oppidum*, sent some Aedui up on the right, and launched a surprise attack from his small camp. The Romans easily crossed the 6-foot wall and captured three of the Gaulish *castra* which it protected, including that of the Nitiobriges whose king, Teutomatus, barely escaped naked to the waist on a wounded horse. Then Caesar, 'having achieved his purpose' (*consecutus id quod animo proposuerat*), sounded the recall. Only the 10th legion heard it and the rest pressed on to the *oppidum*. Here the women, remembering the treatment of Avaricum, made as if to surrender, and L. Fabius, a centurion of the 8th legion, actually mounted the wall. But the Gauls, with their cavalry leading, rushed back from the ridge and Caesar had to commit his reserves to cover the Roman re-treat. Fabius and those who had followed him were killed and so was M. Petronius, another centurion, trying to break down the gates. Additional confusion was caused by the arrival of the Aedui, because their arms were similar to those of the enemy and although their right shoulders were (as agreed) bared, the Romans thought it was a ruse. The legions reformed at the foot of the hill and Vercingetorix withdrew his men within his fortifications (*intra munitiones*).

Roman losses were 700, including 46 centurions. The next day Caesar failed to lure Vercinge-torix out to battle on the plain. The day after he left for the country of the Aedui.

No. 25
Date: 52 B.C.
Reference in Caesar: VII:55
Place: Noviodunum, an *oppidum* of the Aedui
Probable identification: Nevers (Nièvre)
Map reference: 69/3
Summary. Used by Caesar as a supply base, where he had concentrated his hostages from all the Gaulish tribes. Eporedorix and Viridomarus massacred the garrison, sent the hostages to Bibracte, carried off all the supplies they could, and burnt the rest.

No. 26
Date: 52 B.C.
Reference in Caesar: VII:57–58
Place: Lutetia, an *oppidum* of the Parisii
Probable identification: Paris
Map reference: 56/11
Summary. Situated on an island in the Seine (Ile de la Cité). Large forces from neigh-bouring tribes assembled under Camulogenus, an aged but skilful Aulercan. He opposed Labienus some distance away, where a marshy stream (Essonne) drained into the Seine. Labienus tried, under cover of mantlets, to build a causeway with wattles and other material, then withdrew to cross the river higher up, at Melun. When Melun fell, the Gauls sent orders to burn Lutetia.

No. 27
Date: 52 B.C.
Reference in Caesar: VII:58
Place: Metiosedum, an *oppidum* of the Senones
Probable identification: Melun (Seine-et-Marne)
Map reference: 61/2
Summary. Also situated on an island. Labienus built a pontoon bridge with about 50 boats. Such inhabitants as remained (those who had not been called away to war) were terrified by this unusual operation (*rei novitate perterritis*) and the town fell without a struggle. Labienus then rebuilt a bridge which the Gauls had destroyed, crossed to the right bank, and marched on Lutetia.

No. 28
Date: 52 B.C.
Reference in Caesar: VII:68–90
Place: Alesia, an *oppidum* of the Mandubii
Probable identification: Mont Auxois, Alise-Ste-Reine (Côte-d'Or)
Map reference: 65/18
Summary. Situated on a high hill washed by streams on north and south, and surrounded by hills of similar height except on west, where there was a plain. The east slope below the walls was occupied by Gauls, protected by a ditch and a 6-foot wall (*maceria*). Caesar began to construct a circumvallation 11 Roman miles long, complete with camps and 23 redoubts. In a preliminary battle the Roman cavalry, with legionary support, defeated the Gaulish

cavalry and pursued them right up to the outer wall. Here, jammed in the narrow entrances, they suffered heavy casualies, and Vercingetorix had to shut the gates of the *oppidum* to prevent their abandoning the outer lines. After this he sent out all his cavalry to raise support elsewhere, leaving 80,000 people in the *oppidum*, and evacuated the outer position. Caesar then strengthened his circumvallation with towers, *lilia* and other devices, adding a ditch 20 feet wide 400 paces in front of it, and also constructed an outer line, 14 Roman miles long, against any relieving force. In Alesia a council (*concilium*) met. Critognatus recommended cannibalism 'as in the war with the Cimbri and the Teutones', but it was decided to send the old and infirm and the Mandubian women and children out of the *oppidum*; but Caesar refused them passage. When the besieged saw the arrival of the relief army (8,000 cavalry and 240,000 infantry), they made a sortie and covered the first Roman ditch with wattles and filled it with earth (*cratibus integunt atque aggere implent*). Caesar engaged the relief cavalry, who were interspersed with archers, and narrowly defeated them, after which the besieged retired into the *oppidum*. The relief force, having spent a day preparing wattles, ladders and grappling hooks (*harpagones*), attacked the Romans with arrows, stones and other weapons at midnight, shouting to inform the besieged. After some initial success, they came up against the Roman works and were trapped in the *lilia*, and at dawn, having failed to penetrate the defences, they withdrew.

Meanwhile the besieged had lost much time in bringing out the things they had prepared for a sortie and in filling up ditches, and had not reached the main Roman works when the retreat began, and they had to retire into the *oppidum*. The relief force then decided that Vercassivellaunus should take out a force of 60,000 in the evening, to attack one of the Roman camps which was badly sited on the slope of a hill to the north. This he did at noon next day, while the main relief force made a diversionary attack on the main Roman works. Observing this, Vercingetorix sallied out with poles, sappers' huts (*musculi*), hooks (*falces*) and other implements, and fighting became general. The greatest threat to the Romans was at the badly-sited camp, where some Gauls attacked with missiles while others advanced with locked shields (*testudine facta*); all threw earth on the fortifications, which enabled them to mount the rampart and covered the traps which the Romans had hidden in the ground. Caesar sent Labienus with six cohorts to relieve the camp. Meanwhile the besieged, despairing of penetrating the major Roman works, tried to attack another camp on a steep hill. They dislodged the defenders with missiles, filled the ditches with earth and wattles, and tore down the rampart and breastwork (*vallum et loricam*) with hooks (*falcibus*); but Caesar sent reinforcements, and finally went there himself, and they were repulsed. He then moved over to help Labienus. Here hand-to-hand fighting ensued, with the Romans using their swords. Finally, when the Gauls saw cavalry in their rear and fresh cohorts coming up in front, they broke and fled. When the besieged saw this, they too withdrew, and the rout was complete. The next day Vercingetorix was handed over, the Gauls laid down their arms and Alesia surrendered. Apart from the Aedui and the Arverni, whom he thought might be useful politically, Caesar distributed the prisoners as booty among his men, one to each man.

No. 29
Date: 51 B.C.
Reference in Caesar: VIII: 26–27
Place: Lemonum, an *oppidum* of the Pictones
Probable identification: Poitiers (Vienne)
Map reference: 68/13
Summary. Held by Duratius, a pro-Roman Picto, against 'many thousands' of Gauls under Dumnacus. On the approach of C. Caninius, Dumnacus temporarily drew off his forces to

attack the Roman camp. This (no details) was a failure, and on the approach of a second Roman force under C. Fabius he finally raised the siege and made for the Loire.

No. 30
Date: 51 B.C.
Reference in Caesar: VIII: 32–44
Place: Uxellodunum, an *oppidum* of the Cadurci
Probable identification: Puy d'Issolu, Vayrac (Lot)
Map reference: 75/19
Summary. Drappes (a Senonian) and Lucterius (a Cadurcan), with a force of not more than 2,000, were intending to raid the Roman Province, but as Caninius with two legions was close behind them, they occupied Uxellodunum. This was very strong, protected on all sides by precipitous rocks, and so difficult to attack – but equally difficult for the Gauls to evacuate without being noticed. Caninius built three camps and began to construct a circumvallation as fast as his limited forces allowed. Remembering the shortages at Alesia, Drappes and Lucterius left 2,000 armed men in the *oppidum*, while they took the remainder out to forage. In the event they were both defeated some way from the *oppidum*, Drappes being captured, and Caninius, soon joined by Fabius, could concentrate on the siege. When the circumvallation was complete, Caesar himself arrived and took charge. He decided to concentrate on the water supply. First, he denied the besieged access to the river which ran round the foot of the hill by stationing archers, slingers and artillery to command the slopes. This left one spring which gushed out just below the wall of the *oppidum*. Here, under cover of mantlets which only partly protected the men from the missiles thrown down on them, he built a mound 60 feet high and on top of it a tower of 10 storeys in which he mounted artillery, not to reach the wall but to dominate the spring. Tormented by thirst, the besieged filled casks (*cupae*) with tallow, pitch and pieces of wood (*scandulis* – lit. 'shingles') set them on fire and rolled them down on the Roman works. These were easily set alight, and seeing that heavy losses were being suffered Caesar ordered his men to scale the rocks around the *oppidum* wherever they could, to give the impression of a general attack and divert the Gauls from the Roman works; this succeeded and the fires were extinguished. But though many died of thirst, the besieged still held out. In the meantime, however, Caesar's sappers had been tunnelling towards the source of the spring and finally they diverted it. At its sudden drying up the Gauls surrendered. Caesar cut off the hands of all the survivors who had borne arms. Drappes had starved himself to death in captivity: Lucterius had escaped, but was eventually betrayed by Epasnactus, a pro-Roman Arvernian.

BIBLIOGRAPHY

C. Iulii Caesaris Commentarii de Bello Gallico
Editions: Aldine (2nd Ed.), Venice. 1518.
          Fr. Oudendorp. Leyden. 1737.
          Delphin. London. 1819.
          B. Dinter. Teubner (1st Ed.), Leipzig. 1890.
          H. Meusel. Berlin. 1894.
          R. du Pontet. Oxford Classical Texts, Oxford. 1900.
          T. Rice Holmes. Oxford. 1914.
          H. J. Edwards. Loeb, London and Cambridge, Mass. 1917.
          L-A. Constans. Budé, Paris. 1947.
          A. Klotz. Teubner (4th Ed.), Leipzig. 1952.
          F. Kraner and W. Dittenberger. Berlin. 1960.
          O. Seel. Teubner (5th Ed.), Leipzig. 1961.
          M. Rambaud. Presses Universitaires, Paris. 1965.
Translations: A. M'Devitte and W. S. Bohn. Bohn, London. 1873.
          H. J. Edwards. Loeb, London and Cambridge, Mass. 1917.
          S. A. Handford. Penguin, Harmondsworth. 1951.
          R. Warner. Mentor, New York and London. 1960.

Klotz, A. 1910. *Cäsarstudien*. Leipzig.
Merguet, H. 1961. *Lexikon zu den Schriften Cäsars*. Hildesheim.
Meusel, H. 1887. *Lexicon Caesarianum*. Berlin.
Rice Homes, T. 1911. *Caesar's Conquest of Gaul*². Oxford.
Sihler, E. G. 1891. *Complete Lexicon of the Latinity of Caesar's Gallic War*. Boston.
Tierney, J. J. 1960. 'The Celtic Ethnography of Posidonius', *Procs. R. Irish Academy* 60, Sect. C, no. 5, 189–275.
Webster, G. 1969. *The Roman Imperial Army*. London.

HILL-FORTS, A.D. 400–700

By P. J. FOWLER

THE attractions of a hill-top for settlement can transcend cultural and chronological divisions, although any such site can be expected to interact with a counterpart on valley slope or floor below. In Germany and Greece, for example, the multi-phase nature of hill-fort or acropolis resulting from occupation between Neolithic and Medieval (and even later) times on either side of its 'main' period in Bronze or Iron Age is often visible and sometimes still active; while an intimate relationship with a town, alive or decayed, on lower ground is conceptually expected. The Heuneburg (Kimmig 1968), to take an obvious example in Germany, witnesses a discontinuous sequence of occupation from the 14th century B.C. to the 12th century A.D., while many an acropolis still shows obvious Mycenean, Greek, Roman, Frankish and Turkish architecture and relates topographically and historically, as in the Sparta complex, to settlements nearby. On the Continent, as France and Spain further demonstrate, this point is in fact commonplace, while in southern Britain a Maiden Castle and a South Cadbury, or more appositely an Old Sarum with its full Medieval town or a St. Catharine's Hill with full documentation, appear anomalous in their insular hill-fort context. Yet such multi-period sites have barely so far sharpened our intellectual appreciation of hill-fort longevity and its implications; but are they in fact so anomalous?

As a tail-piece to the preceding considerations of hill-forts as prehistoric phenomena, it is not entirely inappropriate to look briefly at the evidence for their role in the late-Roman and immediately post-Roman centuries.[1] It was after all Sir Mortimer Wheeler (1932 and 1943) who showed us at Lydney and Maiden Castle, with their late-Roman temples, that the 4th century A.D. and later could be an important phase in the history of a hill-fort and, conversely, that hill-forts may well have been a significant factor in at least a local context long after their origin and indeed after their prehistoric or early Roman desertion. There, until recently, the matter has rather been allowed to rest, the evidence from these two sites having tended perhaps to be regarded as somewhat exceptional and perhaps largely the product of the familiar Wheeler magic. Until recently, however, these were two of the very few West Country hill-forts – and my remarks largely relate to this area – which had been systematically examined *internally* on some scale.

Relevant evidence has of course come from further south-west, pre-eminently Castle Dore (Radford 1951) and Chun Castle for which Thomas (1956) demonstrated a sub-Roman use by his recognition of Bi imported Mediterranean amphora sherds and grass-marked pottery among the material from Leeds' excavation in the 1920's.

[1] In self-defence, the author must point out that this paper was commissioned at short notice when, as it happened, there were other particularly time-consuming demands in hand. The short interval after the Conference for preparing papers for publication has not allowed any further research, and this text, minus some colloquialisms, is more or less the lecture as given, gilded by a minimum of references. The survey of the evidence is clearly incomplete but it is hoped that the basic point is not entirely invalid. *The editors wish to thank Mr. Peter Fowler for supplying this contribution at very short notice.*

Similarly, to the east, Pitt-Rivers' well-known Cissbury section (discussed in relation to Tom's field survey in Curwen, 1929) showing the late- or post-Roman rampart on top of the pre-Roman defences has for long been almost semi-humourously regarded as a puzzling oddity even though Curwen himself pointed out in 1929 that Cissbury was by no means alone amongst Sussex hill-forts in having late- and/or post-Roman evidence. And in Wessex itself, although some have from time to time toyed etymologically with Vespasian's Camp at Amesbury as an attractive proposition for a 5th century fortress, the extensive and mostly long-available archaeological evidence of late-Roman and actual/potential 5th/6th century hill-fort activity has never been synthesised in print and the obvious and important role of hill-forts like Barbury in the *Anglo-Saxon Chronicle* has not been followed up archaeologically. One may well ask whether all those battles at hill-forts took place on those sites simply because the hill-forts themselves were at strategic spots – as has often been assumed – or whether they took place there because people were in occupation? And if the latter, who was on the inside? – was it necessarily the embattled Britons *inside* the walls of Badon who withstood the ineffectual siege of extra-mural Saxons? – the *Chronicle* does not say so, and theoretically the positions could have been reversed. Anyway, the point is surely that hill-forts are not only the subject matter of prehistorians, and the only real purpose of this paper is to query whether, by concentrating on the pre-Roman archaeology of hill-forts on one hand and the problems of town and villa above all on the other in considering late-Roman Britain, we may not have underemphasised the significance of hill-forts as a factor in the 4th–6th century confusion and, in parallel, have underestimated those centuries as important in the history of hill-forts.

From this criticism I except, of course, Wales, where the Royal Commission, particularly in *Caernarvonshire III* (1964), and Alcock in a series of recent papers (summarised and referenced in Alcock 1963a), have tackled precisely these questions and made us aware in detail, so far as the evidence goes, of sub- and post-Roman hill-fort archaeology. And Scotland too has its cognate material reasonably well-documented (Feachem 1955). What follows here is an attempt, undocumented in detail at this stage and certainly incomplete, to bring this facet of hill-fort archaeology into some sort of focus for central and south-western Britain, bearing in mind the total absence of any discussion of this point in a recent 'standard work' such as Frere (1967). Grinsell (1958, 229) perhaps best sums up the general view: 'Some have discerned in these examples (Maiden Castle and Lydney) an indication of a return to the native strongholds with their tradition of valour as the economy of Roman Britain became more precarious.'

Arising from this are three specific questions:

(i) Just how widespread and frequent was the use of hill-forts for occupation or reoccupation from late-Roman times onwards?

(ii) Depending on the answer, to what extent can we continue to assume that *visible* hill-fort defences are of pre-Roman Iron Age date?

(iii) What interpretation can we place on such archaeological evidence as there is for hill-fort use from the 4th century onwards?

Fig. 39. A Preliminary Distribution of Hill-forts with Evidence of Occupation, A.D. 400-700.

Provisionally, the beginnings of an answer to the first question are on fig. 39.[2] Possibly it shows more dots than expected so a brief word on the criteria is necessary. Overall of course the archaeological evidence is extremely defective: less than a dozen well-reported and reasonably extensive excavations, some inadequate excavations, and the rest mainly chance or surface finds recorded with varying degrees of reliability. Some possible evidence, varying in its non-reliability, has been omitted, despite the temptation to increase the numbers of dots; on the other hand, the map contains a few sites, like Vespasian's Camp and Dyrham where, although at the moment there is no *archaeological* evidence for their inclusion, there are other, place-name or documentary, claims for some sort of use in our period. Most of the examples have of course produced conventionally Roman material rather than specifically 5th–7th century evidence – a point to which I shall return later (see below) – but as far as possible in working partly from secondary sources, only those with some indication of 4th century or later material have been included. On coins, for example, I have only taken Constantinian or later, on pottery only those finds said to be 3rd–4th century or 'late Romano-British', so some selectivity has been exercised.

At the moment the map is no more than a coarse indication of where such sites are rather than what the sites might be. Obviously, to be of use, it must be refined *chronologically*, because a 4th century occupation does not necessarily imply one in the 5th century and, as we can see elsewhere, e.g. at High Peak (Pollard 1966) and Cadbury Congresbury (Fowler *et al.* 1970), a 5th century occupation does not necessarily arise or continue from one in the 4th century nor need it span the whole of the century. The map must also be refined *structurally* because it cannot be assumed that in every case, as at South Cadbury (Alcock 1967), existing defences were refurbished or, as at Cadbury Congresbury, that defences were built *de novo* (Fowler and Rahtz 1970). And it must be refined *contextually* to show what the hill-forts' associations are: how many contain, as at Maiden Castle, or are related to, as at Cadbury Congresbury, temples? How many, as at Cannington (Rahtz 1969), are to be associated with cemeteries? Is there local evidence of a connection, social or tenurial perhaps rather than tangibly archaeological, between any of these hill-forts and adjacent towns, villas or other settlements? Meanwhile, however, pending a considered survey the map can serve as a visual quantitative presentation of much of the relevant evidence.

[2] I wish to acknowledge the timely assistance so readily given in quickly compiling the data for fig. 39 by Professor Charles Thomas (Devon and Cornwall); and the Royal Commission on Historical Monuments (England), especially Dr. Isobel Smith and Bruce Eagles of its staff (Dorset and Gloucestershire). Mrs. Elizabeth Fowler gave much help in assessing the evidence published in the indispensable *VCH Wiltshire I*, i (1957); without the detailed work already completed by Philip Rahtz for other purposes (Rahtz and Fowler 1972), the Somerset basis of this paper would not have existed. Much of the content here derives from the stimulation afforded by our current co-direction of the Cadbury Congresbury excavations and the relationships between that site and Leslie Alcock's results from Dinas Powys (1963b) and South Cadbury.

The data on the map is 100 per cent complete (as far as I know) for Wales, Cornwall, Devon and Somerset; and 75 per cent plus for Dorset, Wiltshire and Gloucestershire. No original work, and a quick search of only the obvious secondary sources, was carried out for Hampshire, Sussex, Berkshire and Oxfordshire. Time did not allow of a search further afield, and it is hoped that someone else may pursue the matter more thoroughly. Northern England, Scotland and Ireland are deliberately omitted, without prejudice to their importance in this context.

In the English area it covers there are, taking the Ordnance Survey (1961) figures, 582 forts. The *c.* 40 non-Welsh examples here represent, therefore, 7 per cent of the total as basal minimum. How realistic that percentage is one can but guess. On the other hand, in Somerset, the one county with reliable data (Rahtz and Fowler 1972), of the 62 forts 12 are on fig. 39 with absolute or only slightly qualified claims, i.e. *c.* 20 per cent, and I personally suspect that to be a much more realistic minimum figure for the proportion of hill-forts in the West enjoying a new lease of life in the late 4th century or later.

Before looking at the Somerset evidence more fully, one or two of the sites in nearby areas can indicate the problems and potential of the present available information. Madmarston in Oxfordshire is now in retrospect of greater significance than was realised 11 years ago (Fowler 1960). Stratigraphically the evidence was impeccable: a cobbled level with post-holes in it overlay the back of the Iron Age rampart and indeed the hoard of ironwork and was associated with typical late-Roman material including Oxford colour-coated wares and 4th century coins. The evidence was little explored but of course one wonders now just how late that occupation continued, whether it included timber buildings, and indeed what was its nature and extent. There was certainly a lot of pottery and not, as at St. Catharine's Hill for example, just a sparse scatter attributable to Roman picnickers (Hawkes *et al.* 1930). Madmarston provides in hindsight a minor classic example of the sort of evidence ideally recoverable in relation to a hill-fort's defences, as previously found at Cissbury and Wandlebury, Cambs. (*cf* Fowler 1960, 30), and subsequently at Cannington, Somerset (Rahtz 1969), but no evidence of new defences or refortification was observed there.

Much more common is the sort of evidence from a site like Oldbury Camp, Wilts. (VCH 1957, 53–4): sundry diggings and many surface finds, the latter not always located precisely and some dubiously attributed and now lost. The material includes Roman pottery, a coin of Valentinian, a bone comb with ring and dot ornament, and the large well-known type G pennanular brooch best assigned to the 5th century, all apparently from inside the hill-fort. One can only remark 'how tantalising' and wonder about the sequence and date of the defences visible on the ground and, even more clearly, from the air.

We can also look at late hill-forts in a context, for example in the Dorchester area with its Roman town, two hill-forts, several villas, other settlements and extra-mural cemeteries (RCHM 1970). Here Maiden Castle can represent hill-forts elsewhere with known temples but what about the smaller Poundbury and the cemetery outside its eastern end? This hill-fort is another with not a little late-Roman evidence from inside it although its interior has only been spot-sampled rather than stripped; the cemetery or cemeteries, currently under examination (Green 1969), instead of being viewed from the Roman town walls as it is by implication in the recent Commission plan, should perhaps, in one of its phases anyway, be viewed from the hill-fort ramparts. It may not be altogether just another, albeit elaborate and complex, extra-mural cemetery for a Romanised urban population but rather related in part to re-use of the hill-fort. It is surely just a matter of time until Mediterranean imported pottery turns up in this area, and meanwhile the apparent or potential similarity of the hill-fort/

cemetery relationship with what we know to be the case in Somerset is striking.[3]

Through lack of evidence from good excavations the situation in Gloucestershire is even more obscure. On its southern borders, Blaise Castle (Rahtz and Brown 1959) almost certainly contained a late-Roman temple, hinting that Lydney further upstream may not be alone along the tidal reaches of the Severn with a hill-fort/temple relationship; while King's Weston Camp in the same area now also has what appears to be a Somerset-type sub-Roman cemetery immediately outside it (Godman 1971), so the hill-fort/cemetery relationship too is not confined south of the Avon. Overlooking the Avon Gorge are three hill-forts which have all produced Roman material too. But what about all those hill-forts along the Cotswold scarp, in the area which looms so large with rather gloomy Romanised paganism in Dr. Anne Ross's survey (1967) and yet contains one of the three densest concentrations of villas in the country (Stevens 1966; Webster 1969). At least 15 of the hill-forts have produced firm or suggestive archaeological evidence of something happening in them from the 3rd century or later onwards but, until the last two years with Crickley and Leckhampton, none have been properly excavated. Coins are the most frequent evidence, for example at Little Sodbury, at Trewsbury, Coates, Beckbury, Uleybury, Kimsbury and the giant Nottingham Hill itself – is there not a likely temple or two somewhere in this list? In any case, where did all the villa-people go because, however long into the 5th century some villas continued, it is quite clear that most did not continue indefinitely (Webster 1969). Admittedly, occupation of some sort continued into the 5th century at Cirencester and Gloucester but the evidence does not yet indicate large urban populations. We know of definite late-Roman occupation, with certain or probable 4th century buildings, in for example Norbury, Woodmancote, and Ring Hill, Haresfield, but really the hill-fort evidence is again tantalisingly defective. Crickley, with its 6th(?) century metalworking, suggests the potential (Dixon 1970).

One other important type of hill-fort evidence is the brand new hill-fort. High Peak, near Sidmouth on the Devon coast, is the best and perhaps the only proven example. Although considerable Neolithic occupation of the site was demonstrated by the several cuttings into and about the remnant defences, Roman material was totally lacking and the defences themselves appear properly to belong to the 5th, probably the later 5th, century on the evidence of imported Mediterranean pottery (Pollard 1966). So we must allow the possibility of hill-forts appearing *de novo* in the 5th if not the 4th century even though, east of Devon anyway, the possibilities are limited if only for the practical reason that many of the suitable hill-tops already had defences on them before 400.

While we can speculate about the numbers of hill-forts affected by late-Roman/early historic refurbishings of existing defences, the number of cases where this has been actually demonstrated is very small. Significantly, a number of reasonably excavated hill-forts where this might have been expected from internal evidence – Maiden Castle, Poundbury, Madmarston, Crickley (so far) – have produced no evidence of refortification. On the positive side, examples with such evidence comprise at the moment only

[3] Since the Conference, Mediterranean pottery has in fact been identified at Dorchester. I am grateful to Professor Barry Cunliffe for this information.

a very short list including Lydney, Castle Dore (probably), South Cadbury, Cadbury Congresbury and Cissbury as the most obvious candidates. But these also are reasonably well-examined instances, at least as far as their defences are concerned, and they hint of a possibly much higher incidence of late refortification, in the West Country anyway, than has presently been realised. Perhaps now that we are all looking for this sort of evidence in or immediately beneath the topsoil instead of naïvely assuming that hill-forts are prehistoric, we shall begin to realise the potential.

It is fair to say this has already begun to happen in Somerset, stemming largely from the lead of Rahtz at Cannington and Alcock at South Cadbury. Furthermore, not only are the relevant structural details of 5th century fortification emerging but studies there are moving to a stage of at least superficial appreciation of what Cunliffe (above pp. 53–70) has called, for an earlier period, the hill-fort and its environment (Rahtz and Fowler 1972).[4] In Somerset the two best-documented archaeological features of that environment are Roman temples and perhaps other later ritual structures, and cemeteries. Temples lie just outside Cadbury-Congresbury and the possible hill-fort on Brean Down, and a temple has also been proposed in South Cadbury (Alcock 1967, 72). A guess would place one on Ham Hill too, and possibly also on one or other of Brent Knoll, Dolebury or Worlebury, all of which have produced late-Roman material.

Inhumation cemeteries of 4th century or later date can of course occur in non-hill-fort contexts e.g. Camerton, where surely the cemetery is not initially of Saxons but of the remnant sub-Roman population of that small road-side town; and Portishead where recently yet another such cemetery was rescued from the site of an incipient petrol station. But they also relate to hill-forts, not only fairly directly by proximity as at Cadbury Congresbury where one overlies the temple and *temenos* ditch in Henley Wood just outside the hill-fort's eastern defences, but also within a rather wider context as Rahtz has argued for Cannington. There the largest of the cemeteries so far discovered is seen as that of a whole local community focused on the reoccupied hill-fort after moving up from the floodlands of the River Parrett around the Roman settlement at Combwich. A similar cemetery also occurs at Brean Down, to complete the trinity there, as at Cadbury Congresbury, of hill-fort (?), temple and cemetery. The large cemetery on the south side of Worlebury – not the well-known one inside reported by Dymond (1902) but one outside which has come up in bits and pieces during Weston-super-Mare's suburban creep (material in Weston-super-Mare Museum) – is another candidate, possible even continually in use from pre-Roman to post-Roman times.

Of the hill-forts themselves, a dozen or so out of five dozen in the county have claims for late/sub/post-Roman use (see above). The most widely examined, South Cadbury, is already well-known because it is so important and has been so promptly reported in interim stages. The significant points for present purposes are that a large hill-fort was refortified the whole way round its inner rampart using a timberwork technique in association with a flat-topped, platform-like bank; that the refortification included a new gateway and a contemporary metalled surface; that the refortification

---

[4] Since Rahtz and Fowler 1972 is a comprehensive and fully referenced paper up to date into early 1971, the reader is referred to it for further information and bibliographical detail. Somerset sites are not otherwise referenced here.

followed the line of an existing defence but did not apparently include remodelling of outer works; that the new inner rampart included late-Roman material in its make-up and was dated by sherds of imported Mediterranean pottery on its tail; and that in the 5th/6th centuries the enclosed area contained occupation features including timber buildings.

Much of this with some additions is repeated at Cadbury Congresbury, a much smaller hill-fort much closer to the sea. Relatively small-scale excavation has shown re-fortification along the probable line of pre-Roman defences and also – this is an important point – a big new defence along an apparently new line. This new defence, which includes an entrance, is also basically a low flat-topped platform behind some sort of façade but, unlike South Cadbury, it has its own newly-cut ditch. Behind the defence are also timber buildings, both rectangular and round. Associated with these buildings was an occupation layer containing thousands of animal bones; hundreds of pieces of pennant stone roof and floor tiles of Roman derivation, probably from the nearby temple at Henley Wood (above, p. 209); many fragments of Roman glass and brick; glass beads, some probably imported; bronze and iron objects of Roman and later date, including three type G pennanular brooches; iron slag and furnace fragments; and several hundred sherds. These included some of late Roman type, but are pre-ponderantly from Mediterranean amphorae and table-ware, with a few from vessels probably of Gaulish origin. Some indigenous hand-made sherds of grass-tempered and sandy wares also occurred. Over much of the site these types were found together, but on the back of the defences, and more particularly in the 1970 ditch section, they were separated stratigraphically. There the Roman sherds were in a primary context; they quickly gave way to a layer which is non-ceramic except for a few hand-made sherds and it was only in the upper levels that imported sherds were found (Fowler and Rahtz 1970).

On the basis of the 1970 sequence at Cadbury-Congresbury, imported sherds are not part of the 'late-Roman' or immediately post-Roman assemblage, but are a secondary feature in the post-Roman activity there and perhaps further afield in Somerset. A date of c. 450 has been suggested for the refortification of Cadbury-Congresbury: it is likely that soon after that Roman ceramics went out of use, and some time later, perhaps c. 500 or in the early 6th century, new ceramics were imported into the area. Such a date is consistent with that suggested in the areas in which this pottery was made. The three hill-forts that have been recently examined, the two Cadburys and Cannington hill-fort (and several other hill-forts whose reoccupation seems likely), are all much larger than the Glastonbury Tor settlement, for example, and represent a scale of post-Roman settlement site for which there are no parallels in areas further west. Their size may reflect the basic economic wealth of Somerset relative to that of places in the 'highland zone'.

Dating these defended settlements is difficult. The evidence from Cannington is only of Roman pottery, with later material and C14 dates from the cemetery. There is a little Roman pottery on Glastonbury Tor (admittedly not a hill-fort but still defensible?), but *not* in a direct association with the buildings. There is late Roman pottery from South Cadbury, which Alcock is inclined to regard as having nothing to do with the refortification, but to be earlier (4th century?) and perhaps associated with a temple. The refortification of Cadbury Congresbury is associated with the use of Roman pottery which, however, quickly went out of use. Cannington and Cadbury Congresbury therefore seem to have begun *c*. 410–450 while the Tor and South Cadbury may have been later, in the period of currency of imported Mediterranean pottery centering on *c*. 500. There is, however, nothing in the evidence from the Tor or South Cadbury to show that they did not originate in the mid rather than the later 5th century: the imports on the Tor only give a *terminus ante quem* and the late Roman sherds in the rampart at South Cadbury only give a *terminus post quem*, both of which could be as early as *c*. 450 or even earlier.

While there is no necessity to find a common date for these settlements, it might be easier to explain their function in relation to historical events if they could be demonstrated to be broadly contemporary. The most usual interpretation is that they represent the strongholds of local rulers, the defended settlements of a political or military *élite* dominating the surrounding countryside. Their defences may have been as much for the personal protection of the *élite* and their retinue from hostile 'subjects' (*cf* motte-and-bailey castles) as for local strongpoints which protect the local population against attack from outside (*cf* the Alfredian/Edwardian *burhs*). The enemy in this latter case could be sea-borne raiding parties coming into the Bristol Channel (especially at Cannington) or, more probably, Germanic groups from the east.

These are two very different concepts. The former need have no common date or cause other than the breakdown of one political system, i.e. the Roman bureaucracy, and its replacement by 'tyrants' or 'kings' dominating small areas. Such a transition might be spread over several decades and vary in time from place to place. The latter might be much more specific and contemporary in the fact of a common threat. If this threat was Germanic, then an occasion in the mid-5th century is clear – the *Adventus Saxonum*, the sudden political and military take-over in the east which made such an impression on contemporary and later writers.

Who were the new ruling class which set itself up as local tyrants or defenders in Somerset? Were they the remnants of the ultimate Roman aristocracy rising from the ranks of the peasantry, the former native farmers or villa labourers? Or were they immigrant Irish or Welsh, taking advantage of the final breakdown of the Roman system to seize land and power in a rich area? Any of these are possible, and much more evidence is needed, though Alcock has suggested that South Cadbury was the military stronghold of an 'Arthur-type figure' who, with his retinue, commanded more than local allegiance.

All of these possibilities imply that the defended settlements were those of rulers. It may be that they should be thought of more as elements of communal defence, organised either on a local or a wider basis as strongpoints in times of crisis, by confederacies of local peasants or aristocrats. This may especially be true of Cannington where the cemetery could be that of a 'normal' community of a hundred or more people. The date for the start of these new settlements may therefore be tentatively placed in the mid or later 5th century, even if their inhabitants are potentially so dramatically diverse. The evidence from Cadbury Congresbury hints that at the time when imports were arriving on the site, perhaps half a century after its foundation, not only had the timber and stone ramparts begun to collapse, but that the ditch was filled up with silt and stones almost to the top. On present evidence, this site could be one which, set up in times of insecurity, continued after the crisis had passed with a new phase characterised by imported material during a time when the defences had ceased to be a relevant aspect of the site.

Obviously, at this stage, there can be conclusions, but the evidence now coming to light is suggesting that some hill-forts anyway enjoyed a possibly very significant new lease of life from the mid-5th century onwards. At the moment, we can but guess to what extent the Somerset evidence is applicable to neighbouring areas, and it is here that the evidence with which I began – those hill-forts with conventionally late-Roman material – is relevant. Such evidence may only indicate occupation in the 4th century but take away the imports from a site like Cadbury Congresbury and what remains? – a collection of ostensibly late-Roman rubbish including metalwork. Maybe we shall soon find imported Mediterranean and Gaulish pottery and glass of the 5th–7th centuries in our Wessex hill-forts, but if the distribution of such material does not extend inland then the occupation of 'Arthur-type figures' will be represented only by the sort of material which some hill-forts are already known to contain, i.e. late-Roman rubbish conventionally dating from a century earlier. Should we in fact be reading '5th/6th century' for 'late-Roman' throughout? – chronological recalibration is not the prerogative of prehistory after all. Meanwhile, let us give those '4th century squatters' and 'late-Roman picnickers' scattered in our hill-fort topsoils a rather more serious consideration – Arthur may not be under every stone, but there were many knights in the Dark Ages.

BIBLIOGRAPHY

Alcock, L. 1963 a: 'Pottery and Settlements in Wales and the March, A.D. 400–700', in Foster, I. Ll., and Alcock, L. (eds.), *Culture and Environment* (Routledge & Kegan Paul), 281–302.

Alcock, L. 1963 b: *Dinas Powys* (University of Wales Press).

Alcock, L. 1967. 'A Reconnaissance Excavation at South Cadbury Castle, Somerset, 1966', *Antiq. J.*, 47, 70–76 (subsequent interim reports annually in same journal up to 50, 1970; full report forthcoming).

Curwen, E. C. 1929. *Prehistoric Sussex* (Homeland Assoc. Ltd.).

Dixon, P. W. 1970. *Excavations at Crickley Hill 1969–70* (Gloucestershire Coll. of Art).

Dymond, C. W. 1902. *Worlebury*.

Feachem, R. W. 1955. 'Fortifications' in Wainwright, F. T. (ed.), *The Problem of the Picts* (Nelson), 66–86.

Fowler, P. J. 1960. 'Excavations at Madmarston Camp, Swalcliffe, 1957–8', *Oxoniensia*, 25, 3–48.

Fowler, P. J., and Rahtz, P. 1970. 'Cadcong 1970', *Current Archaeol.*, no. 23, 337–42.

Fowler, P. J. *et al.* 1970. *Cadbury Congressbury, Somerset 1968* (Dept. of Extra-Mural Studies, Univ. of Bristol).

Frere, S. S. 1967. *Britannia* (Routledge & Kegan Paul).

Godman, C. 1971. *Proc. Univ. Bristol Spelaeol. Soc.* forthcoming.

Green, C. J. S. 1969. 'Interim Report on Excavations in the Roman Cemetery, Poundbury, Dorchester, 1969', *Proc. Dorset Natur. Hist. Archaeol. Soc.*, 91, 183–6.

Grinsell, L. V. 1958. *The Archaeology of Wessex* (Methuen).

Hawkes, C. F. C., *et al.* 1930. 'Saint Catharine's Hill, Winchester', *Proc. Hampshire Fld. Club Archaeol. Soc.*, 11.

Kimming, W. 1968. *Die Heuneburg an der oberen Donau* (Führer zu vor- und fruhgeschichlichen Denkmälern in Württernberg und Hohenzollern, 1).

Ordnance Survey. 1961. *Map of Southern Britain in the Iron Age*.

Pollard, S. H. M. 1966. 'Neolithic and Dark Age Settlements on High Peak, Sidmouth, Devon', *Proc. Devon Archaeol. Explor. Soc.*, 23, 35–59.

Radford, C. A. R. 1951. 'Report on the Excavations at Castle Dore', *J. Roy. Instit. Cornwall*, N.S. 1, Appendix.

Rahtz, P. A. 1969. 'Cannington Hill-fort, 1963', *Somerset Archaeol. Nat. Hist.*, 113, 56–58.

Rahtz, P. A., and Brown, J. C. 1959. 'Blaise Castle Hill, Bristol, 1957', *Proc. Univ. Bristol Spelaeol. Soc.*, 8, 147–71.

Rahtz, P. A., and Fowler, P. J. 1972. 'Somerset, A.D. 400–700', in Fowler, P. J. (ed.), *Archaeology and the Landscape* (Baker).

Ross, A. 1967. *Pagan Celtic Britain* (Routledge & Kegan Paul).

Royal Commission on Ancient and Historical Monuments (Wales). 1964. *An Inventory . . . Caernarvonshire III* (HMSO).

RCHM. 1970. Royal Commission on Historical Monuments (England), *An Inventory . . . South East Dorset*, pt. 3 (HMSO).

Stevens, C. E. 1966. 'The Social and Economic Aspects of Rural Settlement' in Thomas, C. (ed.), *Rural Settlement in Roman Britain* (CBA Rsch. Rpt. 7).

Thomas, C. 1956. 'Evidence for post-Roman Occupation of Chun Castle', *Antiq. J.*, 36, 75.

VCH. 1957. Victoria County History, *Wiltshire I*, i (Oxford Univ. Press).

Webster, G. 1969. 'The Future of Villa Studies', in Rivet, A. L. F. (ed.), *The Roman Villa in Britain* (Routledge & Kegan Paul).

Wheeler, R. E. M. 1943. *Maiden Castle, Dorset* (Soc. Antiqs. Rsch. Rpt. 12).

Wheeler, R. E. M., and T. V. 1932. *Report . . . Lydney Park, Gloucestershire* (Soc. Antiqs. Rsch. Rpt. 9).

INDEX